# BETWEEN
# SUNSETS

## LEAH OMAR

Fulton Books
Meadville, PA

Published by Fulton Books 2022

ISBN 979-8-88505-360-0 (paperback)
ISBN 979-8-88505-361-7 (digital)

Printed in the United States of America

To O and B, D and D, J and J, S and T, Dad and Mom, and all those that have and continue to walk on the shores of this sacred land. May I always feel you in the breeze, hear you in the birds, and see you in the sunsets.

# CHAPTER 1

There is something liberating about owning so little that I can fit all of my worldly possessions in my car. I feel weightless, with nothing holding me down or keeping me in place. I have the freedom to go anywhere. I'm wild and unattached, with hopefully more life in front of me than in my rearview mirror.

And speaking of my rearview mirror, I haven't seen the concrete jungle of Chicago in over seven hours. I exhale as I cross the Mississippi River, where a sign welcomes me to Minnesota. Three more hours and I'll be in Wheaton.

My car slows with the city traffic of Minneapolis. The steel skyscrapers stretch upward, threatening to stab through the feathery white clouds amid the vastness of the blue sky. I drive northwest out of the city, where the land turns flat and expansive, the pastures are the color of emeralds, and the sun sparkles off the surface. The top is down on my Beetle. My long curls dance above me as my car whips in the wind.

I turn my music up and look out at the sprawling farms on both sides of the road. My family used to make this trip almost every summer, no matter where we were living, and with every sight and sound, muscle memory kicks in, and my body senses that I'm getting closer. My parents offered to visit me for part of the summer, but that would have required so much rearranging of their schedules that I agreed to come to them instead. Another reason I'm happy that relationships and things don't tether me down, as now I have the freedom to spend my summer in Wheaton with my grandparents. I can't imagine wanting to be anywhere else.

As a child, I thought the drive to Wheaton was so exotic. My brother and I would count cows, and I would marvel at how remote everything appeared as we got closer to my grandparents' town. Farms would stretch out to the horizon as far as the eye could see. I would imagine what life would have been like had my dad not attended college in Chicago, met my mom, and then later taken a job that required our family to move all over the world every three to four years. What might my life have looked like had I been born and raised in Wheaton?

I pull off the freeway and head west. As kids, this was always the point in the car ride where my brother, Robby, and I lost the ability to sit still. The last hour on a two-lane road meant we were almost to Wheaton, where Grandma Sis and Grandpa Sunny would already be waiting for us in the front yard, watching for our car to roll down Main Street.

I would speak with reckless abandon, and Robby would punch my arm to annoy me. All the while, Mom would turn around and scold us for making so much noise while Dad was trying to concentrate on driving. But I would look at my dad and see half of his mouth turned up in a smile—not upset at all but rather just as excited as I was. He was almost home.

I find myself eager again as the Wheaton water tower appears in the distance. I turn my radio off and laugh as the giant pelican statue welcoming me to Wheaton comes into view. With no cars in sight, I pull off the road and take a picture. Robby will get a kick out of this when I text it to him later. The pelican statue is the gaudiest thing I've ever seen. It's at least six feet tall, its bright orange beak stretching all the way to the ground as it sits on a large wooden stump carved with the words "Welcome to Wheaton."

Every time we would reach it, Dad would turn back to Robby and me and say, "A pelican, a pelican, its beak can hold more than its belly can." When we were young, Robby and I would laugh and ask him to say it again. As we got older, we would groan and roll our eyes, even though I always secretly hoped he would say it.

I turn left onto Main Street. People doing lawn work wave at me. I smile back. Farther along, my grandparents' house comes into view, but because I'm a couple of hours early, I drive past. They're creatures of habit. Arriving early would throw off their entire day. I'll get to see them soon enough.

There's something nostalgic about the historic downtown of Wheaton. The four-block area is stuck in time, preserved to what it looked like a century ago. The modernization of America must have started at the shores, never reaching Middle America and Wheaton. Perhaps someone tried to modernize the town, but the citizens of Wheaton rebelled against the thought of changing this already perfect place. That's what I like to think. Downtown Wheaton is a piece of Americana, a slice of history that reminds me of simpler times. The buildings ooze with character. The largest structure in town is the shiny, steel grain elevator up ahead.

I continue on the road that leads out of town and head southwest a few miles. Lake Traverse appears off to my right. It's narrow at the river basin, then darts out, stretching more than a mile wide. My dad always used to remind Robby and me that Lake Traverse was formed by a glacier. The history of the lake made him proud. My mom, Robby, and I would humor him when he told us this information every time we arrived. Lake Traverse was my favorite place in the world as a child. I've never been able to call any one place home, but if I had to choose somewhere, it would be here.

I turn down the long gravel driveway. Corn sprouts through the dirt on both sides of the road—tiny specks of green with a promise of a future. They're like a clock telling me that Memorial Day weekend is one bookend of summer. The corn will be tall and nearly ready to pick by the other bookend, Labor Day weekend. The driveway stops short of the lake, where there is a fork in the road. I turn right. Big, mature trees create a canopy on both sides.

I pull into the gravel driveway of the cottage, turn my engine off, and sit and stare. I'm here.

The lawn is overgrown, but it looks like someone has been mowing because it isn't as long as the prairie grass on the edge of the yard. The cottage is only about fifty feet from the lake. The view isn't clear because of sumac and ash trees that are overgrown on the shoreline. I go to my grandparents' hiding place for the key and open the door to the cottage. Dust flies out at me. It's obvious that no one has stepped foot in here in a very long time. All the furniture is covered with plastic.

Water droplets bead from the brown spots dotting the ceiling, threatening the floor underneath. The drywall is moldy, and the wood looks rotten. A wave of sadness floods me as I take in the state of the cottage. This had been a place of happiness when I was a kid. I would arrive, and life's worries would fall off my shoulders, if only for a moment. I would pause my concern about where my dad's job in the foreign service would take us next. My grandparents would sit and watch us play in the water or on the lawn for hours, and their cheeks would ache from smiling by the end of the day. I have always tried to convince myself that I liked moving all the time because it meant that I was a citizen of the world. But what it really meant was that I didn't belong anywhere.

As I look around, it's hard to picture those times. There has been no love or care of the place, and it shows on every surface. I can barely stand to be here. The musty odor mixes with the smell of sulfur. I cover my mouth and nose and let out a sneeze. Dust from the table flies into the air.

Outside, the lake glistens in the sun, and the northwest wind brings the waves crashing into the shore. My hair flies in my face, so I tie it back and throw on my favorite Chicago White Sox cap. When I was young, Grandma Sis often said that my hair alone probably weighed more than the rest of me. I smile at the memory. I was a short little thing and all hair. Grandma Sis always called me her wild child, something that became a self-fulfilling prophecy.

This cottage has been an out-of-town getaway ever since Sis's parents built it when she was still a girl, and it's only a few minutes from town. When my grandparents were married, it became theirs. They would spend every spring, summer, and fall day here either fishing, duck hunting, or entertaining family and friends. When my family would visit Wheaton, we would spend our days and nights here. Sunny and Sis's home on Main Street was only visited if we came here in the winter months, which was rare because my dad hardly ever got time off from his job.

I'm not ready to head back to town, so instead, I walk down the road, wanting to explore more of the land I grew up visiting. I reach the fork in the road where I turned right to our cottage and continue walking. Another driveway veers off from the road, so I decide to explore.

On the right is a beautiful A-frame log home that wasn't here the last time I visited Wheaton seven years ago. There used to be a green cottage instead that belonged to my grandparents' best friends, Oscar and Eleanor Abram. The wood of that old place was faded from the relentless sun. It had a screened porch off the side. All the kids would play in the lawn, while Grandma Sis and Ms. Eleanor would sit on that porch and sip iced tea. Now, at this new place, the lawn is manicured to perfection, the green grass mowed into flawless lines that extend from the driveway to the lake. Mature trees stretch toward the sky. A few newer trees have been planted near a shed. Up ahead and to the side of the yard, I happen upon a large pile of wood in all shapes and sizes. The sun beats down, causing a glint of luster in the collection. I investigate further.

The light brown hues of the beautiful pieces of Norwegian pine contrast against the auburn-colored maple. There's so much beauty and possibility in this wood. I love creating splendor and vitality where it doesn't exist. My thoughts are all over the place as ideas pour into my head.

"Can I help you?" a voice booms from behind me.

I jump and turn to find a man standing there in a T-shirt and jeans, with work boots that look like they could flatten a person. My pulse races at his unexpected presence. His baseball cap sits low on his head and shadows much of his face.

"I-I'm sorry. I saw this pile of wood and was looking through it." I stand up straight and point back to the woodpile.

When he takes a step closer, I move backward to put space between us. He's so much taller than me that I have to strain my neck to look at him. His gray shirt is tight. I squint my eyes to read the three lines of a horizontal tattoo that covers a scar on his right arm.

"Oh, you mean this wood here, on my land?" His balled fists rest on his hips as he manages to make himself look even more commanding.

I fiddle with the hem of my shirt, a nervous habit. "I was just leaving."

I take a step toward him, as it's my only way out. He doesn't move, so now I'm much closer to him than I want to be.

"You can't trespass on people's property." His voice is gravelly enough to ignite a fire in me.

Trying to hold my ground, I break into a manic laugh. By the look on his face, he's surprised by the big sound that comes out of me.

"Are you worried I'm going to steal your wood?" I ask.

"It doesn't matter. You're on my land without permission."

"I'm done with this conversation." I let go of the hem of my shirt and try to get around his protruding elbows.

"I saw you poking around the Berglands' place. What are you doing here?" He lifts the cap off his head, wipes his forehead with the back of his hand, and then runs his long fingers through his sandy-blond hair. Then his eyes dart up to meet mine.

I cringe at the recognition. Jake Abram. His eyes are large and turquoise, the color of the Sea of Sardinia, which I was lucky enough to visit once with my family. The most unique eyes I've ever seen. I haven't looked into them in person since I was eight years old when I attended his high school graduation with my family.

"Sunny and Sis Bergland are my grandparents," I concede finally. "I'm Camilla Bergland."

He furrows his brow and takes a step closer to me. A look of amusement comes over his face. "The only granddaughter of Sunny and Sis is still a child. I remember her."

"A funny thing happens as time passes," I drawl, rolling my eyes. "People get older. I assure you I'm their granddaughter. My parents are Rob and Ellen, and my older brother is Robby."

He puts his hand up to his chin and nods. "I remember Robby, but you don't look like his sister."

Jake had meant more to me than I had meant to him. I knew it then and I know it now. He still doesn't seem to place me. Jake is the oldest of the three Abram kids. Robby, my cousins, and I grew up playing with him and his siblings in the summers because their grandparents had the cottage next to ours. Jake was my first crush. I was his shadow for years, right up until he got his license and became too cool to hang out with us kids.

At his graduation, I told Robby that I would marry Jake someday. Sure, eight is young to have such thoughts, but I've never followed societal rules.

To embarrass me, like only an older brother knows how to do, Robby marched me over to Jake and told him that I wanted a picture with him. I don't always remember what people say, but I remember how they make me feel. When Jake agreed, Robby grabbed a disposable camera off one of the tables. Jake stood behind me and put his hands on my shoulders. I'm sure my face was crimson and my heart was visible through my chest. I wonder if that picture still exists.

I yank off my White Sox cap and wipe my brow. My golden curls blow in the breeze. His forehead wrinkles as a look of recognition spreads across his face.

"Although it has been great reminiscing, I have to get going," I say as I pull my cap on and start walking away.

"Be on your way, City Girl."

*City Girl.* I stop and turn to him. "You do remember me then?"

He seems to have no concept of personal boundaries. As he steps closer, I need to strain my neck to look up at him. His lips pucker as he appears in deep thought. His eyes survey every inch of me.

"I guess Sunny and Sis's granddaughter filled out."

I gasp. Before I have a chance to stop myself, I shove his arm. "You're disgusting."

He grabs my wrist to stop me from pushing him again, and I know that if he wanted to, he could hurt me with one slight twist. His fingers are so long that he could probably wrap them around my wrist one more time. When he squeezes, a stare-off ensues.

He lets go of my wrist. I stick up my middle finger, turn back, and stalk down the gravel road. His laugh continues as I walk away. That is not the Jake Abram who let me follow him around everywhere, the one who sat on the floor and played dolls with me and let me take a picture with him at his high school graduation. That boy was kind and considerate. The man he has become is anything but.

# CHAPTER 2

Anger seeps out of me as I drive back to town. It's safe to say that this wasn't how I had hoped my arrival in Wheaton would happen. I wasn't expecting anyone to roll out the red carpet for me, but I also wasn't expecting that kind of interaction. Everyone from this town has always been so nice, and if my memory is correct, Jake used to be a fairly decent guy too.

I pull into the driveway of my grandparents' house on Main Street. They rise from their lawn chairs the moment they see me. Smiles spread across their faces as they approach. I'm struck by how much they've aged since I last saw them two years ago. Dad had flown them down to Chicago a few days after my college graduation from the Savannah College of Art and Design, where I received my degree in interior design, and they spent two weeks with us. After, on a hot June day, we all went to the airport together so my parents could fly back to Wheaton with my grandparents and I could fly to Cambodia to start my two-year stint in the Peace Corps.

My parents had expected me to jump into the workforce after they funded my private education, and although I felt the pressure from them, I didn't want to settle down. Not yet. The Peace Corps would allow me to see more of the world, gain some design inspiration, and mostly feed my feelings of wanderlust. Yes, my friends from Savannah College were landing their dream internships and talking about where to live next, but the idea of being tied down to a career that would keep me in one place made me want to hyperventilate. The longer I resisted jumping into a career, the more I could remain free.

My grandparents had cried after we cleared security, knowing that they wouldn't see me for a while. I brushed those feelings aside and didn't let myself think about how far I was going and how old they were getting. Instead, I let myself get excited about my new adventure. I do recall walking to my gate and praying that this wouldn't be the last time I would get to hug my grandparents.

What feels worse is the fact that I haven't been to Wheaton in seven years. The last time I was here, I was seventeen, living in Washington, DC, and at the height of my teenage angst. I spent three weeks scrolling through my phone and sulking. After that trip, I started college and I never made it back to Wheaton. My parents would fly my grandparents to Chicago, where I would meet them following a flight from Savannah. I loved seeing them and I loved that they came to me. Now, finally, I would be coming back to them.

I run over to Grandma Sis first. Her arms are already stretched out to me. I wrap my arms around her tiny frame as she smiles against my face.

"Oh, Camilla," she says. "We've been so lonesome for you."

"Hi, Grandma. I missed you too." I place a kiss on her smiling cheek as her soft and wrinkly hand wraps in mine.

Grandma Sis remains the most stylish person I've ever known. Today she wears straight-legged black slacks, a red patent-leather belt, and a tucked-in white blouse. Sis has always been my style icon.

With my hand still swathed in my grandma's, I lean over to put my other arm around Grandpa. Sunny, who awaits my embrace. Even though it's a warm, sunny day, Grandpa wears his flannel Pendleton shirt. As I bury my face into his neck, the circular tin of his snuff pokes me through his front pocket. The air around him smells of the mint-flavored snuff he always carries.

My grandpa speaks through his smile. "My little Cammy, how was your trip? Are you hungry? What can I help you carry in?"

Grandpa and Grandma stare at me with anticipation. Their faces are the windows into how much time has passed—each wrinkle a year I didn't see them, each crease a representation of the time that has passed with only phone calls and letters. Regret floods over me at how much time I can never get back.

Grandpa Sunny's hand rests on my shoulder as I pop the trunk open to where all my belongings for the summer reside. I pull my two suitcases out, place them on the ground, and wave off my grandpa as he tries to take one of them. My grandparents lead me through the backyard, where we enter the house through the back door. The siding is brand-new, I notice, finding myself grateful that my dad and Uncle Larry have taken such good care of Grandma and Grandpa from afar.

Even though I haven't been here in seven years, everything in the house looks and smells how I remember. With the windows wide open, the aroma of the lilac bushes bursts through the kitchen window. The inside of the house wafts with the scent of mint from the jar of candy my grandparents keep on top of the refrigerator.

The blue carpet that used to look so vibrant is faded as it stretches beyond the dining room and into the living room. There are waves in the carpet, as it should have been replaced a decade ago. I worry about my grandparents tripping over the unevenness of it. The walls are lined with hanging frames full of memories of my grandparents in their younger years as they raised their two boys in this house.

As a child, I hated when it was time to leave Sunny and Sis. I hated leaving all these memories collected over a lifetime. All in one place. My dad's room growing up. Uncle Larry's. Pictures of them as a family in the house. I've never had anything like that in my life.

"Cammy." Grandpa puts his hand on my shoulder. "We thought you would be hungry after a long trip. I went down to the café and got some chicken and potatoes."

I stretch my arms out in a yawn and try to hide my surprise that we aren't having a home-cooked meal. In all the times I've visited my grandparents, Grandma always did the cooking. I can't remember ever eating out.

"That sounds great. Thanks, Grandpa."

I move my suitcases out of the way as my grandpa takes the food out of the paper wrapping.

Grandma takes my hand in hers. Her hand feels so small. Sunspots darken her pale skin. "Camilla, where do you live now?"

My grandpa's eyes dart to mine, and then he looks down and continues putting food on the plates.

"I flew in from Cambodia a few days ago and stayed at my parents'."

I know that isn't really an answer. Where do I live now? It's a great question. My belongings are in my two suitcases on the floor, so perhaps this is my home. I do have some items back at my parents' loft in Chicago, but that doesn't feel like home.

"Oh, Camilla, you've moved so far away. Why Cambodia, of all places?"

I recognize this as part of what my parents explained to me back in Chicago. Grandma gets confused sometimes. I put my other hand on hers, squeeze, and feel the skin that loosely hangs. "I'm here now, Grandma."

Grandpa puts my food on a plate. "Have you been in Cambodia since you graduated from college?"

"I have." I smile as I cut up my chicken. "I did come back to Chicago for a couple of weeks last summer to see Mom, Dad, and Robby."

Grandpa shakes his head but smiles at me. "You were never one to stay put, were you?"

As Grandma chews her food, she turns to me and speaks with her mouth still full. "Your hair isn't the only reason I call you my wild child, Camilla."

"I guess I want to see as much of the world as possible before I find the place that suits me best."

"You kids have freedoms we never had when we were your age," Grandpa Sunny says before he bites down on his biscuit.

After dinner, Grandpa shows me to my room. It's the large bedroom in the front of the house overlooking Main Street from the second floor. It was Uncle Larry's room as a kid. We called it the green room because of the bright green carpet. My dad had the room in the back of the house, called the orange room because of the carpet. Every bedroom in the house had its own color of carpet and its own personality to match. We called my grandparents' room the red room. All of those carpets were replaced years ago, but the names remain.

The room seemed so big back then, but now that I'm here, I see that it's nothing more than two twin beds with a nightstand between them. The walls are decorated with busy-patterned wallpaper and a framed painting of two ballerinas. It smells the same.

How is it that every house has its own scent that carries every memory? If I close my eyes, I can picture Robby as a child propped up on his elbow as we talked late into the evening.

"I hope this room will be fine for you." Grandpa watches me take it all in. His eyes look tired. The fine wrinkles that used to be subtle have grown with depth.

"This room is perfect. Thank you."

Relief floods his face. "Great. I'll let you get settled, but I thought we'd have ice cream for dessert. I'm hoping vanilla with chocolate syrup is still your favorite."

"That sounds great. I'll be right down."

I watch as he leaves. The stairs groan as he descends. I look down at my suitcases and decide to wait until tomorrow to put my clothes away for the summer. I'm tired, my bones ache from the long drive, and I still feel a bit jet-lagged, seeing that this is only my fourth day on this side of the world. I look into the mirror and run a finger through my long and unruly curls.

It was such a last-minute decision that I would be the one to spend the summer in Wheaton. My parents were here for two weeks in late April, and they offered to come for two more weeks over the summer, but they also wanted to go on a trip with friends to Paris. Uncle Larry and Aunt Diane couldn't get away from their jobs until late summer, so the entire family looked to me. I jumped at the opportunity.

My only stipulation for coming was that Robby had to promise to join me for a few days at some point.

I won't deny the relief on my parents' faces that they could go on their trip to Paris and then visit in the late summer when Uncle Larry and Aunt Diane will arrive. And I was more than happy to come here instead of spending the summer at Mom and Dad's downtown Chicago loft, with them pressuring me to figure out what's next for me. I've missed my grandparents and felt a strong desire to see them. Being here also forces me to face so much of what I've been avoiding—the reality that they are getting older and not as capable as they once were and that I'm going to lose them eventually. I'm a strong person, but I don't think I'll recover from losing Sunny or Sis. Or, for that matter, losing anyone I love. Robby always tells me that I avoid letting people in because I fear loss. I wouldn't go that far. However, I have created a cocoon of self-reliance around my life, and I like it this way.

The door to my grandparents' room is closed, and I hear a bed creak, so I tiptoe down the stairs. There's a noise in the kitchen. Grandpa's back is turned to me as he scoops ice cream into two bowls. He pours chocolate syrup over the ice cream and then grabs spoons.

"There you are. Let's go sit on the sunporch."

Grandpa Sunny hands me a bowl. I follow him out to the porch, where we take a seat on a wicker couch overlooking Main Street. My first bite of the ice cream is cold on my tongue. Ice cream was always my thing with my grandparents. I've never enjoyed it as much in anyone else's company. On the occasions when we didn't have ice cream in the house, my grandparents would send me with their orders to the ice cream parlor down the street. Grandma always wanted chocolate, and Grandpa always wanted crème de mint.

"Look at all the traffic tonight, Cammy."

Grandpa and I watch the street where one car drives by and then another. I think about how different life is in this small town.

"How is Grandma doing?"

The metal of his spoon clinks as it hits his empty bowl. He puts it down on the wicker table in front of us. "Sis has been confused lately. The doctors say it's only going to get worse, but she has good days too."

"Well, I'm happy to be here with you and Grandma."

"Dear, we are so happy to have you here. We have missed you terribly. We love the letters and pictures you send, but it doesn't replace getting to touch you."

We lean back and prop our feet on the wicker table and stare out the window in silence. We have no lights on in the porch, but every time a car drives by, the headlights illuminate the room, if only for a moment.

"I forgot to tell you." I look at my grandpa. "I stopped at the lake cottage before coming here."

His sigh is long and heavy. "Your grandma and I haven't been out there in quite some time."

"The lawn looks taken care of, but the cottage needs some work."

Grandpa pats my knee and slowly stands up. I give him an extra push to help.

"That cottage used to be one of the best things in our lives," he says. "It makes us sad to see the state it's in."

I grab our bowls and stand. "Maybe it could be restored."

"With the money that your dad and Larry insist on sending us, we have some of the funds. What we don't have is the energy to fix it up just to watch it all go downhill again." He takes my hand and leads me out of the porch. "With your dad and Larry living so far away and with us getting older, we just can't do the upkeep."

"I understand, Grandpa. Hey, I've been meaning to tell you."

He pauses.

"I ran into Jake Abram. Does he live out there?"

Grandpa Sunny looks contemplative as he loops his fingers in his jeans. "He does. When Jake moved back to Wheaton, he wanted to fix up his grandparents' place, but it was too far gone. He tore it down, built a beautiful log home, and has created a nice life here."

*Moved back from where?* I wonder. I also don't recall hearing that Oscar and Eleanor, Jake's grandparents, had passed away. They were my grandparents' best friends.

I reach out and wrap my arms around Grandpa's neck. "Thanks, Grandpa. It's past your bedtime. Get to bed. I'll be up soon."

His shoulders rise as he takes a breath. He smiles, but his face looks so tired. He clutches my shoulder and nods toward the stairs that lead to the three bedrooms.

"I'll see you in the morning." Grandpa Sunny leans down and kisses me on the cheek. Then he makes his way toward the stairs.

It's only eight in the evening. I can't remember the last time I've gone to bed this early, but I drove nearly nine hours today and feel like a good night's sleep is what I need. Upstairs, I open the window of what will be my bedroom for the next three months. As I lie in bed and feel the warm breeze come in through the windows, I hear the cars that cruise Main Street. I'll enjoy falling asleep to this sound each night.

Before I shut my eyes, I decide to text Robby.

*Hopefully, you received my earlier text that I got here safely. (Is it really that hard to text back?) All is well in Wheaton. Grandpa and Grandma seem pretty good. I drove out to the cottage too. It's in terrible shape. Makes me sad. Do you remember the Abrams? Yeah, well, I ran into Jake. Remember him? The oldest. We went to his high school graduation. Anyway, he grew up to be a JERK. And by the way, I haven't forgotten your promise of coming here to visit. MAKE IT HAPPEN. I can't be in Wheaton all summer without you. And yes, I realize it's only 8:30, but I'm going to bed.*

# CHAPTER 3

A lthough the house is silent, I sense that I'm the only one still lying in bed. It's been so long since I've lived with others and felt energy apart from my own in a house. I peek outside of my bedroom and see that my grandparents' door is open and their bed is made. I tiptoe into the bathroom and take a shower. After, I go downstairs to find my grandparents.

Sun pours into the large picture window in the living room, illuminating Grandma's face as she stares at the wall, her eyes glossed over. Her gaze cuts to mine. "Camilla, honey, I hope we didn't wake you." She tries to push up from the plush blue chair but then falls back.

I place my hand on her cheek, warm from the morning sun. "You didn't wake me. I had plenty of sleep."

Her face lights up as an idea comes to her. She gets out of the chair and claps her hands together. "Do you still drink tea? I think I put the kettle on."

"Tea sounds great."

We go to the kitchen, where I plan to take the kettle off the burner just before it starts screaming. But when we get there, I see that the kettle is in the sink and the faucet is still running. Water pools out of the kettle.

"That's odd," Grandma says. "I'm sure I put it on the burner. I bet Sunny came in here and removed it."

I run a cloth over the kettle's bottom to dry it and put it on the burner. Grandma Sis first introduced me to tea when I was a young girl. She only drinks black tea, so that's all I drink when I'm with her. We would sit at this table in the mornings while everyone else was off and doing things, and we would plan out our day. Sis would still have her hair full of rollers but would be impeccably dressed and ready to take on the day.

When I agreed to come to Wheaton, my parents sat me down and warned me about how far Grandma's ailment had progressed. Dad always calls it her "ailment," or sometimes it's her "condition." The word of what Grandma faces seems too harsh to put out into the universe, so we rarely utter it as a family. My mom is 100 percent Italian, the granddaughter of immigrants who came here seeking new opportunities. She's one of the most direct communicators I've ever known, and I love that about her. However, my dad is 100 percent Norwegian, and he prefers a more passive approach to communication. Since Grandma Sis is his mom, he wins the argument when it comes to what to call Grandma Sis's condition.

"Camilla, the whole town knows you're here because it's all Sunny has talked about at morning coffee. There was also an article about you in the *Wheaton Happenings*."

I put my hand up to my mouth and laugh. Robby and I always used to think we were royalty because the news of our visits always would be in the *Wheaton Happenings*. It only took me a few years to realize that everyone who visited made the paper, but it still made me feel special to see my name in print.

My grandpa shuffles toward us, his legs too tired to lift his feet completely. "Look at this. My ladies having tea, just like the old days." He leans over and kisses Grandma on her cheek.

Grandma places her hand on his and smiles into his kiss.

My grandparents celebrated their sixtieth anniversary a few months ago. My parents and Robby came to Wheaton for the long weekend, as did Uncle Larry, Aunt Diane, and my cousins, Liam and David. I couldn't leave Cambodia for such a short trip, so I was the only family member missing. It wasn't the first time that everyone had gathered except me.

My grandparents met in Wheaton as school children and dated all through high school. The summer after their high school graduation, they got married and used all their savings from working odd jobs as teenagers for a down payment on this house. I can't imagine having a history with someone that expands sixty years.

"Cammy, it's up to you what you do today," Grandpa says, "but I like to be at the café by eight thirty for coffee, and I know my friends would love to see you. Our friend Annie comes to visit your grandmother every morning. The two of them cross-stitch and knit."

Grandma swats Grandpa in the shoulder. "Oh, we do more than that, Sunny."

Grandpa's lips turn up in a smile as his face reddens. "Yes, they also gossip and solve all the problems of Wheaton, and sometimes even the world."

I grab the empty teacups from the table. "Well, Grandpa, I never turn down a coffee date. Let me throw some clothes on."

As my grandpa looks at me, he's probably thinking the same thing I am: that as a child and teenager, I always turned down going to the café. He would ask me every day. He would tell me that his friends would love to see me, but I was always too busy or too tired. Why can't we know what we're gifted with when we have it?

Before I head upstairs, there's a knock at the door and then footsteps in the mudroom. "I'm here, Sis and Sunny."

In walks Annie, who is larger than life, just as I remember. Even though she's pushing eighty, like my grandparents, she dyes her hair fire-engine red and wears a full face of makeup. Annie went to school with my grandparents. She has been their best friend ever since grade school. She married a few times, but none ever worked out and none resulted in children. When I was young and visiting Wheaton, she was part of every gathering. I always considered her a favorite aunt, even though we aren't related. She lives on a farm outside of town. Grandpa says she's the richest farmer in the county, and maybe even the state.

I jump up and wrap my arms around her.

She plants a kiss on the top of my head. "I've missed you, Camilla. Welcome home." Her makeup is impeccable, I notice, though now it settles more into the cracks of her face than it used to.

"I've missed you, Annie. It sounds like Grandpa and I are going to get coffee, and you and Grandma are going to solve the world's problems."

"Welcome to the life of old people, honey. This is our daily routine, and it rarely changes."

I chuckle at the sight of Grandpa looking at his watch as he stands by the door. "Sorry, Grandpa. I'll be ready in five minutes."

Annie pulls me in for another hug before I run upstairs to put clothes on. "I suggest you find some kids your age to hang out with while you're here, or it'll be the boredom that kills you before summer's end."

\*\*\*\*\*

Grandpa and I walk down Main Street with my arm entwined with his. We pass by the gas station he used to manage when he and Grandma raised my dad and Uncle Larry. I used to think Main Street felt larger than life, with the department store, grocery, theater, and all the other storefronts that made this town. But now there are so many vacant stores as we walk. A few of the staples still exist, like the bakery. The smell of fresh bread and doughnuts seeps out onto the sidewalk. The liquor store is still there and the pool hall where we used to go as kids with Dad and Grandpa. The shop owners are busy sweeping the sidewalks outside the stores that are about to open. They greet us as we pass.

On the corner at the end of downtown is the café. A handful of trucks are parked out front. Grandpa holds the door open for me, and I'm met with the smell of coffee and maple syrup. Everyone looks up from their newspapers and discussions to look at Grandpa and me.

"Over here, Sunny. I saved you and this beauty a seat."

Grandpa smiles. We make our way to a table where three men about his age look anxious for us to join them.

"Camilla, I would like to reintroduce you to some buddies of mine, as it's been a while." He gestures at the men staring at us. "This is Walt here and then Juan, and over there is Lawson."

I assess my grandpa's friends and remember them immediately. They were always popping by the cottage and fishing with Grandpa. "The four musketeers," I called them. Walt is a thin man with a gut. He wears a pair of rainbow suspenders holding his jeans up, and when he smiles, it lights up the room. Juan has pale yellow hair, not one of them gray. People pay big bucks at the salon for that color. I laugh inside as I admire Lawson's all-gray tracksuit. He keeps his long hair braided down his back, mostly brown still with a few white strands throughout.

I stick my hand up in a nervous wave as my grandpa scoots a chair over to me. "It's so nice to see you guys."

Walt speaks first. "Oh, Camilla, you were just wee big the last time we saw you." He holds out his hand to show me. "You visiting Wheaton is all Sunny has talked about."

Juan leans over and places a kiss on the top of my hand. "What Sunny didn't tell us is how beautiful you are. You look just like Sis did at your age."

"Ah, thank you."

My grandma was a beauty. When I was young, I would spend so much time looking through pictures and albums of her. Grandma's parents moved to the United States from Norway when she was a young girl to join other family members that had moved here. By the time Grandma was five, they had settled in Wheaton. My grandma's real name is Signe, but I can't remember the last time I've heard anyone call her that. To everyone in her life, she's Sis.

Grandpa's family also moved here from Norway. His real name is Sven, but I've only ever heard him called Sunny. He says he got the name as a young boy when he was fishing on Lake Traverse with his buddies and caught five sunfish in a row, which isn't that common. I wonder if their names were changed through the years because immigrants are always trying to find a way to appear more American. Either way, my Scandinavian grandparents are Sunny and Sis to everyone who knows them.

Lawson brings me back to the present. "People at the reservation say the fish are biting at the south dam. I may go with some crawlers and see if I have any luck."

"Do you live on the reservation, Lawson?" I interject.

"No, dear. Georgia and I moved off shortly after we were married, but many of my family is still there, and people on the res know how to catch fish."

The Lake Traverse Dakota Reservation lies on the South Dakota side of the lake. As a kid, I loved hearing about the Native Americans, their history, and their traditions. Wheaton is a unique small town in that it has always been a melting pot of different cultures and people. It has always had a large Native population, but during the civil rights movement of the sixties, it also gained a large Black population. It's a smorgasbord of people and ways of thinking, and from the outside looking in, it seems to work.

"That's the stupidest thing I've heard all morning, Lawson." Juan puts his hand on the table. "You need to go to the bait shop and get yourself some leeches. That's the only way you'll catch any fish at the south dam."

"Ope," my grandpa says. "I hear people are having a lot of luck at the dam with minnows. You may want to try those."

Walt leans into us and speaks while his eyes roam the room to make sure no one else is paying attention. "I think we'd have more luck in the boat. I hear people are catching their limit of walleye at Skunk Island. Anyone up for a fishing trip this afternoon?"

Grandpa takes a drink of his coffee and shakes his head. "Not today, boys. I'm going to help Camilla get settled."

Crumbs fly out of Lawson's mouth as he speaks. "I'll be at the south dam with my crawlers, and anyone can join me."

Juan puts his fist on the table, trying to look tough. "I'll meet you at the dam with my leeches, and we can see who catches more fish."

Lawson and Juan have a stare-off as the rest of us watch it unfold.

Walt puts his hand up for a check. "You're all the most stubborn men I've ever known."

Juan once again kisses the top of my hand and then puts his hand up for a check as well. I can't imagine having the same friends my entire life. As much as my family moved around, I was never afforded long-term friendships.

"I promise I'll get in the boat with you soon." Grandpa puts his hand up for a check, and before I know it, we're walking back down Main Street toward their home.

A white truck passes by and slows in front of us. The man takes his hat off and tips it at us. "Hi, Sunny."

Grandpa's face lights up. "Hi there, Jake."

I groan at this latest evidence of the law of life. The moment I don't want to see someone, that's the exact person I won't be able to get away from. Jake glances in my direction before continuing by.

"Do you and Grandma want to drive out and see the cottage with me today?" I ask.

"Oh, Cammy, we'd like to, but the last time we went, it upset Sis too much." He gives me a heavy look. "I just don't know how to keep it running while also taking care of our house in town."

"Grandpa." I pause as I look at him. "Do you mind if I do some projects on it this summer?"

He shrugs. "Help yourself, but I think it's a waste of your time."

We walk in silence for a bit longer, arms wrapped in each other's, in no hurry.

"You're going to have a lot of free time here, you'll realize," he says after a time. "We keep to a tight schedule. I hope you don't get bored."

"I promise I won't get bored. I'm so happy to be here with you and Grandma."

And although I've only been here for a day, I am indeed happy. For whatever reason, I'm not focused on what's next. I'm in the present, enjoying this walk down Main Street with my grandpa and loving the simplicity of life in Wheaton.

We get back to the house to find Annie and Grandma sitting on the front porch with their yarn out. They're probably on their third cup of tea by now. Grandma's eyes light up when she sees us, but I know that most of her happiness is meant for Grandpa. I imagine that he feels like the safest thing in the world as her brain continues to fail her.

Annie drops what she's doing and packs up her knitting materials. "Well, I'll leave now but I'll be back after dinner." She pats my hand and kisses my grandma on her cheek. I'm starting to get the impression that Annie is part babysitter and all friend.

"You don't have to come back, Annie," I say. "I can help out tonight."

Annie takes my arm and winks at me. "Tonight, you and your grandpa are shooting pool."

# CHAPTER 4

I've never witnessed such punctuality, but at five in the evening, there's a knock at the door and then footsteps.

"Sis, Sunny, I'm here," Annie's voice rings out from the back door.

Between the whistle that blows twice a day for the farmers—at noon and six o'clock at night—and the visits from Annie every day at eight thirty and five, I may never need to look at my watch this summer.

"Cammy, you and I need to make up for lost time, so I thought I'd take you on a date tonight." My grandpa's expectant eyes look at me.

"Grandpa, I'm happy to stay in," I say. "We could play cards or see if there's a baseball game on."

Annie coughs and speaks into my ear. "Your grandpa needs to get out of the house."

"Never mind," I say. "I'll get changed and be right down."

I change clothes in my newly organized room that I worked on all afternoon. Almost every piece of clothing I own hangs neatly in the closet. I hadn't considered that Grandpa needed to get out, but I can imagine the routine gets boring. So much of what he does is to take care of Grandma Sis. I wouldn't have thought that taking me to the pool hall would be such a highlight for him.

Annie and my grandma are already in the living room having a conversation about what to watch tonight as I come downstairs, ready to go. Grandpa has changed into a fresh Pendleton shirt and clean jeans. He leans in to kiss the top of Grandma's head. No one notices me as I take out my phone and snap a photo, wanting always to remember this moment.

"You clean up nicely, Grandpa."

He tucks in his shirt and admires his outfit. "You too, Cammy. Every man in the pool hall will be envious of me."

When I travel, one of my favorite things is finding the biggest dive bar off the beaten path, sidling up to the bar, and getting to know the people and their stories. Most of the cities my dad's job took us to were large and sprawling, but I always gravitated more toward the small towns and how at peace I felt in them. My personality has always been too laidback to love the hustle and bustle of a city, but I've never quite found the small town that has suited me either.

We walk down Main Street, where the pool hall sits about halfway down the first block. We enter, and the smell of stale cigarette smoke flies in my face. It has been illegal to smoke indoors for a while here, but they would have to tear this building down and rebuild it to get rid of the smoky, pungent smell. My feet stick to the floor as I walk—decades of spilled beer stuck to the wood, a permanent fixture that couldn't be removed even if someone scrubbed the floor twice a day.

It takes a moment for my eyes to adjust because of the high sun outside and the dark, dingy space inside. I squint and blink, and finally, everything comes into focus. Every single pair of eyes is looking at my grandpa and me.

The bar is surrounded by stools full of people chatting with the bartender and one another. Square tables line the rest of the pool hall, with an opening that leads to a room with the pool tables and arcade games. When I scan the room, it doesn't take me long to spot the rude Jake Abram. He's in a chair facing me, but the other three at his table have to strain their necks to observe me.

"Let's go to the bar, and I'll get us both a beer," Grandpa says. He puts his hand on my back and guides me toward the bartender, who's already anticipating us.

"Hi there, Ron," Grandpa says to the bartender. "My granddaughter and I will both have a light beer, please."

The bartender puts two napkins down, followed by two bottles of beer that drip with condensation.

"How's Sis doing, Sunny?" Ron says from behind the bar.

"She's great. She and Annie are back at the house tonight."

Ron nods as Grandpa hands him money. "Here's five dollars, Ron. You can keep the change."

We go through the narrow entrance where the room expands and the pool tables come into sight. The place is just as I remember it. There are four worn pool tables and a few arcade games pressed against the wall. A popcorn machine stands in the corner, making the room smell like salty, burnt popcorn. When my parents would take Robby and me here as kids, they would sit in the other room where the bar is. Whenever Aunt Diane and Uncle Larry were in town with my cousins, Liam and David, it was even more special. We felt so grown-up getting to play in a real pool hall.

It's loud in the room. A foursome plays pool at the farthest table, and a couple of teenage boys play the arcade games. The sound of the arcade bounces off the walls.

Jake approaches us. "Hey, Sunny. How are you?" He reaches his hand out and shakes Grandpa's hand. There's tenderness as he places his other hand on Grandpa's arm.

"Hey there, Jake. I don't know if you remember my granddaughter, but this here is Cammy. She's staying the summer with Sis and me." Grandpa wraps his arm around my shoulders.

"Camilla," I interject. There's only one person in this world that I allow to call me Cammy, and it's Grandpa Sunny.

Jake smiles so big I can see nearly every one of his teeth. He sticks his hand out in an exaggerated manner. "Hello. Welcome back to Wheaton. I read in *Wheaton Happenings* that it's your first trip back in seven years."

He looks back at my grandpa while still holding my comparatively small hand. His are rough and calloused. Mine disappears in his grip.

"Camilla and I ran into each other yesterday at the cottage," he tells Grandpa. When his eyes lock with mine, I'm tempted to slap the smugness off his face.

Grandpa is oblivious to my tense body and Jake's mocking tone. "I'm so happy you two have become reacquainted."

The two of them start talking, and I lean against the wall and observe. Jake towers over my grandpa. It's clear that they're fond of each other. Jake has cleaned up a lot from when I saw him before and has shaved his stubble. By some people's standards, he may be considered good-looking. He's insanely tall, his turquoise eyes are some sort of beautiful, and he either works out or does manual labor because his shoulders are broad and his muscles are visible through his clothes. His tattoo peeks out from below his shirtsleeve. Too bad his personality makes him so repulsive.

Handsome or not, tall and muscly has never been my type. I think it's because I've done so much traveling alone as a woman who's on the petite side. Not that I'm easily pushed around, but big men have always intimidated me. The men I've dated have been less overwhelmingly large, which has helped

me not to feel extraordinarily small. I always gravi-
tate toward worldly intellectuals who can talk about
how European colonization in Southeast Asia greatly
affected the economic and cultural environment.
Someone who reads and can discuss a good book
with me. Not muscly brutes.

My memory is oddly specific as I think about
my ex-boyfriend Leif, with his long dreadlocks and
cutoff jorts, a combination of jeans and shorts. I
can still picture his dirty toes sticking out through
his Chacos, his backpack nearly as big as him as we
wandered all over Europe a couple of summers back.
I met him at a hostel in Amsterdam called the Last
Watering Hole. And it was. It had one large room
over a bar with twenty sets of bunk beds. He and I
both had the misfortune of having top bunks, though
we were right next to each other.

The bar under the hostel had live music every
night, so there was very little sleep to be had. We
talked and realized that we were planning to travel a
similar route through Europe, so we decided to do it
together. He was a hippie type from Newfoundland.
We ended up spending the next few weeks together
traveling through eleven countries.

Near the end of the trip, he told me he loved
me and asked me to come back to Canada with him.
I didn't even need to consider it. Leif was fun, but it
wasn't love for me, and I don't believe it was for him
either. When I told him no, he said he couldn't be
around me if I didn't feel the same way. He continued
heading east through Europe, and I went west toward

home. We could have continued having a great time, but Leif went and messed everything up. Why can't men be satisfied with casual?

Jake doesn't strike me as someone who could have a real conversation, and his muscles intimidate me more than they attract me. And as short as I am, I never consider a man attractive if he's several inches over six feet. If I could go back, I would tell my eight-year-old self that Jake wasn't the right person to have a crush on and that he isn't the man I'll marry someday. What do eight-year-olds know, anyway?

My grandpa pulls up his jeans and then pats his pockets. "I need to go and get quarters. I'll be right back, you two."

Grandpa pulls a few wrinkled dollar bills out of his pocket and walks to the bar. I avoid looking at Jake but can sense his sneer.

"Hey there, City Girl. I didn't think I'd have the pleasure of seeing you again so soon." He lowers his gaze and brings his hand up to his chin. "I'm curious, do you always flick off people when meeting them?"

I roll my eyes as his smirk continues to grow. "You were rude first."

His laugh is gruff as he throws his head back. "You'll find that people in Wheaton aren't very trusting of new people."

"Must be hard to get to know new people if you greet them like you did." I assault my cue stick with the blue chalk. "I haven't seen you since your high school graduation. Did you ever go to college and make something of yourself?"

"Something like that." The cocky smile leaves his face. He picks up a cue ball, tosses it in the air, and catches it with a smack. "I guess I didn't place you at first because you haven't visited your grandparents in nearly a decade."

The heat starts in my belly and spreads across my chest and face. I ball my fists and try to keep them at my side. "Hopefully, you and I can avoid each other while I'm here."

Jake laughs again. "Three thousand people live in this town. I think avoidance will be difficult."

"Then if we do see each other, ignore me."

"Ignoring you won't be too hard," Jake says as he steps closer to me. "I could practically fold you up and put you in my pocket."

I didn't think I could feel more anger, but now I'm sure my heart is going to crack my sternum as it beats against my chest wall. Heat floods my face.

"Is this what you do on a Friday night in Wheaton?" I lean against my cue stick. "Hang out at the local watering hole and get drunk off Boone's Farm?"

Jake's face becomes a shade darker. "Says the girl who's shooting pool with her grandpa on a Friday night."

"Yeah." I throw up my arms, and the cue stick falls to the sticky floor with a thump. "But I'm here visiting. This isn't my everyday life."

"So you're better than me?" The words trickle from his mouth.

"Obviously." I take a step closer. "And not because I don't live in Wheaton, but because I don't go around being rude to people."

Each insult fuels the fire, each offense spoken more quietly until we're whispering. We keep stepping toward each other until we can't get closer. Jake smells like sandalwood soap. Our faces are red. He looks at me like he's never liked anyone less, and I feel the same way about him.

He leans his hand on the pool table. "Perhaps Wheaton isn't big enough for both of us. Maybe you should go back to where you came from."

My neck aches from looking up at someone who's probably fifteen inches taller than me. "I think I'll extend my stay in Wheaton just to annoy you."

My grandpa's sliding feet approach us, the quarters jingling in his hand. "Jake, would you play a game of pool with Cammy and me? We'd love the company."

Jake's mouth opens, but before he has a chance to speak, I clear my throat. "Grandpa, Jake was telling me that he has to get back to his friends, as they have other plans for the evening. What a bummer for us." I shrug my shoulders as I look at Jake.

Grandpa nods, oblivious to how much I loathe this friend of his. "I understand. Next time, Jake. I don't get to see you enough."

Jake looks at me, and even though he scowls, his eyes have a sparkle in them. "Next time for sure, Sunny. It was so great to see you." He pats my grandpa on the shoulder, then steps away slowly. He looks back at me over his shoulder before he reaches the opening to the bar. The smirk is the last thing I see before he disappears into the other room.

*I've only been in Wheaton for a short time*, I think, *and I already have an enemy.*

Later that evening, I send Robby another text.

*Robby, remember me? Your sister who is in Wheaton all summer? And only because you PROMISED you'd visit too? My update for you. Grandpa Sunny seems in great health, but sometimes I catch Grandma Sis blankly staring at the wall. Annie comes every day, which helps a lot. Also, I want it on record that Jake Abram isn't just a jerk. He's an ASS. I don't let anyone under my skin, but he's under it. Wheaton isn't big enough for both of us. Write me back, or I'll tell Mom and Dad on you. J/k. But for real, text me!*

# CHAPTER 5

My eyes blink open as I smell something burning. I hope it's my imagination, but the stench is stronger when I open the door to my room. I race downstairs. A towel lies on the burner in the kitchen, orange and red flames flickering at its corner. My grandma looks small, pushed into the corner. Her hands cover her face. Grandpa reaches the kitchen right after I do.

I push the burning towel into the sink and turn on the faucet. Gray and black smoke starts filling the kitchen. I cover my mouth and cough, then rush over to the kitchen window and shove it open. I rest my hands on my knees and try to catch my breath. My heart skips a beat as it palpitates in my chest. There doesn't appear to be any damage, but this could have been so much worse. By the looks on my grandpa's and grandma's faces, they know it too.

Grandma lowers her hands from her face and wraps her arms around Grandpa. "What did I go and do now?" Her voice trembles.

Grandpa Sunny strokes her head as they embrace. "Oh, Sis, it was an accident. It looks like there was a kitchen towel on the stove."

I stand tall as my heart rate begins its return to normal. The two of them hug. My grandpa's back is to me. Grandma Sis wrinkles her eyes closed. Tears spill down her face. Grandma Sis is stuck in something that I imagine is like purgatory. She has enough awareness to realize that she's slipping away into a world where we're all strangers and nothing makes sense, but she has no control to turn back the clock. She's powerless over this disease, and she's cognizant enough to know it. She tries so hard to fight against time, but she's losing, and she's scared.

Grandpa leads her out of the room as I clean up the mess.

Annie is at the door. I give her the details of the last few minutes, and although my voice sounds calm, I feel anything but.

She embraces me, and her flaming red hair smells like a meadow of flowers. "Camilla, I'm afraid it's not good at all. I don't know how much longer Sunny can keep Sis and himself safe."

"I know," I say. "I'm worried about both of them. I don't know what they would do if you weren't here for them."

Annie pulls away and places her hand on my cheek. "You're here too. Don't forget that. The best thing you can do right now is go to coffee with Sunny and let Sis and me stay in our routine."

"I'm worried they won't be able to stay in this house for much longer," I confess.

"That's a real possibility," Annie says in a lowered voice. "Sunny's waiting. We can talk more when you're back."

After a morning of coffee with Sunny and his boys, where I do my best not to think about Sis almost burning down the house, I decide to drive out to the cottage. Gravity always pulls me out of town and toward Lake Traverse. Time stands still there. I can live in the present and not worry about what comes next. The lake reminds me that I'm a small part of this earth, and when I feel small, so do my problems.

I hear the lawnmower before I see it, but then it becomes visible on the side of the cottage. Jake doesn't see me. I glare as he rides the lawnmower in meticulous rows on the lawn. His jeans look out of place, as it's nearly ninety degrees today. His black T-shirt hangs from his back pocket, and his backward cap hides his hair. I try to look away, but instead, my eyes get stuck on his bronzed skin. Every inch of him comes together to create a kaleidoscope of symmetrical muscles, all perfectly in place.

I march over to him, and when he sees me, he turns off the lawnmower's engine.

"Now look who's trespassing." As soon as the words leave my mouth, I wish I could take them back. After all, he's here mowing my grandparents' lawn. My ears continue to hum even though the mower is off.

"Hey, City Girl, I'm happy to stop. Perhaps you can start mowing your grandparents' lawn yourself, and I can quit spending my time doing your family's work."

He steps off the riding mower and stands in front of me with his hands in his pockets. I curse to myself that I didn't get the Bergland height. What I lack in size, I try to make up for in personality. He takes his cap off and wipes his brow before placing it back on his head. I take a step back from him.

"Why are you mowing their lawn, anyway?"

Jake puckers his lips. "Because you've been gone for the past seven years."

"Why do you find it necessary to remind me that I'm not here a lot?" I ask through gritted teeth. "It's not my fault my dad got out of this town and raised his family elsewhere."

Contempt for each other pulls us closer. The sweat glistens on his chest. On his right shoulder is a defined scar that starts at his scapula and stops just short of his elbow. The scar is red, a victim of the fierce sun. It stands in contrast to his golden skin. I squint and try to get a better view of the tattoo covering it, in three horizontal lines, the cursive too small to read from where I stand.

"Because I continue having to do your work," Jake says.

I reach toward the scar on his shoulder without thinking. "What's this from?"

He brushes my hand away. "Where I'm from, we don't touch people without permission."

I bring my hand to my side, warm from where he just touched me. "So what happened to your shoulder? A work injury?"

"You are seriously asking me this?"

"Or did you trip and fall? Yes, that's it. You fell trying to protect your beloved woodpile from another intruder. Am I getting closer?"

Jake stares at me blankly.

"A lovers' quarrel gone wrong." I laugh, amused at myself. "Am I at least getting close?"

Jake shakes his head, unimpressed. "Everyone knows what happened to my shoulder."

"I'm not everyone." I cross my hands over my chest. "Forget it. I don't care what happened to your shoulder."

He turns on his heels and looks back at me as he yells, "I'm going to assume you don't know how to run a riding lawnmower. So if you don't mind, I'm going to finish mowing your grandparents' lawn."

I don't miss his emphasis on the word *your*. The truth is, none of us are helping Sunny and Sis enough. Sure, my dad and uncle send money for expenses, and now that my parents are back Stateside, they visit at least three times a year. But none of it's enough. I don't need the reminder.

Stubbornness has never been my most attractive trait, but I feel compelled not to let Jake get the last word in. Before he manages to start the mower again, I yell, "Was it a lawnmower accident? Is that what happened to your shoulder?"

I can't see his face, but his head shakes side to side, and his laugh echoes into the day. The lawnmower starts up again as I walk into the cottage.

When I was in town, thinking of the necessary projects the cottage needed, I felt hopeful that I could fix the place up. But now that I'm here, I'm overwhelmed by how much there is to do. It will take hours to clean the place, but even after it's clean, that doesn't solve the issue that the ceiling seems to be caving in and all the floorboards and drywall are rotten.

I get why this place makes Grandma sad. I barely recognize it anymore. It's not the happy place I used to come to as a child. I look at the table where Grandma and I would play card games for hours. My favorite was crazy eights. Grandma would play a few hands with me, but then she would always pull out the Parcheesi board. We would then move onto checkers.

Grandpa Sunny would sit in the rocking chair, going through his tackle box and talking to anyone who would listen about the best way to catch fish. "The Berglands don't need big and expensive boats. It's all about choosing the right bait and lures. And no one knows better than me." He would try to teach me how to rig a pole and tie off the line, but I was never interested in it back then.

My mom would be in the kitchen baking either cookies or a pie because every afternoon at three, it was pie and coffee time. She would take breaks and mow the lawn. She said it was her therapy. Dad would sit in the other rocking chair and read the *Wall*

49

*Street Journal*, front to back, not missing a word. And Robby, he would roam from person to person, deciding what activity he was most interested in. I can still feel the energy of those days.

I open the large window to let in the fresh air. Warm air that smells like sunshine and freshly cut grass mixes with the cottage's stale rottenness. I open the cleaning supplies I bought at the hardware store, but I don't know where to begin. I grab a pen and paper and start making a list of all of the things I need to do to get this place back into working order.

I also make a list of people I'll need to call. Who in town can fix a leaking roof? Will I need to replace Sheetrock? How much would replacing a floor cost? How do I make sure the toilet can be used? Whatever the answers, I love getting my hands dirty, and I'm confident that I can make some positive changes at the cottage.

I turn on the bathroom faucet, but as expected, nothing comes out. I'm guessing that the water hasn't been on out here in years. The shower has a large crack down the middle. When I was a kid, my dad would fuss with the pipes the moment we would arrive to the cottage. The water is from a well source, but at the end of the season, he would drain the pipes so they wouldn't freeze. I regret not watching him do it, as I have no idea how to turn the water on.

As I enter the great room, I see Jake standing at the table examining my list. I rush over and try to grab it out of his hand, but he holds it over his head, well out of my reach.

"This is a mighty big list." He looks down at it. "Do you have any idea what you're getting into here?" His smirk disappears when he sees my expression.

I stare at him and notice that his shirt is now on, covering his scar. "Give me the list."

Jake holds it high over his head again and looks around the place. "I haven't been inside this cottage for years. It's in worse shape than I realized." His words sting, but he's right.

I jump and reach for the list, but instead, I chest-bump him on my way down. I pull the chair out from under the table and stand on it. I'm just slightly taller than him standing on a chair, so this is the closest I've been to his eyes.

"Give me my list," I say under my breath.

Jake puts his arm down, glances at the list again, and places it in my hand. I breathe out and stay standing on the chair as I smooth out the piece of paper.

"I know it's none of my business, but what's your plan here? You're going to get this cottage fixed up, and then what? You'll go back home, no one will be here to maintain it, and it'll go downhill. I don't want to see Sunny and Sis get their hopes up."

"I don't want that either."

Jake's gaze beats into mine. "Cottages go downhill fast on Lake Traverse without the proper care. This lake can be harsh."

For the first time since becoming reacquainted with Jake, I see a glimmer of sincerity in his eyes. I don't fully understand his affection for my grandparents. I know Wheaton is a small town, and everyone knows every person, but it's like Jake has assumed a caretaker role for my grandparents as it relates to their cottage.

"I appreciate you mowing their lawn," I say, "but you have no right to question my motives here."

"It's not your motives I question. It's your follow-through. You don't seem like someone who understands all that's involved."

"I haven't thought everything through yet, but I have some ideas. None of this is your business, anyway."

Jake puts his hands under my arms and lifts me off the chair. He holds me at eye level with him for a moment as my legs dangle in the air.

I flail my legs like a crazy woman. "Put me down!"

Instead, he laughs. My face is so near his that I can see the golden blond stubble on his chin. His turquoise eyes are so close. He makes it seem like holding me is the easiest thing he's ever done. He grips me with his arms extended, holding me at a distance. I stretch my arms out and place them on his shoulders to balance myself. His body tenses at my touch. He puts my feet back on the ground.

I shove him in annoyance, but my push doesn't even cause this brute of a man to flinch.

He laughs again. "You clearly don't want my advice, City Girl, but I'm going to give you some, anyway. Don't spend time fixing anything until you get the roof sorted out first." He points at the water stains on the ceiling.

"Do you know how to fix a roof?" I shout, still out of breath from being held in the air.

"You can't afford me, kid." He purses his lips and hits the table next to me. I jump at the sound of it.

Jake doesn't say anything else as he walks out the door. The mower starts up again with a growl and a hum.

*He's so infuriating*, I think as I look at my list, not even sure where to start. I fold it up, put it in my back pocket, and head back to my grandparents' house. My phone beeps as I pull into the driveway. I read Robby's text.

*Jake Abram? Really, Cam? You do realize he's Wheaton's golden boy, right? And you do know that he played professional football? What rock have you been hiding under? I haven't forgotten my promise. I'll start looking at flights. Although I don't think I should defend your honor by fighting Jake. I mentioned he played professional football, right? Love you, Cam!*

I reply,

*Do you know how many football games I've watched in my life? ZERO. Figures though that he'd play a sport I hate. YES! Look at flights. I need you here. Also, Grandma nearly burned the house down. Okay, not really, but it is probably time for the family to discuss how safe it is for her and Grandpa to remain in their home. It makes me cry just thinking about it.*

# CHAPTER 6

I walk around town to get fresh air. I told my grandparents that I would be home in the next hour because they want me to go to a fundraising social for a woman in town who has cancer. I keep thinking about Jake. He's right about the cottage. I kick a rock down the sidewalk as I think about the source of my annoyance. It's that he's right about everything, especially that I'm a bad granddaughter, rarely coming to visit Sunny and Sis.

All I know is that my grandma isn't doing well, restoring the cottage would bring her joy, and it will give me something to focus on this summer. And anyway, if not now, when? I've never really been able to sit still, and with no friends in town, I have so much free time every day. The other problem is money. Yes, Grandpa said he had some money from Dad and Uncle Larry, but I don't have a clue what fixing up the cottage will cost. Calling Dad or Uncle Larry would probably just lead to them trying to talk me out of this. They would remind me that it's not a good investment and that Sunny and Sis won't be able to take care of the cottage once I leave. It's not worth the risk of looping them in. So for now, I'll move forward and see how far Grandpa's funds and my savings can get me.

I'm learning that living with older folks, everything happens early in the day. By seven in the evening, I'm usually alone as my grandparents go up to bed. But this time, as I enter the house, Grandma and Grandpa are standing by the door as if waiting for me.

"Am I late?"

Grandpa puts his arm around Grandma and shakes his head. "Not at all, but we're ready to head to the fundraising social whenever you are. Do you want to change first, Cammy?"

I glance down at my tank top and cutoff shorts and shrug. I think I look fine, but my grandpa's expression tells me to change. "I guess I can. Give me five minutes."

I put on a flowy black dress. I look in the mirror and decide to take my hair out of its messy bun. My blond curls lay calmly for once. I spray them with a leave-in conditioner to soften the curls even more. I put on a little lip gloss and don't need much makeup, as my face is already sun-kissed.

"We're going to the Main Street Diner," Grandma says as I come down the stairs. "They have a large back room."

Grandpa Sunny pats her hand and takes it in his. "We know Carrie Soleta from the Main Street Bank. She's the nicest gal. She has the good kind of cancer, if there is a good kind. But she'll still have lofty medical bills."

The walk is short, and cars line the street in front of the diner. We go to the back room, finding it already full of people. Music plays, and a few people line dance. I see Annie off in the distance. When she spots us, she comes over and greets my grandparents and then pulls me into a hug. I'm mesmerized by how many people from the town are here—people of all ages—to support Carrie. If I ever got sick, I could never fill a room with supporters. I don't have that many people in my life.

"You all look great," Annie says. "I'm so happy you made it."

Annie glances toward the bar and takes my grandma's hand. "Camilla, why don't you go sit at the bar and try to meet some kids your age. It's not good to hang out with us old folks all the time."

I go to protest, but Annie pushes me away and winks as she takes my grandma's hand. The three of them make their way over to a table as people wave at them.

At the bar, I slide onto a stool and watch the bartender as she serves another customer. She looks familiar to me, but I'm not sure why. She's tall, with an athletic build, and wears her straight, sandy-blond hair in a ponytail that hangs to the middle of her back. We make eye contact, her beautiful blue eyes a little big for her face.

Her lips turn up in a smile. "Camilla, right?"

I turn my head, studying her, knowing that I've met this woman before. "I'm so sorry, but do I know you?"

Her smile is warm as she leans on the counter. "You do, but it's been more years than I care to count. Jenna Abram. My family had the cottage next to your grandparents' growing up."

I throw my hands over my mouth. Jenna and I always seemed to be in a similar situation during the summers at the cottage. She was the youngest sibling of her older brothers, Jake and Dax. Even though she's a couple of years older than me, she and I were always partners in crime. She never treated me like she was too much older and cooler than me.

I stand up and stretch over the bar as she does the same. "Jenna, it's been at least…" I think about how much time has passed. Even though I came out to the cottage for the last time when I was seventeen, I didn't make any effort to see anyone because that would have meant looking up from my phone. "Well, it's been a long time."

Jenna laughs, and even though she's a grown woman, I can still see her as a ten-year-old girl taking me under her wing and showing me the ropes. She has turned into a beautiful woman.

"It's so good to see you, Camilla. My brothers will be here as well. Both Jake and Dax live here now."

I do my best not to groan at the mention of Jake's name.

Jenna stands on something behind the bar and waves someone over. "I'm not sure where Jake is, but here's Dax. I'll catch up with you soon. I have to go serve the thirsty patrons." She winks and then starts taking people's orders but not before she puts a glass of wine in front of me.

It was always Jenna and me in a field of boys. Between Jake and Dax, my brother, Robby, and my cousins, Liam and David, we were the only two girls.

When Dax approaches, I recognize him immediately. He's tall but not as tall as Jake. His hair is also a shade darker than Jake's or Jenna's, but as he gets closer, I can see that he has similar blue eyes.

He pulls up the stool next to me. "Hey, I'm Dax. My sister waved me over here." He looks across the bar to Jenna, and his shoulders slouch. "She thinks I need to get out there and start dating."

My drink nearly sprays out of my mouth. "I assure you, Jenna isn't trying to set you up with me. Apparently, we used to know each other." I reach my hand out to shake his. "I'm Camilla Bergland."

Recognition spreads across Dax's face. "Camilla Bergland!" He refuses my handshake and pulls me into his chest for a hug. "I didn't recognize you." He leans back and checks me out. "And now I feel stupid for thinking Jenna was trying to set us up." His hand goes to his head as he shakes it. "Although it's all she talks about, so you have to understand my mistake."

"Don't worry about it." I laugh. "Well, I probably haven't seen you in over a decade, so I suppose we all look a bit different than we used to."

Jenna slides a beer bottle to him. We turn our stools so they face each other, and his knee brushes against mine.

I quickly take a sip of my wine. "Do you live here?"

Dax nods. "As of a few months ago, Kylie and I live here." He grabs his phone from his pocket and scrolls through it until he stops on a picture. "She's five."

A child with gorgeous brown eyes stares back at me. Her hair is curly, the smile on her face warm. I hand the phone back to Dax. "She's beautiful."

"Yeah, she really is. Zari—my wife and her mom—died when she was four. We tried to stay in our house in Minneapolis because I wanted to give Kylie consistency, but I needed to move closer to my family. She and I sold our house and moved to Wheaton this past winter."

"Dax, I'm so sorry." I reach out and place my hand on his. "I can't imagine how hard that must be."

"Yeah, no one prepares you for it." He looks down and scratches at his jeans. "I was able to get a teaching job here, and now that it's summer, I help Jake out with his contracting business. Kylie and I will find a house eventually, but right now, I like living with my parents and having Kylie surrounded by so many people who love her. Zari's parents are in Atlanta, so staying in Minneapolis didn't make sense. Enough about me, though. Where are you living these days?"

No matter how many people ask me, that question always catches me off guard. "I'm between places. But I'm thinking about heading to Chicago when the summer is up. My parents retired there, and Robby lives there now too." I shrug. "I'm staying with my grandparents now. They're right over there." I point to Sunny and Sis, who sit at a table with Annie and Walt. They seem to be having a lively conversation. My heart swells when I see Grandma Sis laughing. According to Grandpa, she's had a good day so far. We all look forward to her good days. Juan and Lawson are at a table near theirs. Lawson is impossible to miss in his bright red tracksuit.

A woman with a silk scarf covering up chemo's effects goes from table to table, hugging people. She smiles as people pull her in for hugs. From here, she looks like she couldn't be much older than me. My eyes continue to scan the room as Dax talks to me about what he's doing these days for work.

I spot Jake sitting at a table with a woman and two men. His eyes follow Dax and me, and when I look at him, we hold each other's gaze for a moment. I glance at Dax as he tells me about his move to Wheaton and how he's excited for Kylie to start school in the fall.

"Camilla, do you want to come over and meet a couple of my high school buddies? They're waving me over."

"You go ahead," I say, not wanting to crash a reunion of high school friends. "I'll stay at the bar and catch up with Jenna."

Dax puts his hand on my shoulder. "Will you be here long?"

"I'm at the mercy of Sunny and Sis, so I'll be here until they decide it's bedtime, which I warn you is usually early."

Dax chuckles and hugs me again. "I look forward to having you around this summer. It'll be great to spend time together. And I can't wait for you to meet Kylie."

I look into his blue eyes. "I'll be here."

Dax makes his way over to his expectant friends.

For so many years of my childhood, seeing the Abram siblings was the highlight of the summer for Robby and me. They felt like an extension of our family, made even better when my cousins visited the cottage at the same time. Although a lot of time has passed, there's a part of being here and seeing them again that feels like home.

The nostalgia redoubles when I think back to how much I adored Jake. When the other boys would leave me out, he always came to my rescue and made sure I was included. I would demand to sit by him when our families would get together for meals. I also remember when I stopped being cute to him, and his interests shifted to hanging out with friends. I would sit on the shore and watch him cruise around in his small boat while he and his friends fished for walleyes and the younger kids played at the sandy beach. Whenever Jake would see me, he would rub the top of my head. It always made me feel special. He had a sensitivity about him that appealed to me. I didn't see that in other boys.

Dax was the brother who was always too busy for me. He would run around with Robby and my cousins. But he seems to have grown up to be the nice brother. Dax is also closer to me in age, but he was never the one that caught my eye.

I feel a presence next to me. Jake takes the seat his brother just vacated.

"I've been sitting here while you looked off into space," he says. "Were you thinking about me?" He puts his elbow on the bar and smirks in my direction.

I refuse to give him the satisfaction of knowing the truth. "You wish I was thinking about you."

He snickers and then turns his stool toward me. "I see you've become reacquainted with my siblings."

I turn my stool as well. "I have, and the nice gene must have skipped you because Dax and Jenna were nice and happy to see me."

Jake looks back at the woman at the table he just left. She watches his every move, only taking breaks to glare at me. Guys like Jake always end up with girls like her—hair a little too blond, makeup a little too severe, shirt a little too low-cut. They're probably perfect for each other.

"You're impossible, City Girl."

I lean into Jake to make sure he can hear me. "You've been the impossible one."

He's right again, though. I am being impossible. I know it. It's out of my character to be this contentious toward someone. He has a way of reminding me of the shame I already feel about not visiting enough and not being a good granddaughter. And a voice in my head is telling me to stay clear of him.

Jake looks down at my legs dangling from the barstool and smiles. "Let me know if you want me to get you a chair more suitable for your size."

The inside of my cheek takes the punishment as I bite it. "I thought I asked you to ignore me. Why are we speaking to each other?"

He hops off the barstool, leans against the bar, and puts his hand up to get Jenna's attention. "Jenna, would you get your big brother three beers and a soda water?"

He grabs his drinks and turns just as my grandma approaches and then puts them down when her arms extend in his direction.

"Rob, I can't believe you're here," she says to him. When she pulls Jake into an embrace, he towers over her, his hands clutching his drinks as he looks at me over her head. "I didn't know you were going to be here, yet here you are, son. How are you? Was your drive okay? Will you stay for a while?"

As Grandma Sis keeps her rapid-fire questions on Jake, my eyes scan the room for my grandpa, but I don't see him anywhere. Annie sits at a table, but she's not looking.

"You must be so proud of Camilla, Rob. Graduating from design school and moving to the other side of the world."

Jake looks at me and then to my grandma.

"I'm very proud of her," Grandma Sis adds.

"Grandma." I take her arm. "This isn't my dad. This is Jake Abram." I point to Jake, and Grandma rips her arm from my grip.

"Don't tell me who this is. I know my son." She's agitated in a way that I've never witnessed as she wraps her arm more firmly around Jake. Her eyes are glossy. She stares blankly at him, which means she doesn't see him at all.

I make eye contact with my grandpa. He must read my face because he quickens his shuffle toward us. He takes Grandma's arm. "Okay, Sis, it's time to get home. Camilla, are you coming?"

I stand up, but Grandma grabs Jake's arm again. "Sunny, now you let go of me. I'm not going to leave unless Rob leaves too." Her voice has a desperation to it.

Jake motions toward the door. "Let's go. I'll walk out with you."

I follow and watch Jake hold Grandma's arm as Grandpa stands on the other side and holds her other arm. The sun slaps us in the face as we walk outside, reminding me how early it still is. Jake lets go of Grandma's arm.

She stares at him for a moment. She squints and then opens her eyes again. They get less glossy, and she looks at him instead of through him. "You're not Rob."

"I'm sorry, Sis. It's me, Jake Abram. It was dark in there, so you probably couldn't tell."

Her expression contorts as tears pool in her eyes. The street fades around me, and my heart thumps out of my chest, and all I see is Sis, looking small and lost. She looks at me, then at Grandpa, and the tears flow freely down her cheeks.

"Let's get you home, Sis." Grandpa puts his arm around her and heads in the direction of home.

I follow a few steps behind them.

"Camilla, wait." Jake hurries over to me and grabs my wrist. "I'm sorry. I didn't realize things were so bad."

I pull out of his grasp. "This isn't your problem."

"What can I do to help?" He looks over my head at my grandparents, who have already reached their front lawn.

"Nothing. Go back to the party, Jake."

He stares at me, but when I refuse to crack, he gives up and turns to head back inside.

\*\*\*\*\*

As I lie in bed later that night, tears stream down my cheeks, and I feel nauseous thinking of Grandma Sis. I send Robby a text.

*I saw that you called, but I can't talk now. Sis had an episode tonight. What broke my heart most is how devastated Grandpa looked. You should have seen him, Robby. Get here.*

# CHAPTER 7

After Grandma's latest episode, Grandpa made an appointment for her at the Wheaton Community Hospital. I have promised I'll go with them, but I also don't think there's anything the doctors here will be able to do. The hospital in town is great, but there aren't specialists equipped to handle something like this. For anything on this level, people usually get referred to the nearest cities—the Twin Cities in Minnesota or Fargo in North Dakota.

Grandma Sis was diagnosed two years ago with this awful disease. My parents and aunt and uncle flew in and took them to the university hospital in Minneapolis. After two days of tests, the doctors confirmed the deterioration that we'd been seeing for years in Sis.

We sit in the waiting room as the only people here. Grandma paces back and forth. Her shoes clink against the shiny linoleum floors. When she snapped out of her spell the other night, she looked so embarrassed by the entire mix-up. I keep thinking about how Jake handled the situation. There might have been a big scene had he not deescalated things and gotten my grandma outside. I've read it's best not to correct someone when they are in a spell like Grandma was.

A doctor in a white coat walks out to the waiting room. His hair is grayer since the last time I saw him, but I recognize him immediately. "Hi, Sis," he says. "You can come on back."

Grandma goes to the door. Grandpa motions for me to follow, and we go into the room. Grandma sits on the bed as Grandpa and I take a chair. The room smells like those wooden sticks doctors use to check if a person has strep throat.

"Hi, Sunny," the doctor says. "It's good to see you." He smiles as his gaze turns to me. "And, Camilla, it's been years since I've had the pleasure of seeing you."

"Hi, Dr. Abram. It's great to see you too."

He pats my hand, then goes to Grandma.

I had forgotten that Jake's dad is one of the doctors in town. I've now seen almost all of Jake's family except for his mom. I used to think that Dr. Abram was the most dapper man. Besides aging a few years, he looks the same.

He turns to my grandma, who sits with her hands in her lap. "How are you feeling today, Sis?"

She picks at lint on her light-blue pants. "Well, I don't know if Jake told you, but I got confused the other night. I don't remember all the details. Please apologize to him for me."

"Jake mentioned it to me because he was concerned. You have nothing at all to be sorry about, Sis."

The examination continues as Grandpa and I watch. When he finishes, he pats her on the knee and takes a seat in front of his desk.

"Physically, Sis, you're doing great." His voice trails off. "I'll have some bloodwork ordered, and you're due to go back to Minneapolis to see the neurologist in November."

Grandpa gets up, puts an arm around Grandma, and kisses her forehead. Dr. Abram looks down at his folded hands and then up at both of them.

"Alzheimer's is progressive, and unfortunately, there's nothing medically to stop this. But some things can be done to slow the progression. I recommend staying in the same routine as much as possible every day. Try not to add too much stimulation." Dr. Abram shifts in his seat. "Social events can be overwhelming. Don't cut them out entirely but know that it may throw you off, Sis. Keep doing all the things you're doing, such as knitting and cross-stitching with Annie. Try to exercise and get plenty of sleep. Eat healthily. And as things progress, rely on your family to know when it's time to consider bigger changes."

I pinch the bridge of my nose as the tears nearly seep out. My grandma nods as she wipes at her wet face.

Dr. Abram hands me pamphlets before we head out of the office. "Let me know if you have any questions."

I look at the guides on Alzheimer's, caring for loved ones through the diagnosis, and when it's time to look into long-term care facilities. I want to hold them and tell them it will be okay, but I also want to give them space and cry in private.

"Grandpa, Grandma," I say, catching up with them just as they reach their car. "I could use some fresh air."

"Why don't you go for a walk," my Grandpa says.

"Are you sure?"

"Yes. You've been so helpful, Cammy. Sis and I are going to lie down."

Life feels heavy as I make my way down the street. We're nearing the end of a stage, and I'm not ready to enter a new one. I want time to stand still, or at least slow down. But with each day, we keep strolling toward the inevitable aging and death. Every day, we wake up and hold our breath, hoping that today will be a good day. But when the bad days come, and they will, it makes me think that it's time to consider arrangements where Grandma Sis will have more support.

Alzheimer's disease. My family rarely uses the words. We carry on as if we don't address it, we can keep it at bay. That's how I cope too. Denial. The fear has kept me away and built up impenetrable walls. Loving Sunny and Sis too much scares me. But if I stay away and don't witness the degeneration, perhaps I can continue pretending that none of it is happening.

"Hey, Camilla."

I look up as a black truck parks on the road near me. I force a smile when Dax gets out of the truck. "Hi, Dax."

"Out for a morning stroll?" he asks as he starts walking with me. "You left the social before we had a chance to hang out."

"Yeah. I told you, Sunny and Sis don't stay out late." I wonder if he knows about Grandma Sis's episode. It's Wheaton. Everyone probably knows by now. "Did Jake tell you what happened at the benefit?"

Dax shrugs. "No. Is everything all right?"

"You ready, Dax?" The voice belongs to Jake. He's stepping out of the bakery with a white bag in hand.

As he comes closer, my mouth waters at the smell of the pastries in the bag.

"Oh, hey, it's you," he says as he comes up next to Dax. As he clutches his bag of goodies, he looks like he would rather be anywhere else than talking to me.

Dax stuffs his hands in his pockets and glances at Jake, then me, waiting for someone to say something.

"I was heading back to Sunny and Sis's." I pause and point down the road. "So I'm going to keep going."

I start walking and only get a few steps before Jake catches up to me.

He turns back and calls out to Dax. "I need to discuss something with Camilla. I'll meet you at the site." Jake falls in step with me. We pass several stores before he breaks the silence. "I'm sorry that Sis has gotten so bad."

"You have nothing to be sorry about. It's not your fault." I keep walking as I stare straight ahead.

As we pass a few more shops, the awkward silence returns.

"You wanted to walk with me to tell me you're sorry about Sis?" I ask him finally.

"No." Jake stops. "I know you want to fix the cottage up, and although I think it's a waste of your time, I can help."

I scrunch up my face. "And how can you help?"

"I'm a general contractor. I own my business. I know how to fix a place up." Jake puts his hand over his forehead to block the sun. "But like I said, I worry about the investment if no one will maintain it."

I try to look like I'm pondering the offer, although I already have my answer. "I don't want your help."

His voice becomes agitated. "Why are you so stubborn?"

"Why are you willing to help if you think it's a bad idea?" I want to say yes, but I don't know how. I want to admit that things got off to a bad start but that I could use his friendship right now. But I don't say any of that.

"Look, my business is booming. Summer is our busiest time of year, and I don't have any extra time. But I'm standing here offering to help." He throws his hands down and the bag of pastries falls to the cement.

We both look at the open bag. Doughnuts spill onto the sidewalk. Not salvageable. I try not to smile, but I can't help it.

Jake whips down to pick up the bag. "Forget I offered." He starts to walk away.

"Deal," I say to his back. What I'm thinking, though, is that I probably can't afford to pay him, anyway. Plus, I don't want to rely on someone only to be let down. I do feel bad, as his offer would solve some of my problems. And he might have been the one who was rude first when I arrived in Wheaton, but I'm aware that I'm doing nothing to improve the situation.

Back at my grandparents' house, it's silent except for the hum of the square fans they keep throughout to keep the air-conditioning prices down. I pack myself some food and drinks, tiptoe out of the house, and drive out to the cottage.

When I get there, I open up every window and turn a fan on, as it's hotter in the cottage than it is outside. I work in silence and feel Sunny and Sis in everything I touch.

I nearly gag a few times as I clear cobwebs and find some unwanted visitors. I use Windex and newspapers to wash the windows. I'll need to leave the rest of the washing for another day, as there's no running water in the cottage. I remove the plastic covering from the furniture and assess whether any of it is salvageable. I pull my shirt up and wipe my face, which is covered in dirt and sweat.

Hours later, I've done what I can in terms of cleaning. The cottage looks and smells better than it did, but the roof still needs to be attended to, and there are so many things that need to be replaced. I have no idea how to do any of it.

Jake. I should have heard him out, and now I may be forced to swallow my pride and plead to him and admit that my pride is hurt still from the day at the woodpile and him pointing out that I haven't visited enough.

I grab a pen and paper and sit outside in a lawn chair. I've spent a lifetime in places around the world, but nothing is as spectacular as here. Lake Traverse looks out at South Dakota, where the rolling hills are green and stretch as far as the eye can see. As a child, I thought it was so cool that we went from Minnesota to South Dakota once we hit the middle of the lake. I would holler over the boat motor, "We're in South Dakota!"

The lake glistens from the sun. Waves hit the rocks, causing a splash of water. A boat trolls by with two fishing lines in the water. The older gentleman waves. When his line bends, he reels in a fish. A minute later, he throws it back in the water.

A car door slams behind me, causing me to jump. I see that it's Jake, the realization hitting me that my groveling may have to happen sooner than later. His hands are tucked in the pockets of his jeans as I stand and put my list down on my chair.

"What are you doing here?"

"Good to see you too." He opens the back of his truck and starts putting material on the lawn— long, copper-colored metal and plywood, one after another, until there's a stack nearly as tall as me. "Listen to me, City Girl, because I'm only going to say it once." He leans against his truck.

I go to speak, but he holds his finger up and silences me.

"I wasn't joking when I said how busy I am. I don't know how I'm going to manage to help you and keep up with my day job, but I'm going to try. And rest assured, this has nothing to do with you. I love Sunny and Sis like they're my own grandparents. I'm doing this for them." He puts his finger down and continues. "But I see you aren't good at accepting help, so I was thinking, this won't be for free. You give me what money you can at the end of the summer. In the meantime, I expect your help too."

My face flushes as Jake pushes off his truck and puts his hands on his hips.

"But what about you saying it's a bad idea?" I ask.

"Someone will need to be responsible for turning the water off and on each year. Having repairs done, having the septic tank emptied. Things like that. I get the impression that that may be too much for Sunny and Sis right now. That's all I'm saying."

He's not wrong.

"How much will this cost me?"

Jake looks at his pile of supplies. "I can get a lot of the material for free or reduced cost."

"Yeah," I say. "But the labor?"

"I won't be doing it alone. You'll help, and we'll do it on my schedule. I'll work on it with you when I can. You're going to have to do the majority of the work."

"Again, how much?"

Jake brushes his hair out of his face. "We can discuss payment later. But now for what I want from you."

I'm speechless. I've managed to hold my own with Jake since being reacquainted with him, but he's making all the rules, while I'm the obedient puppy who stands here, nodding my head.

"Sis said you're an interior designer. I need some help with my home. I built it three years ago, and besides a bed for me and in my guestrooms and a couple of chairs in front of a TV, I have no furniture."

I scrunch up my forehead, offended. "I have a bachelor's in interior design. It sounds like you want a decorator."

"Semantics," Jake says as he crosses his arms. "Are you up for it or not?"

I don't share this with Jake, but choosing the aesthetics is what I like best about my job. "I'm in."

Jake sticks his hand out. "So we have a deal?"

I hesitate. My mind spins. Why is he doing this? What's in it for him? None of it makes sense. His large hand envelops mine as we shake on it.

"Why do I feel like I just made a deal with the devil?"

Jake laughs but doesn't let go of my hand. "Because the manual work is about to start."

We study each other—his turquoise eyes, wide open, looking at me. I hate needing people, but this plan may work. I'll be able to put some of my design touches on Jake's place, and I'll have help with the cottage. I turn around to look at it, knowing that I could never fix it up on my own.

Jake lets go of my hand and hops in his truck. He rolls down the window. "Meet me here bright and early in the morning, and we'll rip the old shingles off."

Before I have a chance to respond, Jake backs up his truck and leaves.

I shake my head and say, "I hope this doesn't end badly."

# CHAPTER 8

I'm nervous as I drive out to the cottage this morning. Skepticism aside, today is the perfect summer day. The sun is high, not a cloud in the sky. I roll my window down. The warm breeze hits my face as Lake Traverse once again comes into view. It's like the lake has healing power because I start to catch my breath the moment I see it.

I pull up to the cottage and see the white truck. Jake appears around the front of the cottage. Our eyes meet. It occurs to me suddenly that our plan to ignore each other while I'm in Wheaton will be a lot more difficult if we're fixing up this place together. I need to focus on everything I'm getting out of our agreement. The cottage has the potential to be transformed. To my left, near the tall grass at the edge of the yard, is a massive dumpster that wasn't here yesterday when I left the place.

I walk toward Jake. "I still don't feel great about accepting your help," I say as I look at his material.

"You're helping me, too, don't forget," he says. "Think of it as if we're using each other to get what we want."

I sigh. "How can we help each other if we're supposed to be ignoring each other?"

"It won't be hard for me to ignore you and your tiny self, City Girl."

*I hate this nickname*, I think as I roll my eyes. "The beginning of wisdom is to call things by their proper name."

Jake laughs as he pulls his shirt over his head. "Do you always get away with quoting Confucius and playing it off like they're your own intelligent words?"

"I wasn't pretending those were my words." My body flushes with heat, and I imagine my face is bright red. This man, of all people, called me out on quoting Confucius.

Jake continues to laugh at me. "I don't think that's what Confucius meant."

Eager to change the subject, I look around and don't trust that any of this will work out. "Will you give me a ballpark of what I'll owe you? I'm nervous that the amount I'm thinking won't be anywhere close to acceptable."

"Quit worrying about it. It'll work out."

I look at the cottage, at the material on the grass, and then at Jake. He reaches his hand out to me, and I hesitantly take it.

"Are we good?" he asks, shaking my hand.

"I guess." His hand is warm, and its roughness tickles my palm. Now we have shaken on this twice. There's no backing out.

Jake goes to his truck, pulls out some things, and holds them up for me. I recognize them as some type of kneepads. Next, he grabs a rope and walks over to the cottage. I feel out of my element as I follow. He motions for me to put on my kneepads. I stop and pull them up over my shoes.

He glances at my legs. "No more shorts. You have to wear long pants."

Everything is happening so fast. I don't want to pause and ask more questions for fear that Jake will change his mind. I scroll through the few things I've learned about him. Former football player, business owner, and general contractor. All roads in Wheaton lead to Jake.

"Next, City Girl, I'm going to tie this rope to you. Before we can roof, we need to remove the shingles."

Jake manipulates both of my arms with his hands until they're fully extended. He pulls me toward him and wraps the rope around my waist. His breath warms my neck as he bends over to tie the rope.

He finishes and pats me on the top of my head. I grab my wrist to fight the urge to swat him.

"This is for your safety," he says. "I won't have anyone hurt on my watch."

The ladder hits the side of the cottage with a thump. Jake motions for me to climb up first, with him right behind me. Once I reach the top, he ties the other end of my rope to the anchor. He explains what we'll be doing and gives me the tools.

The view from up here is beautiful. Even if I fall off the roof, I wouldn't go far. I work side by side with Jake. He hands me something that looks like a giant metal spatula. He motions at me so I know what to do. I pull out exposed nails and drop them into a bucket. After a couple of hours, the only thing left on the roof is plywood. My achy knees and raw hands throb. There's no need to fill the space with words, as Bob Dylan blasts from the truck.

Jake takes many trips up and down the ladder. This latest time, he brings wood up with him. "Next we deal with the leaks. We need to bring up this wood and get rid of the rotten boards, City Girl."

I nod, lift my shirt, and wipe my sweaty face. I'm covered in dust and dirt from head to toe.

"Camilla. Camilla," I repeat with emphasis on each syllable.

He continues to demonstrate what to do as he pulls his shirt out of his back pocket and rubs the sweat off his face. His jeans hang off his hips, and his skin looks tan and smooth as it glistens with sweat. I squint my eyes as I try to read what his tattoo says. I make out the words "moving from one" before he catches me.

"Stare much?" he asks as he moves his tattooed arm out of my vision.

I look down at the roof, and when Jake looks away, I wipe my mouth in case there's drool.

I hold the board as he uses a nail gun to put it in place. We do this a few times until all the bad wood has been replaced. I have no idea what time it is, but the sun continues to get lower in the sky. Jake lies back and puts his shirt over his head.

So much can be learned from working beside someone, especially in silence. Jake is meticulous. He takes no shortcuts. He concentrates so fully on what he's doing, but at times he looks to be deeper in his head than the work we're doing. Sure, he usually gives me sarcasm and terseness, but I often catch him watching me work, and he brings me water throughout the day.

My skin is many shades darker than when we started, but it's from the dirt covering me, not the sun. "How long have we been up here?"

Jake takes the shirt off his head. He looks at the sky and smiles. A real smile. "Hours."

I lie back. "Why do you look happy? I can barely move. My muscles hurt so bad."

"Because seeing results brings me a sense of accomplishment."

I rise, move to the ladder, and lower myself slowly to the ground. With each step, my muscles cry out in pain, especially my hamstrings. I pull my shirt up again and wipe at my face, but there's no fighting the deluge of sweat. The ladder moans as Jake comes down next. I feel gross, but Jake is one of those people where sweat looks like a glistening mist causing his honey-shaded body to shine. Life isn't fair.

"Have you ever worked this hard?" He eyes my wet tank top and clingy cutoff shorts.

"I painted schoolhouses in the humidity of Cambodia," I admit. I don't let him further in, though. Jake knows I'm an interior design by education, but what he doesn't know is that I've spent my short adult life everywhere in the world, doing everything I can to not settle down.

Surprise spreads across his face. "Then laying a roof should be nothing for you."

I look toward the lake and then at Jake. "I can't shower when I get to town because it'll wake Sunny and Sis."

"That's a bummer for you."

"How about a dip in the lake?" I ask as I bite my bottom lip and smirk.

"Umm, no." Jake crosses his arms over his chest. "I have running water at my house."

"Speaking of water, do you know how to get the water turned on at the cottage? I have no clue."

"Yes." Jake rests his hand over his lips as if he's in deep thought. "But even once I get it turned on, until that broken shower is fixed, there are no showers out here for you."

Before I have a chance to think too hard, I throw off my shoes and then peel my sweaty and soiled tank top and shorts off my body and run to the dock. I'm wearing my swimsuit under my clothes because I had an idea that a lake bath was going to be the best I could get this evening. I hear Jake's gasp as I go sprinting toward the water. The dock vibrates under my feet. I reach the end and launch myself into a cannonball, just like when I was a child.

The water is cool as I plunge in. I lie back, the salt from my face running over my lips. I float face up in the water and smile at the setting sun.

Movement on the dock causes vibrations I can feel. Jake stands there, watching me float. "I didn't think you'd actually jump."

I stand up and wade toward the edge of the dock, where I use the wheel to pull myself up. "The water feels incredible. Hop in."

"As amusing as it is to watch you, I think I'll take a warm shower when I get home."

The water drips off me as I stand in front of him, a puddle forming at my feet. "Are you always this uptight?" I whisk my head in his direction and splash him with lake water.

He jumps back. "City Girl, I let loose in more ways than you can imagine." He turns away from me and walks off the dock.

I follow close behind. The wood of the dock jiggles beneath my feet. "Will you quit calling me City Girl?"

Jake turns around and watches me as I continue to wring out my hair. "But that's who you are, right?"

"What? A city girl? You don't know anything about me." I lean against the cottage.

Jake closes the space between us. A bark of laughter comes out of him. He puts his hand on the cottage and leans in. "You aren't the first out-of-towner who's come to Wheaton and judged our small town—how we live—thinking you're better than everybody else."

His words sting. I don't think I'm better than anyone here, although from Jake's perspective, I can see why he has deduced that. My internal struggle about Grandma Sis, deciding what I want for the next chapter of my life, like where to live, all of it has made me come off as a closed-off person.

"The only thing I've figured out," I say, "is that you've changed." I poke my finger into his chest.

Jake puts his other hand against the cottage. Our arms touch, and I'm boxed in. The only way out is to duck under him. I'm tempted. Our contempt for each other must exhaust us because we both breathe heavily. He's so close to me I can smell the mint on his breath.

"If you're trying to intimidate me, it's not going to work." I lean back harder on my hands, nowhere else to go. My heart feels as if it will leap out of my chest. I find it impossible to catch my breath.

"You think I'm trying to intimidate you?" His body nearly presses into mine. "Why would I do that?"

"I don't know," I whisper. "But you are."

The man is a giant, even hunched over.

"Camilla, I wasn't trying to—"

My lips part as we hold each other's gazes. A car door slams, causing Jake to jump back. I clear my throat, walk around the corner of the cottage, grab my soiled, wrinkled shirt on the grass, and put it on. A woman gets out of the car. At first, I can't place where I've seen her before, but then I recognize her as the woman I saw at the benefit sitting next to Jake.

Her hair is so blond it's nearly white, her makeup severe against her fair complexion.

Jake hurries toward her. I follow. She looks at me, then Jake, and then back to me. Her skirt is short, her shirt low-cut, her heels tall. One of the heels gets wedged in the soft grass. "I don't believe we've met. I'm Tiffeny, Jake's girlfriend."

As I see Tiffeny up close and note how Jake responds to her—or rather, doesn't respond to her—I can sense that they aren't a good fit for each other.

"I'm Camilla. And I'm sorry to hear that." My joke falls flat under the stone-cold face she gives me. "I mean, I'm sorry for you, Tiffeny." I look to Jake, who avoids my eyes altogether.

Jake brushes me off and goes to his truck. "Be sure to clean up this mess and throw the scraps away," he calls back to me. He gestures at the old roofing material lying all over the lawn.

I sigh, as I don't think my body can handle any more manual labor.

Tiffeny gets in her vehicle, Jake gets into his truck, and they pull out of the driveway. I look down at my wet clothes clinging to my body and smile. The cottage will get its repairs, and I have someone who knows what he's doing to help. I've been so busy punishing Jake for making me feel like a bad granddaughter that I went out of my way and made him not like me.

I grab my phone from the picnic table and send a text to Robby.

*Okay, so I have kind of big news. I've decided to fix up the cottage. I asked Grandpa if it's okay, and he doesn't seem to care one way or another. Guess who's helping. Any ideas? Okay, I'll just tell you. JAKE! Grandpa says he's like a grandson to them. I'm helping him with something, too, but it's still pretty nice of him.*

# CHAPTER 9

K eeping a routine for Grandma Sis isn't difficult in a town like Wheaton. I wake up in the mornings and have a cup of tea with her, and at eight thirty, Annie walks through the door. Then Grandpa and I stroll to the café and have coffee with Walt, Juan, and Lawson. By nine thirty, I've consumed enough caffeine for a week.

Now two weeks into my time in Wheaton, I'm officially a regular at the cafe. I think I've heard every fishing story that Lake Traverse has to offer. It reminds me of the sign that used to hang in my grandparents' cottage: "Early to bed, early to rise. Fish all day, tell big lies." The quote must have been based on Grandpa Sunny and his buddies.

After coffee, I try to catch up on internet time at the boutique coffee shop. I look at job openings back in Chicago almost daily, even though I'm not entirely sure I want to end up there. I also explore reenlisting in the Peace Corps, but something about that doesn't feel right either.

By the time I get back to my grandparents' house, the Meals on Wheels service is there. Dad and Uncle Larry set up that service right after I told them how little Sunny and Sis cook these days. I make a sandwich for myself while the Meals on Wheels lady finishes her drop-off. Grandma and Grandpa then head upstairs for their afternoon nap.

At this point, I usually head out to the cottage for some manual labor. Later, I will drive back into town to help my grandparents with dinner, which consists of leftovers from lunch or something that I cook. I've enjoyed making them meals. Many nights, Annie pops over, as well, and we cook together while Sunny and Sis sit in the kitchen and we all talk and laugh. Then I'm back at the cottage no later than seven in the evening for more work. I never thought I would enjoy a routine this much, but there is ease in the predictability.

\*\*\*\*\*

This morning at coffee, Walt's mouthful of toast doesn't stop him from speaking. "Now that Lawson can't be in the fishing tournament, how are we going to find a fourth? Everyone's already teamed up."

As Lawson shakes his head, I admire today's tracksuit—a bright orange one spanning from neck to ankle.

"Georgia's making me go to Fargo to sit around and wait for my oldest granddaughter to have her baby," he explains to me mournfully.

Juan slurps his coffee and plays with the end of his mustache. "Didn't your granddaughter consider the fishing season when she decided to have a baby?"

"Oh, you better believe I brought this up to her," Lawson says as he slaps his hand down on the table. "She says I should be grateful she avoided duck and deer season."

It isn't rare for me to find myself lost when these men have conversations like this. It's also not uncommon that they talk about the same thing several times in a single week.

I put my coffee down. "Is someone going to explain to me what you're talking about?"

Everyone puts their cups down simultaneously, each of them donning an expression of shock.

Grandpa pats my hand in a patronizing manner. "Sorry, Cammy. Wheaton Days are coming up in two weeks. I don't know if you remember, but you came once or twice as a child. There are events all week, and one of the events is the walleye tournament. You can only enter with four people. One person drives the boat while the other three fish. Every year for the past few years, the young kids have won. But this year, we think we have a shot."

I look around the café, which is full of men that I imagine would like to be part of their foursome. "There's no one else who could join your team?"

"We're saying everyone else already has a group," Walt says, food again flying everywhere. I'm almost positive a piece ends up on my hand, but I refuse to look down and draw attention to it.

I pull my bottom lip into my mouth and look at Walt, then Juan, Lawson, and, finally, my grandpa. "What about me?"

89

My grandpa speaks first. "Oh, Cammy, I'm sure we all appreciate your offer." He looks around at his friends. "But walleye fishing takes a lot of skill."

"I used to fish with you all the time, Grandpa."

He laughs. "And you were the cutest fisher-girl on the lake, but this is a serious competition."

"Maybe I could drive the boat," I suggest.

"Oh no, Cammy," Grandpa Sunny says under his breath like it was the most provocative thing he'd heard all day. "That is a job just for Juan. He knows this lake like the back of his hand."

Walt swallows the last of his bread. "It's not a bad idea, Sunny." Walt looks at me. "And think of all the single men that Camilla could meet. We have a couple of weeks to prepare. Why don't we drink coffee out at your cottage and teach this girl how to fish?" He winks at me like we're in on this together.

I look at the others, hoping they'll go along with the plan.

Juan takes my hand in his and then leans in to kiss it. "*Mi amor*, I think with our help, we could make you ready for this competition."

Lawson stands and stretches his hands over his head. The orange tracksuit rides up, exposing a belly full of hair. "Camilla may be the last one left not in a group. It's better than forfeiting, I suppose."

"True," Walt, Juan, and Grandpa say at the same time.

*I'm only slightly better than forfeiting*, I think. At least they don't lie to make me feel better.

"When do we start?" I ask as I clap my hands together.

Walt threads his thumbs through his suspenders. Today, he switched the rainbow ones for navy blue ones full of bulldogs. "Let's meet at the Bergland cottage at nine tomorrow. We'll start off the dock and work our way up to the boat."

I say goodbye to the men, excited that I'm going to learn how to fish again.

*****

After lunch, Sunny and Sis lie down for a nap, so I drive out to the cottage to see if there are any projects. A blue car that I don't recognize is parked in the driveway.

"Hey, Camilla, sorry to just pop in like this." It's Jenna, and she's holding a platter of food.

Jenna bobbles a platter in her hand, and I rush over to help her.

"I've heard Jake is working you pretty hard," she says. "I figured you guys would want to eat."

I lead Jenna into the cottage. "Thanks so much. I've been living on leftovers from Meals on Wheels, so this is a welcome change." I place a platter of sandwiches covered in plastic on the table.

"I also brought drinks. They're in the car. Let me grab them."

Jenna heads back out to her car for sparkling water and slings a duffel bag over her shoulder. "I know you have a lot to do, but it's so beautiful out.

Do you want to just lie in the sun for a while and catch up?"

"Yes!" I practically scream. I enjoy hanging out with my grandparents, but I've missed being able to talk to someone my age. "That came out more desperate than I was intending."

I've started keeping some items at the cottage, so I change into a swimsuit and pull a couple of lawn chairs out for us to lie on. We find the sunniest spot on the lawn and put our towels down on our chairs.

Jenna fills me in on her life. After college, she was engaged for a short time and lived in North Dakota, but the engagement ended last year, and she moved back here. Her degree is in journalism. She wants to live in a larger city and try a hand at writing.

"I'm jealous that you've gotten to live in so many places." Jenna studies me. "I don't think writing a column in the *Wheaton Happenings* is going to get me where I want to go as a journalist."

"Yeah, it's been great to travel." I decide not to share the part about how the older I've gotten, the lonelier I've felt. I've never thought this way before, but I'm starting to feel alone in this world with nothing tying me to a place.

Jenna sits up and applies sun lotion. "Where do you think you'll go next?"

"Who knows? My parents have settled in Chicago. My brother recently moved there too. The four of us haven't been in the same city in almost a decade, so that would make sense." The pit in my stomach returns. I don't think I'll ever be ready to leave Sis and Sunny. Not this time. They need me, but I need them too. I also don't share that the loft my parents bought is downtown and screams "empty nesters." They aren't exactly asking for me to move in with them.

"How do you like it here?" Jenna asks.

The sun warms my closed eyes. "It's hard being back and seeing my grandparents getting old. I've been away so long. I had no idea how bad things had gotten."

Jenna reaches her hand out and grabs my dangling fingers. "I'm sure they're both happy that you're here now."

I chew at my lip, contemplating whether to ask what I want. I decide to go for it. "Jenna, I don't want this to come off the wrong way, but was Jake always kind of—"

"A jerk?" she interrupts.

My hand covers my mouth to stifle a laugh. "Okay, you said it, not me. I know it's been about fifteen years since I've seen him, but he isn't the Jake I remember."

"Life has hardened him," Jenna says as she rolls over and lies on her stomach. "After his football career ended, he made one mistake after another. He's been home for a few years now, but he can't get over the downward spiral he was in. He's his own worst enemy."

"Yeah," I say as I sit up in the chair. "Robby mentioned that Jake played pro football. I had no idea." It occurs to me then how odd it is that I have never heard this news, even in passing. But then again, Robby loves basketball, my dad and I are big baseball fans, and I've never seen my mom watch a sports game. The Berglands lost touch with the Abrams so long ago that if Jake and his football career had ever been discussed in our family, it wasn't something I overheard.

Jenna sits up, crosses her legs, and looks at me. "I already like you almost better than everyone in this town. People in these parts all know he was a professional athlete, and a lot of them are users."

I grab my ball cap and pull it lower on my face. "People can suck. I haven't lived Stateside much, and I'll be honest, I've never watched a football game in my life."

"I haven't shared this with Jake because I don't want him to get a big head," Jenna says, "but having him here is great. Between me calling off my wedding, Zari dying, and Dax and Kylie needing us all to step up, Jake has been taking great care of us. In more ways than one."

My arm starts to fall asleep under the weight of my head. Zari. Dax's late wife. The Abrams have been through a lot, it seems.

As if Jake knows we're talking about him, he pulls up in his truck. I stand up and pull my cutoffs over my bikini bottoms. Jenna does the same. We head toward his truck, where he has loads of material in the back.

Jake's gaze isn't subtle. My skin pebbles from his stare.

Jenna looks at her oldest brother and then me. "Well, I hate to bow out, but I have no interest in helping, so I'm out of here." She goes back to the lawn chairs and grabs her things.

When she returns, I pull her into a hug. "Thanks for coming. I can't tell you how much I needed girl time."

She gives Jake a punch in his gut. "I like this one, Jake, so you better be nice to her." Jenna laughs and heads to her car as her brother waves her off.

Jake pulls boards out of his truck. "You're not going to wear that, are you, City Girl?"

I look down at my cutoffs and bikini top and shrug. "What's wrong with my outfit?"

"Besides the fact that it's distracting, I don't want to have to pull splinters out of your skin."

"As if I'd ever ask you to."

"You can pick up some overalls at the hardware store. You know what those are, right?"

"Of course." I've seen my grandpa wear them many times.

"Maybe you can find some designer bibs made for city girls."

I huff but decide that line of conversation has gone far enough. Besides, he's probably right. Bib overalls would be better than shorts and a T-shirt for this kind of work.

But that's all I have for now. In the cottage, I pull a white T-shirt over my swimsuit. I put on my sturdy tennis shoes and stand with my hand on my hip as I watch Jake and wait for instruction.

"Well, I have good news and bad news," he says. I nod at him as he speaks.

"The bad news is, there's a lot of rotten wood that will need to be removed. The good news is, you're going to learn how to drywall. And because we're going to take this place down to the studs, we're going to insulate and make the cottage livable year-round. I'm going to put in some ductwork in case you guys decide to install a furnace."

"Should we run this by Sunny?" I ask.

"He and I already talked. He's game for anything."

I look down at my hands that are already raw and throbbing. As difficult as Jake can be, none of this would be happening without his help. I need him, and he knows it.

"Okay, tell me what to do. I'm ready."

Jake turns on the old cottage radio, and music fills up the space. At his instruction, we start removing rotting wood and tearing the walls apart. With every bang of the sledgehammer, I cringe. I know that things look worse with demos before they get better, but I feel like we're tearing this beautiful cottage down.

The rotten boards are almost completely gone, revealing the studs. I wipe my brow. This is so much work.

Jake seems to read my mind. "Let's take a break."

I pull drinks and the sandwiches Jenna brought out of the fridge. "Should we sit outside?" I want to get out of this dusty cottage and not have to look at the destruction.

We sit on the lawn on the towels that Jenna and I were using earlier. I remove my T-shirt, which is now more brown than white.

Jake leans back on his elbows and closes his eyes, our legs inches from each other.

"So I heard you played professional football," I say.

"And?" His gaze snaps toward me.

"And nothing. I didn't know. I'm making conversation."

Jake sits up and stuffs half a sandwich in his mouth all at once. When he's done chewing, he deflects. "It doesn't look like Sunny has turned the water on for years because the pump was rusted, along with some of the rubber gaskets. They'll need to be replaced before you can have running water again. And pumps aren't cheap."

I open my sandwich and take the tomatoes out. "I get it. You don't want to talk about it."

"There's nothing to talk about," Jake says through gritted teeth. "I also want an electrician to inspect the wires. I guarantee it hasn't been done in a while."

The hint is taken. Jake doesn't want to talk about football. "When do I get to see your place? I want to start sketching design ideas."

Jake leans back and appears to relax. "Whenever you want to see it." He takes a drink from his water bottle. "Except for right now. We have more work to do."

"What's my budget? I mean, you make it sound like you don't have much furniture."

"I'm going to give you my credit card." He nudges his leg against mine. "But don't go crazy."

I rub my hands together as I lie back on the towel. "Jake's credit card. This'll be great."

"Yeah, yeah." Jake stands, his body shading me as he puts his arm out to help me up. My muscles ache as I come to my feet. I try to remind myself that I've done manual labor before. I painted new schools in Cambodia. When I spent a summer in Botswana, I would sometimes walk over ten miles a day to manage outreach in the local communities. But nothing I've done has prepared me for overhauling the cottage. No wonder Jake is all muscly.

"Your girlfriend seems nice." The words slip out.

He lets go of my hand, throws his head back, and laughs. "Girlfriend is a debatable term."

I raise an eyebrow.

"She doesn't like you and me spending so much time together," he continues. "But I assured her that you dislike me as much as it's possible to dislike a person."

"Ha!" I head into the cottage with Jake on my heels. I look back at him over my right shoulder. "You can also let her know that you aren't my type."

Jake shakes his head. "Any other insights about how you feel about me that I should share with Tiffeny?"

"That should cover it."

I put on my work gloves and spend the next couple of hours side by side with Jake, removing all the rotten wood from the cottage. I look at the time and realize that I missed my cue to return for dinner. Hopefully, Annie was able to help out.

With each rotten board removed, the cottage gets a bit fresher. I look out the window to the rolling hills of South Dakota, just catching the last rays of the sun as it disappears over the horizon. I can't wait for the day when I can sit by the lake and enjoy the scenery instead of working inside.

# CHAPTER 10

There is no way to bring Grandpa and his friends to the cottage without telling them the extent that Jake and I have been fixing it up. Walt, Juan, and Grandpa all stand with hands in their pockets, looking up at the roof.

Walt speaks so fast I can barely catch all of his words. "The roof looks great. It was smart to go with metal. And Jake is helping? What time do you guys work? We should start taking our afternoon coffee out here, right, boys?"

"We spend most days during the weekend out here," I say. "The weekdays are less predictable. But you should have your afternoon coffee here."

"How nice of Jake to help you," Juan says with a wink. "We'll come by at three daily. Maybe you could serve us pie, Camilla."

I look toward Grandpa Sunny, who hasn't said a word. "Grandpa, any thoughts?"

"It looks great, Cammy. It was in such shambles. I trust Jake."

They take turns giving me fishing tips as we walk to the dock.

Grandpa hands me my fishing rod. "Before we get into the boat, Cammy, we need to work on casting."

"I still don't understand why you don't just let me drive the boat," I say.

"This lake is shallow and rocky, so we can't take any chances. Juan will drive."

It has been at least ten years since I've cast a pole. Walt and Juan give each other a knowing look as they back off the dock, not wanting to take any chances of getting caught by a misfire.

"You're going to want to put your pole behind you," Grandpa says. "And as you move forward, push this button to release the line. Watch me do it."

He casts the line out effortlessly. After doing it a second time, he hands me the pole. On my first try, I don't release the line the right way, and I nearly hook my face.

"Ope!" they all yell in unison.

I cast again. This time, I've got the hang of it. By the third try, I'm a professional.

"Come out here every day, Cammy," Grandpa says. "Keep casting, and you'll be perfect."

Juan walks back onto the dock with a tape measure. "Okay, Camilla. The only walleyes that we can count have to be between fifteen and nineteen inches. We'll be working against the clock, so you need to be able to eyeball if the walleye is a keeper or not."

He shows me how big the fish needs to be as I watch on. Walt comes back on the dock and starts explaining how a walleye strikes the line compared to other fish. "Stripers, for example, will vibrate the pole as they get closer to the boat. And a northern pike will try to take the line under the boat. But a walleye, Camilla, will be an even and steady drag. You'll know. If you're a fisherwoman, you'll know."

They all talk fast as they give me instructions simultaneously.

"Should I be taking notes?"

My grandpa looks toward the cottage and waves. I turn to see Jake approaching the dock.

"Hi, guys," Jake says. "Mind if I join you?"

Grandpa waves him over. "The more, the merrier."

Walt and Juan look at each other, panicked, clearly not wanting Jake in on our secret.

"The dock is pretty full, Jake," I say. "I don't think we can fit one more." I wave him away.

Jake puts his hands out and then rolls his eyes and heads into the cottage.

Grandpa leans into me. "Cammy, that wasn't very nice."

"Grandpa, we can't let Jake know our secret strategy. His team are the enemies."

Walt puts his hand on my shoulder. "She's right, Sunny. He and his buddies are our biggest competition."

Juan walks off the dock, and we all follow. He turns to me. "This is enough of a lesson for one day. Next, we need to fish from the boat. We'll teach you how to spot what a keeper walleye looks like and how to take a fish off the hook."

"I have to take my fish off the hook?" I scrunch up my face at the thought.

Juan jumps in. "No one will have time to do it for you. You'll have to learn."

Usually I'm not squeamish, but there's something about touching a fish that makes my skin crawl.

Jake seems to have dropped something off. I watch as he gets into his truck and drives away. I say goodbye to Grandpa and his friends, who have somehow become my best friends in Wheaton. I laugh to myself at Walt's cat suspenders and Juan's socks pulled up to his knees. The socks have red and black stripes on the sides.

I wave as they drive away. Then I decide to walk down to Jake's to see if he's there and can tell me what's next on our list. The breeze doesn't reach the gravel road because of the thick canopy of trees on both sides. I spot the apple tree that Grandma Sis and I would walk to and pick apples for pie. We would fill buckets with the apples to replenish Grandma Sis's fruit cellar. We would use last season's apples for baking while the boys went out fishing. Already a few small and green apples have begun to grow on the tree. I make a note to come back in a week to see if more apples have appeared. Usually, they aren't ready to pick until the end of the summer.

Next to the tree sits a beautiful iron bench that my grandparents found on the side of the road when I was young. My grandpa fixed it up and painted it. In small letters on the back, it says, "Sis and Camilla's bench." I smile at the memory of him presenting the bench to us. Over the years, we spent hours sitting there, looking at the tree and enjoying the breeze off the lake in the background.

Next, I see the Point. This was where I would sit and cast with Dad and Grandpa. According to them, it's the best fishing spot on the entire lake. Everything here is sacred. Every sight sparks a memory of happiness and nostalgia.

I keep walking until I reach Jake's cottage, where I find his truck parked out front. His lawn is obnoxiously perfect. The original cottage I remember in this spot has been replaced by Jake's massive structure. It doesn't feel accurate to call this a cottage. It's more of a huge home on a lake.

When no one answers my knock, I try the door handle. It opens. I yell into the house, "Hey, Jake, are you in here?"

I slip off my shoes and enter. The space is even larger on the inside than it appeared from the outside. I enter into a mudroom with locker shelves, neatly hung life jackets, and a row of fishing poles.

Next is a great room. My mouth hangs open. I'm happy to be alone because I wouldn't want Jake to have the satisfaction that I find this space incredible. It's better than perfect. The entire wall facing the lake is windows from floor to ceiling. The walls are knotty pine. Like Jake said, there is almost no furniture, though it looks like he already worked with an interior designer or an interior architect. I would never have designed anything this good.

Everything looks new and smells like fresh wood. The living room extends into the kitchen, which boasts the biggest island I've ever seen. I take out my phone and start snapping pictures of the space. Off the living room, there's a short hallway that leads to a bedroom and a bathroom. The bedroom has a queen bed but nothing else. The bathroom looks unused.

I walk out of the hallway and through the kitchen. On the opposite side of the cottage, I find an identical hallway that leads to a bedroom and bathroom. A double staircase leads to a top floor that can be entered from the open living room or kitchen. The stairs float and are completely open to the great room. I get to the top landing, a balcony with a knotty pine railing overlooking the west-facing windows. I snap more pictures.

Behind me is a sliding barn door that traverses the length of the balcony. It opens from the middle. I slide one door open and then the other, leaving an opening that must be about twenty-five feet wide. Behind the doors resides Jake's beautiful bedroom. It has a king bed and two nightstands but nothing else. I sit on the foot of the bed. With the barn doors open, a panoramic view of the lake awaits me. Jake's bed has one of the best views of the lake I've ever seen. The attached bathroom boasts a large soaker tub and an adjacent walk-in closet.

This gorgeous house is like a blank canvas of beautiful wood and architecture. The aura is peaceful, as if I have wandered into a sanctuary. Even though the place is new, I can sense Jake's grandparents, Oscar and Eleanor. This space is sacred.

Jake's scent is strong in the closet as I run my hand across the shirts that hang in an orderly fashion, organized by color and type. There's a folded Stanford University sweatshirt among some mementos of Stanford football.

The pieces begin to come together. Jake left Wheaton to attend Stanford. Then, at some point after, he started his professional football career.

I'm just beginning to examine the pictures and articles hung on the far end of the closet when I hear footsteps coming up the stairs. My heart leaps, as I know there is no way to escape without being caught.

I run out of the closet as Jake comes into his bedroom.

He shakes his head when he sees me. "Hey, stalker. What are you doing in my house?" He sounds not at all surprised that I would let myself into his space.

My face reddens. I yank at my shirt. "Okay. Hear me out. I knocked first. I did. But no one answered, and the door was unlocked. I didn't plan to walk through your entire house, but I fell in love with it and couldn't stop." As the words pour out of me, I kick myself for admitting how much I love the place.

"And you ended up in my bedroom?"

I chew on the inside of my cheek and look back at the closet. "Well, technically, I ended up in your closet. But look, I took so many great photos. I mean, your place was designed to perfection. I may want to add some built-ins in the great room. But, wow, besides decorating your space, it will need nothing else." I take a breath and pivot. "Where were you?"

"Since you so rudely didn't let me join your crew, I was fishing off the dock."

I shrug and start scrolling through my phone and showing the pictures to Jake—proof that I entered his space for a purpose. The warmth of his body causes my skin to tingle as I lean across him to make sure he looks at my pictures. He smells like sandalwood and sunshine.

When he hands back my phone, his eyes captivate me.

"Did you design the floor plan?" I ask. "It's so perfect. The way you separate the bedrooms and bathrooms downstairs, the views, the sliding barn door so if you don't need privacy, you can keep the doors open and get panoramic views of the lake from your bed."

Jake laughs. "Yes, I designed the floor plan. And as you noticed, I need furniture for it to feel like home."

"I can do that."

Jake walks out of his room.

I follow. "So you went to Stanford?"

"You went through my stuff?"

"Not purposely. I saw some Stanford stuff in your closet."

"Yes."

He stops on the last step and turns to me, causing me to break my rhythm and trip over my feet. I grab onto his shoulders for a brief moment before letting go of him. His hands grip my waist before he drops them.

"And if I remember correctly," he says, "you came to my high school graduation."

"I did." I startle at the idea that he really does remember me. "My family was on a month-long holiday and visited from Dublin. We spent the month in Wheaton and attended your party."

We stand at the bottom of the steps as he turns his head in thought. "So you would have been about eight?"

"You remember that?" I ask, perplexed.

Jake walks toward the front door and opens it. "You don't remember, do you?"

I shake my head, unsure of what he's referring to. "Remember what?"

"We share a birthday. I'm ten years older than you to the day. You don't remember the pictures our parents made us take together?"

"Weird." I furrow my brow. "I didn't think you remembered me at all."

"Memories are starting to come back to me." Jake looks back at me as he admits it. "Ten years. I've lived a lot more life than you. Remember that next time you give me attitude."

I step down from the bottom step. "Sure, but—"

Before I have a chance to finish my sentence, Dax enters through the open door. He smiles when he sees me, steps past his brother, and hugs me. "Camilla, I didn't know you'd be here."

I look at Jake and then his brother. "Didn't Jake tell you I'm helping decorate his place? I came over to get ideas."

"I'm glad you're here," Dax says as he strides over and puts his arm around Jake. "My parents took Kylie to a movie, so Jake and I had plans to go to the pool hall. We're meeting a lot of people. You should come. It beats hanging out with Sunny and Sis, right?"

Before I have the chance to answer, Jake speaks. "Camilla was just telling me she has plans tonight, so she won't be able to join us."

Inwardly I scowl, remembering how I'd said essentially the same thing to Grandpa when he invited Jake to play pool with us.

Dax takes his arm off Jake. "Are you sure, Camilla? Even for a bit?"

Jake looks at me, stone-faced, and I can tell he does not want me joining them for the night. I can take a hint.

"Thanks for the invite, but I'm going to finish a few things at the cottage before I head to town. You guys have fun, though."

I make sure to glare at Jake as I pass him on my way out the door.

# CHAPTER 11

I look in the mirror and barely recognize my body. Muscle has appeared in places I never knew muscles existed. I never thought I would be one of those women who could see definition in her abdomen, but my individual abs are now visible. Hours at the gym wouldn't have had the same results. All of this manual work at the cottage makes me feel healthier than ever before. It seems like maybe this small-town living is starting to wear off on me, and I haven't even been here a month.

My fishing buddies are mad because I demand that I take the day off from my lesson. For the past few days, for two hours straight, I've learned the art of catching walleye. I know how to rig my pole, I know what lure to use depending on the water clarity, and I've almost mastered knowing what kind of fish is on the line before the fish breaks the water. For a while, I would get confused over the difference between smallmouth bass and a walleye, but now I know how to identify a walleye 100 percent of the time—big eyes, golden-speckled body, top fin. I've almost mastered netting my own fish, but I still have major work to do related to getting the hook out.

Today, though, I blocked my entire morning to bake an apple pie with Grandma Sis. She was so excited when I asked her to show me how to bake pies like hers that she practically ran to the basement to get last fall's apples from the cellar. I want to study each step so that someday I can make these amazing pies as I tell my children all about Grandma Sis. If I want these traditions to continue into the next generation, it's up to me to keep them.

"Camilla, the most important step, and the one people seem to skip, is that the apples need to marinate in the butter and cinnamon all night long. It helps so much with the flavor." Grandma pulls the bag of marinating apples out of the refrigerator. "And I make my own butter. But don't share that with anyone."

I write all this down in the notebook I'm keeping.

Grandma puts the bag of apples aside and grabs her bowl of dough. "Next, my dear, homemade crust is best." She kneads and stretches the crust she prepared the night before. She pours the ingredients onto the crust, then creates a lattice effect with it. She brushes a thin coat of butter and cinnamon onto the crust and puts it in the oven.

As I watch, I wonder why it is that I've waited until the end of my grandparents' lives to learn all of these skills. It's like I never had the time before, but now I feel rushed to get everything in before it's too late. I want to know how to fish, I want to be able to bake Grandma Sis's pies, and I want to fix up the cottage.

My mind flashes to my European literature class in college. We were studying George Bernard Shaw, who said, "Youth is wasted on the young." In the lesson, we learned how Shaw was asked to elaborate. "Youth," he replied, "is the most beautiful thing in the world—and what a pity that it has to be wasted on children!" I didn't understand that back then. Now I think I do.

Grandma Sis pours us both a cup of tea. We sit at the kitchen table and wait for the pie to finish.

"When I was a young girl," she says, "my mom and I used to make this pie together. I tried to get my boys into baking, but it was never their thing. I always hoped to have a granddaughter I could bake with."

Her eyes glisten as she takes my hand in hers. Everything makes Grandma Sis emotional these days.

"Things are getting confusing for me," she says. "But please don't forget how much I love you—how much I've always loved you."

I stand up from the table, take my grandma in my arms, and hold her. "Grandma, I could never forget." My face is wet with tears, and I'm not sure which ones are mine and which ones are hers.

"I remember when you were a young girl," Grandma says, "and we would walk down to the apple tree on the road. You always wanted to be with the older boys, but they'd leave you behind when they went out on their adventures. But, Camilla, I loved that time with you. We'd talk about where we wanted to travel that evening on the moonbeams, and we'd fill our baskets with apples and then take the supply from last year's batch and bake those boys the best apple pies. And when they'd come in from their adventures, we would be their heroes."

"That's how I remember it too, Grandma."

When the oven beeps, I rise to take out the pie. It smells like everything good in this world. The crust is a beautiful golden brown.

"Grandma, the Wheaton Days festival is coming up. They have a pie contest. I think we should enter."

Her face lights up. "Let's do it! We'll bake many pies between now and then to perfect the recipe."

The rest of the day, I run around doing errands. I make an appointment to get internet at the cottage so I can spend more time there and less time at the coffee shop. I reach out to Jenna about a picture idea I have for Jake's new home. Jenna confirms that she has what I'm looking for. She promises me she'll bring some of the pictures to the cottage, where she and I plan to fire up the grill to make dinner.

When I arrive at the cottage, it's clear that Jake has been here and gone. The drywall is finished, with the mudding around the boards perfectly smooth. Everything is coming together. The next step will be to paint the walls. I start rummaging through old pictures that have lived in drawers out here for decades. They're covered in layers of dust. My idea for Jake's home has also given me some ideas for things I could do here. I want to honor and remember the past by bringing it to the forefront of the design.

A car door slams. Through the window, I see that it's Jenna. Right behind her is Dax, who's holding hands with the most adorable little girl.

At the door, Jenna hands me a bag of pictures. "I brought company."

Dax pulls me into a hug.

"Hey, Dax." I kneel. "And you must be Kylie."

She looks up at Dax. "Dad, she knows my name." Then she turns to me. "Do I know you?"

I reach my hand out to her. "My name is Camilla. I knew your dad when he was your age."

Her brown eyes go big. "That's so cool!"

When I stand, Jenna loops her arm in mine. "Hey, so," she says, "there may be one more. Jake and I were texting, and he wants to come over and grill with us."

I try not to groan.

Jenna wastes little time in getting started with setting the food and wine on the picnic table. As I help her prepare for the meal, it occurs to me that part of the reason Jake and I have been doing all this work is because I'm trying to recreate the past on some level. Whatever the future might look like, it feels good to be using the cottage for fun again.

Dax fiddles with the grill. I can only hope that it still works because it doesn't look like it has been turned on in years. He seems to have the magic touch, though, because it comes to life. "Are you surviving Wheaton?" he asks me.

"I am." I look down and kick at the grass. "But time is moving too fast."

"I've never heard anyone say that about their time here," he says as Kylie runs up and hugs my leg. "Kylie seems to like you."

"She's beautiful, Dax."

"I know. I'm going to be batting the boys away when she's older."

Jenna pours us all a drink as I go inside and put on my swimsuit. A few minutes later, Jenna and I dangle our feet in the water as Dax swims with Kylie. She wears a bright pink suit and an orange life jacket. She dunks her head under the water and squeals.

Dax laughs at Kylie and then turns to us. "If only Robby were here. And Liam and David. We always had so much fun."

"Guys, I forgot to tell you," I say. "Robby will be here in a few days."

A car door shuts. We all look back to see Jake getting out of his truck. He carries a bowl and a bottle of wine, a guitar case slung over his shoulder. "I brought a salad," he yells from across the yard.

Jenna and I get up and meet Jake at the picnic table. Kylie comes out of the water and sprints toward him as she unzips her life jacket. Jake puts down the guitar case before she gets to him. When she reaches him, she launches herself into his arms. He spins her, leaving wet spots all over his shirt.

"I'm so glad you're here, Uncle Jake." Her arms wrap around his neck. She looks so tiny in his arms.

"Well, I heard there was going to be a pretty girl here, and I was right." Jake kisses her forehead. I'm embarrassed when his gaze cuts to mine, and he catches me staring.

He puts Kylie down. Dax wraps her in a towel and dries her off. Jake's shirt is now soaked, but he doesn't seem to care. He pops the cork on the sparkling wine and pours me a glass.

"Try this," he says. "It's my favorite."

I hold the glass to my lips. The bubbles warm my throat. "What is it?"

"It's Penedes Espumoso."

Wine nearly shoots out of my mouth as he pours a glass for Dax and Jenna.

"From the Penedes region of Spain?" I ask.

"Do you know any other Penedes?" Jake asks as he grabs a can of sparkling water.

"I'm surprised, is all. I went to the Penedes winery when I was doing an internship in Barcelona. I've never met anyone else who's heard of it. Aren't you going to have a glass?"

"I'll stick to sparkling water." Jake winks at me as he moves the bottle aside so Dax can refill his glass.

Jake and Dax grill the meat as Jenna and I finish setting the picnic table. We laugh as we retell childhood stories. Kylie seems to enjoy hearing about her dad when he was younger. I think about how much I wish Robby were here. With as much fun we're having, it's almost like no time has passed at all. I barely recognize Jake as he tends to the steak, laughing. He looks happy. His guard is down more than I'm used to.

Dax brings a plate of steaks to the table. "All are medium rare. I hope that works."

After we all choose our places at the table, Dax cuts up small pieces for Kylie. She has planted herself next to me. Jake sends around the salad. I put a fork in the steak and bring it to my plate. It's cooked to perfection and juicy. I can't help the moan that escapes my lips.

After I finish my first exquisite bite, I nod to the guitar case leaning against the cottage. "You play?" I ask.

"Some," Jake says as he concentrates on cutting his steak. "Kylie likes when I play around a fire. Don't you, Kylie?"

"Uncle Jake is the best at guitar," Kylie says with a mouthful of food. "He taught me the G and C chords."

"Wow, Kylie." I smile. "It sounds like maybe you're the best."

She shakes her head. "No, Uncle Jake is still better. He can play whole songs."

After dinner, we all sit around the fire. Kylie crawls into my lap, and I welcome it. When I was in Cambodia and Botswana, I got to be around so many children. I miss it. She leans back on me, and I wrap my arms around her to warm her bare arms. No one speaks at first. Instead, we all stare at the dancing flames against the lake.

Jenna is first to break the silence. "I wish Grandpa and Grandma could see us all together. I bet they're smiling from heaven."

"They'd love that we're having a fire at the Bergland place," Jake says, "just like they used to do."

A car door slams. We all sit still, waiting to see who will appear. I don't need to look because I recognize Tiffeny's voice as she rounds the corner.

"There you are, Jake. I've been looking for you."

Jake slowly glances at Tiffeny. He appears indifferent, if maybe a little less than excited to see her. It's not what he says but what he doesn't say as he stands up and brings another chair to the firepit. The mood and energy shift with Tiffeny's presence. I don't know why I care, but I don't want her here. She looks ready to go out on the town. A severe eyeliner trims her small blue eyes, and her hair is pulled into a high ponytail.

She doesn't bother greeting any of the rest of us before she starts grilling me. "It must be hard to give up your life to come to a place like Wheaton."

I stretch my legs out toward the fire and pull Kylie in closer. "Not so hard."

"Well, you've sure kept Jake busy since you arrived."

Jake looks down when I glance at him.

"I mean, every free minute, he seems to be with you."

"Well…" I pause, not sure how to respond. "I definitely appreciate his expertise. I couldn't do this without him."

"Well, I'm sure your type can't wait to get out of this place."

My face flushes. Biting my tongue has never been one of my strengths. "My type?"

Before Tiffeny can answer, Kylie lifts her head and chimes in. "Are you leaving?" she asks between yawns.

Everyone except Jake looks to Tiffeny. Jake only has eyes for the fire.

"I don't mean to sound rude," Tiffeny says. "It's just...the whole world is your oyster. Why would you let Wheaton hold you back?"

I cross my legs and readjust Kylie on my lap. I've met people like Tiffeny before. They tend to be threatened by me. I take a slow and deliberate breath so my annoyance doesn't show. "I appreciate your concern, but I assure you, Wheaton isn't holding me back."

Jake leaves us for a moment before returning with his guitar case. He takes out the guitar and starts stringing the chords. I'm happy the attention has refocused to someone else. He starts playing, and after a few chords, his baritone voice rings out into the night with the song "Have You Ever Seen the Rain," less in the style of Credence Clearwater Revival and more in the style of Willie Nelson.

Jenna joins. They have beautiful voices that blend together perfectly. Jake sits erect in his chair, legs apart as his fingers strum. Watching him does something to my stomach. Even though I want to, I can't look away. The way the words drip out of him like honey and the way he subtly glances at me when he sings.

Kylie puts her lips up to my ear and whispers, "Do you know how to do hair?" She runs her fingers through mine.

I plant a kiss on her beautiful brown curls. "I do. What do you have in mind?"

"Anything," she whispers. "My dad brushes my hair wrong, and it gets all frizzy."

"You have to tell your dad that you can't brush curly hair when it's dry. I know many hairstyles. Would you want it braided? I'm pretty good at that."

Kylie screams into my ear. "I'd love braids!"

"If your dad says it's okay."

Jake and Jenna continue singing.

"Maybe later," Kylie says sleepily. Her eyes close and her head leans against me.

The song ends. None of us says a word as we watch the sun hit the rolling hills and start to disappear. I grab my phone to take a picture. Jenna and Dax do the same.

Jake grunts. "How many pictures of this sunset do you all have on your phone?"

I don't say anything, but I already have a few.

"I don't get why people want to watch the sunset through a screen," he says. "Just look at it."

Dax stifles a laugh, but Jake has a point. I put my phone away and watch as the sun disappears behind the hills. A sliver of the orangish yellow sun lingers. I've seen the sunset on the Mediterranean

Sea and over the Great Wall of China. Nothing even comes close to rivaling the sunsets on Lake Traverse.

Jake starts playing again.

Dax gets up and takes Kylie out of my arms. He whispers over the guitar, "I'm going to get my baby girl home."

I seize the opportunity to slip out of my chair and go to my car to grab a few things that I wanted to drop off at the cottage. Warm summer sprinkles begin to fall from the sky just as I sense the presence behind me. I turn to see Tiffeny following me.

I open the car door and grab a bag. "What's up, Tiffeny?"

"I needed to get something from Jake's truck," she says as she opens the door. "The cottage is starting to look great, Camilla. Jake's happy with the progress and what it will do to property values."

I slam the door and look at her. "Jake's interested in property values related to my family's cottage, huh?"

She looks back toward the fire and then to me. "You didn't know? Jake's only helping you fix it up because he wants to buy it from your family when you're done." She smirks. "It's funny because you probably thought you were getting free labor out of him. But it's actually Jake getting free labor out of you."

Heat prickles my entire body. I've never been so happy for the darkness, as I'm sure I've turned five shades darker. "Well, Tiffeny, I assure you that Jake and I are both using each other equally."

She laughs and walks back to the fire. I stand there paralyzed. Jake has been so helpful, but now it all makes sense. And what reason would Tiffeny have to lie about this?

I decide to text Robby.

*I had to text you so I won't say something I regret to anyone else. Jake is a jerk. We're at the cottage, and his little girlfriend just informed me that he's only helping me because he wants to buy the cottage from our family when we're done fixing it up. Can you believe the nerve of him? As if we'd ever sell it. Also, he plays the guitar. How pretentious, am I right? Okay, see you soon.*

# CHAPTER 12

Today's list is long. I need to master the art of taking a fish off the hook with my grandpa and buddies, then go through pictures and design ideas for Jake. I must paint the inside of the cottage and inquire about a water heater. Every time I cross something off the list, I seem to add two more things.

What consumes me most is trying not to think about what Tiffeny told me last night. I had just started to think he was helping me out of the goodness of his heart. I blame the guitar playing. It softened me. And my guard was down. Now he's right back where he started at the beginning of the summer—a temperamental jerk. At least I'm getting help. That's what matters.

We're all sitting around in chairs in front of the cottage when Walt shakes his head at me.

"It's settled then," he says. "Camilla doesn't have to touch the fish. She can wear a glove and push on the gills while dislodging the hook with needle-nose pliers. There will never need to be any fish-touching."

I look at Walt, then Juan, and finally at Grandpa. "Are you sure I'm still worthy of being in your boat after this concession?"

Grandpa pats me on the knee as the other two give me reassuring looks. "It's your last thing to master. We'll have to move forward with this plan."

Suddenly, I'm full of confidence as I stretch out my legs. "You guys. I've got this. We're going to win this tournament."

Walt leans in as if there may be someone listening to us in the trees. "We don't need to enter our group until Saturday morning. We can't let anyone know that Camilla is our secret weapon."

I pucker my lips and give Walt a knowing look. "I haven't told anyone. I promise."

We all look beyond the cottage as a car pulls up. All of us sit back in our chairs with our cups of coffee. Everyone tries to look nonchalant, but instead, we draw more attention to ourselves. Walt puts his hand up to his chin like he's deep in thought. Juan puts his cup down, digs both of his hands in his jeans pockets, and studies the grass. Grandpa looks at the sky and whistles.

Jake turns the corner and sees us all sitting there. "Am I interrupting something?"

Grandpa jumps up faster than I've seen him move since I've been back. "Well, the boys and I are having a cup of coffee out here. I hope you don't mind if we stay."

Jake puts down the paint. "You can watch Camilla and me paint."

I prop the door of the cottage open. Grandpa, Walt, and Juan position their chairs in front so they can see us work. I fill their cups with fresh coffee and then get my brush ready.

Jake shakes his head as he opens the first can of paint—a color called Grey Owl. He yells back toward the door, "You guys have been fishing a lot out here."

Grandpa's voice chimes back from the other side, "Cammy wanted to learn how to fish, so us boys have been teaching her a thing or two."

Jake's paintbrush glides across the ceiling as I work on the trim at the baseboards. "This doesn't have anything to do with the fishing tournament, does it?"

"Ope!" Walt sounds like he's choking. "Of course not, son."

Jake looks at me as I trim near his feet. "Sounds like you're up to something," he says quietly so the men can't hear him.

I stand up and stretch my back. Jake quits painting and squints his eyes.

"Do you know why Walt never married?" I ask him, eager to change the subject away from the fishing tournament.

He hands me a roller and leans toward me. His breath is warm against my ear. "You know, he and Annie have been together since…well, since before I can remember."

"What?" I shout.

Jake puts his free hand over my mouth.

"What is it, Cammy?" Grandpa yells through the door.

"Nothing, sorry." I turn to Jake and lower my voice. "How did I not know this? Do my grandparents know?"

"Almost everyone knows. I'm not sure why they're secretive about it, but everyone knows, and zero people care. They seem happy."

I get back to rolling paint, side by side now with Jake. "My mind is blown."

Juan walks in, followed by my grandpa and then Walt. They stride around as if examining our progress. Juan puts his finger on the wet paint, leaving a mark I'll need to fix.

"We're going to drive back to town," Grandpa says as he stretches his arms up in the air. "See you later, Cammy. And thanks again for helping, Jake."

We say our goodbyes, and then it's just the two of us again.

This cottage isn't large, so progress happens fast. Because the floors are being replaced, anyway, I mostly don't have to worry about working so fast that paint drips on them. It's nice to smell fresh paint instead of mildew and stale air. We finish the great room. The floors are still hideous, but the walls are starting to look nice. I love the color. Jake moves on to the bedrooms, where he maneuvers the furniture to the rooms' center so he can paint.

After a time, Jake returns to examine my progress. He opens the refrigerator, pulls out two bottles of water, and hands me one. Somehow, we've already been painting for hours. Time flies when working on this cottage. The smell of paint seeps from my pores.

Jake goes to the door. I follow, my gaze trained on his back. My foot gets stuck on the tarp draped over the couch, and before I know what's happening, my bottle of water shoots out of my hand. I tumble and land face-first in the paint tray. Miraculously, I don't have paint in my eyes, but I'm now covered, the paint having splattered everywhere.

I rise to my hands and knees and look at Jake, whose mouth is wide open. He does the worst possible thing. He bends over, puts his hands on his knees, and laughs harder than I've ever heard anyone laugh. I stand up, rage coursing through me, on a mission to make sure Jake Abram ends up with as much paint on himself as I have. Before he knows what's happening, I grab the rest of the paint tray and dump it on him. He looks at me in disbelief as paint drips down his shirt and jeans.

I wipe my hair back, now covered in gray paint, and wait for his reaction. He holds his shirt, which is so saturated that the paint runs off him. He reaches his arms out and puts them around me. He wiggles in a way that manages to get me covered in more paint. Now it's not only in my hair and face but all over my new bib overalls. He continues to laugh as he presses against me.

"Jake!" I yell.

He stops but keeps his arms around me.

"You looked like a puppy." He snickers as he takes my hair in his hand and gathers it into a ponytail. "On your hands and knees, looking up at me with those big eyes. I mean—"

"I'm glad I amuse you." I run my finger down his wet T-shirt and rub the excess paint on his face. "It's almost dark, and I can't go into town looking like this."

Jake lets go of my hair and shrugs. "Jump in the lake."

"Alone?" I ask, lips puckered, hands on my hips. "It's getting dark outside. Come with me?"

"I have a shower. With soap. And warm water." Jake likes to remind me of this.

I look down at myself. I'm a mess. In the bathroom mirror, I confirm that the paint is everywhere. It's on my face and neck and starting to get hard and crusty.

Jake enters the bathroom and looks at me. I give him my most pitiful look.

"Ugh, fine," he says. "You can use my shower."

"Yes!" I scream as I clap my hands.

I put an old towel down on the driver's seat of my car and drive to Jake's house so I can leave for town from there. For fear of getting paint everywhere, I avoid touching anything except for placing two index fingers on the steering wheel. My knees are caked in paint, my face feels like I'm wearing a facial mask, and I don't know if this mess will ever leave my hair.

At Jake's, we take our shoes off outdoors before entering.

"Let me grab you something to change into," he says as he goes up the stairs.

I stand there waiting for him, wondering if I should stay put or follow him. I decide to stay put.

He returns with some clothing balled in his hands. He gestures at the bathroom nearest me. "You can shower in there. I grabbed my smallest clothes, but they aren't going to fit you." He holds up a red Stanford shirt and a pair of black shorts and throws them at me.

"Can we shower at the same time?"

"Are you asking me to shower with you?" His expression contorts as he scratches his stubble. "I'd usually say yes, but you know, that could complicate things—really go against us not liking each other, you know?"

"I don't want to shower with you!" I put my hands on my hips, exasperated at his interpretation of my words. My face turns hot under the paint. "I meant because of water pressure. I was asking if you can have two showers running at the same time."

He laughs and walks away. "I knew what you meant, but seeing you get all worked up was worth it."

I go into Jake's guest bathroom—one of two on the main floor. It's nice and clean, with white tiles and a grayish stone countertop. The shower and tub combination looks brand-new. It's full of unopened body washes, shampoos, and conditioners. I tell myself that I should make a deal to shower here every day after sweating all day at the cottage.

I use the brand-new loofa to scrub at my skin until I'm raw. I rub the shampoo into my hair, hoping that the water-based paint comes out. Then I stand under the rainfall showerhead and enjoy the tremendous water pressure. This is by far the best shower I've had in Wheaton. My grandparents don't even have a proper shower. They have a tub with a removable shower head that I have to hold. But this shower is heaven. I moan as the warmth reaches me everywhere.

In Jake's clothes, I look as ridiculous as both of us expected. I pull the drawstring on the shorts as tight as it'll go and then roll the waistband three times. I put on my bra even though the paint oozed through my clothes and stained it. Finally, I tie the oversized shirt on the side. The mirror confirms that I look every bit as twelve years old as I feel in this outfit. My hair is still speckled with gray paint.

When I leave the bathroom, Jake isn't down yet. I go into his kitchen and search for a bag I can throw my bibs into so I don't make a mess everywhere. I open some cupboards but don't see anything.

"Can I help you find something?" Jake asks from the top of his stairs.

"A bag or something for my messy clothes."

"Come here, City Girl." He waves me upstairs.

I take my time on each step until I reach his bedroom.

Jake steps out of his closet while he towel-dries his hair. He's wearing only a pair of shorts. "Give me your clothes. I'll throw them in the wash."

I meet him in front of his closet and hand him my bibs. He throws them in the washing machine in his closet. He grabs a shirt to put on, but before he does, I take his arm to examine his tattoo. He freezes at my touch.

"What does your tattoo say?" I turn his arm to get a better view. Three cursive lines. Black ink.

He rubs his tattooed arm and then puts a shirt on. "It says, 'You can't get away from yourself by moving from one place to another.'"

I raise my eyebrows. "That's one of my favorite lines from *The Sun Also Rises*. Was that on purpose?"

"Was what on purpose? That I quoted that book?" His body goes still. "How did you know from such a small quote that it's from that book?"

I grab my shorts, as it feels like they're about to fall off my hips. "I love Hemingway. And I love that book especially."

"Yeah, me too." He looks at my outfit and shakes his head. "You quote Confucius, and I tattooed Hemingway. I guess we're both pompous."

I laugh. "What does the quote mean to you?"

"A ton."

"Did you put the tattoo over your scar for a reason?" I follow him out of the closet and out of the bedroom.

"Do you always ask this many questions?" he asks.

"It seems like a good way to get to know someone."

"Yes." He turns back to me as he reaches the bottom of the stairs. "The placement was on purpose. Any other questions?"

131

I follow him downstairs and toward the door. "Is it true that you're only helping me with the cottage because you hope to buy it someday?"

"Is that what you think?"

"That's what I was told."

He corners me between the door and him. "You weren't lying when you said you didn't like me. Especially if that's what you believe."

He puts his hand out and leans in. I feel out of my body, as if I'm watching him get closer in slow motion. I still myself, waiting. His breath is against my face. His eyes pierce into mine, our lips a hairsbreadth apart. My stomach is in tingly knots. I can smell his shampoo and the sandalwood scent on his body.

Then he reaches the doorknob and turns the handle. I jump out of the way so he can open it.

"You deny it?" I say as I bend over to grab my shoes. "Because Tiffeny told me, and I feel like I'm at least owed an explanation."

"I don't owe you anything."

He closes the door on me. I'm left outside alone.

# CHAPTER 13

The third week of June marks Wheaton Days, which is all the town can talk about. Everything and everyone buzzes with energy. I sit around with Walt, Juan, and my grandpa, the four of us enjoying a cup of coffee at the cottage after our daily fishing lesson.

I ask Walt a follow-up question. "So wait, the tournament this Saturday lasts for one hour?"

Walt shakes his head. "The competition starts at nine thirty in the morning. We have to sign in at nine. This is when we'll surprise all the other entrees with our ringer." He points to me.

I nod, though I'm surely not a ringer.

Grandpa puts his hand on his knee. "Once we're in the boat, Cammy, we have one hour to catch as many keeper walleyes as possible. At exactly ten thirty, all boats need to be lined up near the dam to count and measure fish. The boat with the most keeper walleyes wins the competition, and all those fish are handed over for the fish fry the next day."

I laugh at how excited my grandpa is as he explains this all to me. "Yes, so like I said, we only fish for an hour."

Juan sighs, as though I should already know all this. "No, kid. That's the prize we want to win, but then we fish until three in the afternoon. There will be prizes for the largest walleye, the largest fish—usually a catfish or a carp—and the smallest fish. Guys, am I missing any?" He looks at Walt and my grandpa.

Walt puts his cup down and pats his knees. "It would be great to win biggest fish, too, but all the glory comes with catching the most walleyes in an hour."

I stand up. "Do you guys think we have a chance? I mean, I've seen some of the boats on this lake. They are a lot fancier than what we have."

"We have something they don't have, Cammy," Grandpa says. "We know this lake better than anyone. I think we have a real shot."

"And who's our biggest competition?" I ask.

Simultaneously, they all say, "Abram Contracting."

Then Juan says, "They've won the past three years. Jake knows this lake as well as we do, unfortunately."

I look over at Walt, his gut protruding out of his shirt. I've learned a lot about fishing, but our only hope of winning this is if these old men can keep up with the competition. Everyone gets up. I gather their coffee mugs as they walk to Juan's car.

Walt hangs back and puts his arm around me. "Things are looking great out here, Camilla. I know your grandpa doesn't say much, but he's so proud of you."

Before I can say anything, he takes off. He catches up to Juan and my grandpa, and they drive away, leaving me to my work.

\*\*\*\*\*

The task I was given today was to start hauling everything out of the cottage so Jake and I can lay the floors. I love my choice. I went with a laminate that looks like hardwood floors, and I can't wait to see the fresh look they give the cottage. The color is breezy in a way that will make this small cottage look like a beachfront home. I haul the light items to the shed, trip after trip. Sweat pours out of me. I can't wait until the new water pump Jake ordered comes in so I can take a shower out here. Well, I'll need the pump and also to replace the shower. I'm starting to doubt if I'll ever be able to shower out at the cottage.

Like clockwork, I hear Jake pull into the gravel driveway after his work shift. A part of me always expects him not to show, especially since the last time we saw each other ended in a fight. But he has proven himself reliable. I feel bad that he spends most days on job sites and then comes here and does the bulk of the heavy work, but I need him too much to offer him an out.

He pulls off his shirt and throws it on the grass as he walks across the lawn. His jeans are full of paint stains. They sit low on his waist, probably from the weight of the toolbelt he wears.

I open the door for him. "Do you ever wear a shirt?"

"It's like a million degrees out, and I've been working since eight in the morning," he says as he glances at my outfit, which consists of running shorts and a tank top. He's right about the heat: it's way too hot for bibs. "Do I make you nervous, City Girl?"

I wrinkle up my face and turn away from him so he won't see me blush. "Not at all."

He laughs as he looks around the cottage. "Decent progress. Let's start hauling out the bigger items."

My relationship with Jake is the easy kind. It never progresses. The relationship spins in a circle and never penetrates too deeply below the surface. I get the sense that, like me, this is Jake's favorite kind of relationship. I'm aware of how much he and I seem to be alike. We are Leos to the core, we both like Hemingway, and neither of us is keen on letting many people in. I need his help with the cottage, and he needs me to design his home. Nothing more.

I grab one end of a dresser, and Jake grabs the other. Silence. We watch each other as we sidestep, moving the dresser to the shed. Muscles protrude out his arms as he carries more than his weight. Sweat drips down his face. I jump when his gaze cuts to mine, catching me staring.

We put the dresser in the shed and walk back into the cottage together, where we grab the dresser from another bedroom. Again, we haul it out in silence. This time, I avert my gaze. We make a total of four trips to the shed.

Next, Jake shows me what to do with the laminate floor. We measure, Jake cuts, and then he pounds it in place with his mallet. Repeat. Besides a grunt here and there, we continue to work in silence. When I glance in his direction, he seems a million miles away. He never looks up from what he's doing.

He stops working and grabs a bottle of water from the fridge. I lean against the wall and pull my knees up to my chest.

"I would never try to buy this cottage from your grandparents." He sits next to me, knees folded, elbows rested on them, the sweet smell of sweat coming from his body. "So we're clear."

I continue to stare ahead. "I don't care if you were planning to or not. Sunny and Sis would never sell to you anyhow."

"Is that so?" Jake turns to me. "Then why did Sunny once ask me if I was interested in buying the cottage?"

My blood boils. "You're lying."

Jake bumps his knee against mine. "I don't lie."

"When?" I ask as I bang my knee against his even harder.

"It was a few years back. He wanted to gauge my interest. He said the upkeep was too hard and that your dad and uncle live too far away to use it regularly enough to justify keeping it."

"You're a liar, Jake Abram."

Heads turned toward each other, our arms touch. It feels like fire is going to come out of me.

"And you, Camilla Bergland, see things how you want to see them and not how they are. And you're usually wrong."

"Am I wrong about you?"

He laughs. He puts his hand on my knee, causing shivers up my spine. He goes to stand, and I catch his belt buckle and propel myself up with him. He looks at me, caught off guard.

"As for what you think about me," he says, "that may be the one thing you're right about."

I keep my hand looped in his belt. "And what did you tell my grandpa?"

"I told him I would help him in any way I can, but I felt like the cottage should stay in the Bergland family."

"Good because you can't have it."

Jake stuffs his hands in his pockets, and we both look outside at the setting sun. I release my grip on him. It seems like a waste to miss the daily ritual of the sun retiring for the evening just so we can fight with each other. We stand so close that I can feel the heat of Jake's body.

"The only reason I even considered your grandpa's offer was because no one in your family lives remotely close enough to give this place the love it deserves. Your dad and uncle throw money at it and visit a couple times a year for a week or two, but who do you think takes care of things the other forty-something weeks—"

"Stop!" I practically yell as I push Jake in the chest.

He doesn't flinch. "Sunny told me you've never stayed in one place very long, so it's not like you're going to keep this place up. I've told you how much work is required out here. Sunny was ready to throw in the towel. Don't be mad at me for being honest with you."

I don't cry often, but the tears are right there behind my eyes, threatening to poke through and spill down my cheeks. "Quit acting like you know my family. You make me so mad."

Jake furrows his brow. "Camilla, I'm not trying to upset you."

"Answer this one question." I bend over to crank the window open and let in some fresh air. "If you're not trying to buy the cottage from my family, why did Tiffeny say that to me? Are you calling her a liar?"

Jake leans forward and puts his hand on the table. "I admit, I said that to Tiffeny, but I didn't mean it. And I didn't think she'd say it to your face."

I shut my eyes and shake my head. "So you're saying you're the liar. Why even say it then?"

His laugh is guttural as the cottage gets a shade darker from the setting sun. "Because I spend every free minute of my day with you, you're hot as hell, and Tiffeny is jealous. Telling her I'm using you seemed to please her."

I freeze, my hand on the doorknob, and shake my head, unsure I heard him correctly.

"You look like you've seen a ghost, City Girl. You know you're gorgeous, but you're annoying as hell, so quit acting repulsed by my honesty."

I still can't seem to form any words.

"I'm much more interested in a person's mind than their looks," he continues. "And well, you and I haven't liked each other since day one."

I hold up my finger to him. "Not from day one. As kids, you were my favorite. But from the moment I got here, I realized you aren't the person I idolized as a kid."

He grabs the arm I have raised to him and holds it over my head. His other hand grabs a fist of hair behind my neck. The cold door pushes against my back as Jake presses into me, his body against mine, his knee between my legs. I close my eyes, but he's so close that when he speaks, I can feel his breath against my neck.

"We're not kids anymore, are we?"

I open my eyes. He lets go of my wrist and slides his fingertips down my raised arm until they're at my side.

Now that my arm is free, I push him away. "No, we aren't kids anymore, which is a shame because that was a better version of you." I step aside and open the screen door. "Now go."

Jake pauses, as out of breath as I am. "No problem for me, City Girl."

"Good," I huff.

"Good," he replies.

His chest rises. He lets out a sigh, but then he leaves. I slam the door behind him. Then I slide down, wrap my arms around my knees, and let myself cry.

My dad has been the best son. He calls my grandparents every day. He sends money and he visits every chance he gets, whether it's with my mom or alone. He calls Annie to check in. He calls Walt at least once a week. Uncle Larry is the same way. Sunny and Sis raised two independent sons who went on to marry and have children and lead successful lives. Why is this a bad thing?

The cottage becomes darker as dusk sets in. I stay unmoved from my spot, leaning against the door. Finally, I collect myself and start my drive back to town. I need to stop caring even a little about what Jake thinks about my family or me.

*Hey, Robby. I just called, but you didn't pick up. I miss you. Safe travels, and I can't wait to see you. I need you here.*

# CHAPTER 14

The morning of the fishing tournament, I peek my head through the curtains. There's not a cloud in sight. I know that even though the cottage is only ten minutes out of town, the weather can be very different at Lake Traverse. I'm excited about the fishing tournament today, but I'm even more excited that my brother Robby is making his way to Wheaton and will hopefully arrive before the street dance begins tonight. When I get downstairs, Grandma Sis is cutting sandwiches and putting them in bags.

"Hi, Grandma. Can I help with anything?"

She turns to me. "I was about to wake you up, Camilla. Sunny has been pacing for hours already."

We share a laugh. I'm not surprised at how excited Grandpa is for today. Grandma licks peanut butter off her finger, and her lips smack together.

"I'm going to give you the food, Camilla. If I give it to the boys, it'll be gone in the first ten minutes."

As I help Grandma put bags and drinks into the cooler, I hear the screech of the back door open.

Annie enters, bags and sowing material in hand. "Get ready, ladies. The fishermen have arrived." She looks toward the back door and laughs.

A minute later, Walt and Juan walk through the door. Walt greets Annie first and then throws a bright yellow shirt in my direction. I hold out the oversized, shapeless shirt in front of me. It reads "Coffee Crew." There is a large cup of coffee on the front. On the back, they have printed my name as *Cammy*.

When Grandpa joins us, Walt throws him his shirt. I'm speechless about the whole thing, as we never discussed matching T-shirts. They are so bright that I'm positive they could be seen from space.

Walt looks at me anxiously and points upstairs. "Go on, Camilla. Get changed. We need to go."

I decide to wear a bikini under my clothes as an excuse to take off the T-shirt at some point. The shirt is at least two sizes too large. I do my best to tie the side, but it's no use. Paired with my cutoff shorts, it looks like I'm wearing an oversized T-shirt and nothing else.

The men are all wearing their shirts when I come back downstairs. I break down laughing when I see them all standing around nervously in the kitchen. Walt wears his suspenders splattered with fish photos over the tucked-in shirt. Grandpa and Juan wear their shirts untucked.

Grandma puts the lid on the cooler and pulls me over to her. "Camilla, I don't think Sunny was this excited even for our wedding day."

"I hope I don't ruin the competition for them. And, Grandma, I've gotten all the ingredients for the pie, so we'll make that in the morning." I squeeze my grandma in a hug. Then I grab the cooler, and we're on our way.

Juan's boat is tied to the dock at the cottage, so we head there first. With Juan behind the wheel, the drive to the lake takes longer than usual. At one point, I'm convinced that a combine trundling along the two-lane highway is going to pass us.

We finally arrive to the dock, where we do a pole check and a gas check, and then get in the boat and head to the dam. Juan drives the boat. I sit closest to him, with my grandpa next and Walt at the far end.

Juan looks at me and points to the waves. "We call these waves the walleye chop, kiddo. It's the best weather for catching walleyes. And it will also make it difficult for some boats to navigate all the rocks."

Walt must feel left out of the conversation because he yells over the motor. "Lake Traverse is a shallow lake, kid. The deepest it gets is about eleven feet, and it's rocky. We have the advantage of knowing where every rock pile is."

Grandpa smiles. "That's right. We don't need the fancy depth finders those other boats have. We have decades of knowledge of fishing this lake."

"The waves are on our side," Walt yells over the motor.

All the men nod in agreement in a way that makes me think they're trying to convince themselves that they have a shot this year. Up ahead, several boats are lining up to get registered. Someone with a clipboard comes over and takes our team name: Coffee Crew. Team captain, Sunny Bergland.

Once we register, we anchor out in the open water and wait for the horn to blow. A boat pulls up right next to us, and of course, it's Jake's team. I don't recognize the man driving the boat, but both Jake and Dax are there, as well as a friend I always see Jake with. Jake's judgmental eyes take in my outfit.

"Hey, City Girl, are you wearing a dress?"

I shake my head and take a deep breath. "You're jealous 'cause your team doesn't have matching shirts." I pull my shirt out further so he can get a full look.

To add to how ridiculous I already look and feel, Grandpa feels the need to defend my honor. "My Cammy is as cute as a button."

Jake looks at his teammates and laughs.

"Yeah, Jake, what my grandpa said." I can't hear what anyone on their boat is saying, but they are all laughing and looking in my direction, so I have no doubt I'm the butt of their joke.

Dax smiles and waves. I wave back, grateful that one of the Abram brothers is nice.

Our boat is a lot smaller than Jake's and the other participants'. The motor is a fifty-horse, while the other motors look much larger. When I arrived a month ago, I wouldn't have said that I would end up liking the simplicity of Wheaton, but I do. And part of that simplicity is knowing that every morning at a certain time, I get to see the same faces and usually have the same conversations. I don't want to let Grandpa, Walt, and Juan down, but more than anything, I don't want our friendship to end after the competition.

Dax stands up in the boat and yells over to me, "Are you still going to the street dance, Camilla?"

I try to answer, but Grandpa beats me to it. "Cammy will be there with the best-looking date in town."

Jake coughs.

Dax squints and yells over the running motors. "Well, I'll see you there. And also, if you don't have plans tomorrow, Jake is having a huge bash at his house. He does it every year. It starts in the afternoon and goes late into the evening, so you should stop by."

Jake looks away as soon as our eyes meet.

"Kylie is hoping you'll be there," Dax adds.

"I'll be there!"

A horn sounds in the distance. I grab the side of the boat as we take off.

Juan yells over the motor, "We're headed right to Skunk Island. With this walleye chop, that will be best. And I know of every hidden rock in that ridge."

Juan steers our boat toward the hills on the South Dakota side of the lake. Of the twenty-five boats in the fishing contest, Jake's heads right in the direction of Skunk Island as well. The motor slows, and as we practiced so many times, we cast our lines and troll. The water is choppy, but when I look carefully, I can see the top of a couple of rocks that displace the water ever so slightly.

A boat I don't recognize moves to the other side of the rocks. We hear a screeching metal-on-metal sound, and the motor shuts off.

Grandpa turns to me. "See? Even with their fancy boat, no one knows Lake Traverse like us."

My pole bends before I feel the drag. "I have a fish on my line!" I yell louder than I'm intending.

Walt whispers back, "The Abrams' boat is nearby. We can't let them know every time we catch a fish. We're trying to fish like a game of poker."

Grandpa Sunny puts his hand on my shoulder. "But we are allowed to say 'tuna' ever so quietly." He winks at me and I laugh.

"Tuna," I whisper as I continue to reel in the fish. It feels steady like a walleye should feel, with a constant drag. I have to work to bring the fish to the boat, so I feel confident that it's not a small fish. Juan reaches for the net, and I catch the first glimpse of a fish. It's definitely a walleye. Juan helps net the fish. As much as I'm trying to become a real fisherwoman, I can't stomach to touch the fish, so I put a glove on. The hook is really in there, so I take out a needle-nose pliers and force the hook out. Then I hold the fish up to the measuring tape on the boat's inside. It's a sixteen-incher. Team Coffee Crew has their first fish, and somehow, I'm the one that caught it.

The hour goes by in a blur. I have the hot lure for a few minutes with my bright-green Rattlin' Rapala. After that, Walt gets hot with a blue Shad

Rap, and finally, Grandpa gets the hot fishing line. We catch, we measure, and, if it meets the criteria, we put the fish in one of the two live wells and get our line out into the water again. One boat remains stuck on the rocks. The only other boat in our view is Jake's. I try not to watch too much, but they're also doing a lot of reeling. I know that they're only one competitor, and the other boats might be doing even better than us, but I don't care that much if we lose. I just don't want to lose to Jake.

"Okay, Juan," I yell so he can hear me over the motor. "How much time do we have left?"

He looks down at his timer. "We have twenty minutes, but it'll take five minutes to get back to the dam on time, so we have fifteen minutes of fishing."

I pull at my shirt nervously and bite my lip. We're now on the west side of the rocks at Skunk Island as Jake's boat cruises closer. Suddenly, I want to win this so badly, if only so I can have this experience with my grandpa. Walt nervously looks over his shoulder and then back at his pole.

Now we're down to ten minutes of fishing time. Grandpa gets a walleye on his line. As I look at Jake's boat, so does his friend. When Dax and I make eye contact, he shrugs. I pensively look at Juan driving the boat, then at Dax. I hear the ten-minute warning horn go off from the dam.

"We only have five more minutes of fishing," Juan yells.

A minute passes, then two. My line has gone cold. I haven't caught anything but stripers in the past thirty minutes. I glance at Dax again. Our boats are so close they're almost touching.

"How many fish do you guys have?" Jake says through a grin, but none of us answers.

My deep breath sits in my chest for a moment before I exhale. Dax nods at me and then puts his pole between his legs, freeing his hands. He spreads them, all ten fingers elongated against his knees. Ten fingers. My eyes meet his, and he nods again. As if it all happens in slow motion, Jake and I look at each other. His eyes go to Dax's fingers and then dart back to me.

Ten. *Ten*. Dax is trying to tell me something.

"Walt," I whisper. "How many fish do we have?"

"Ten," he says as he leans into me. "And it's time to head back to the dam."

I look at Dax again, and he's once again holding his pole. But he tried to tell me. I'm not wrong about this. He was giving me a sign.

Everyone in Jake's boat starts reeling in. Walt and Grandpa start reeling in as well.

"One more minute, guys," I whisper. "Just one more minute."

Jake and his friends pull away in their boat, heading toward the dam. I know if we don't get there in time, we're disqualified, but if I'm right and Dax was trying to give me a clue, then we're tied with them.

Walt looks at me, panicked, line still in the water, trolling north. Before I have a chance to sec-ond-guess my decision, his pole bends. I grab the net, the fish gets up to the boat, and I land it. It's a beautiful walleye. Our eleventh.

"Let's get to the dam!" I scream.

Juan puts the boat in full throttle and heads toward the dam as Grandpa works to get the fish off the hook and into the live well. I hope I'm right. I hope I didn't misread Dax's clue.

We're the last boat to pull into the dam just as the final horn blows. We idle right behind Jake's boat. He continues to look at me and then Dax, suspicious.

A judge approaches our boat. We hand her our fish from the live wells. We caught eleven keeper walleyes in the hour. The number seems good, but I have nothing as a point of reference. The judge then goes to the next boat, which is Jake's. They hand over their live well, and the entire time, I can feel all eyes on me, burning holes into my back.

It takes a few minutes, and we all sit on the edge of our seats. I exchange glances with my team. No one says a word, and it has become so quiet that I can almost hear all of our breathing.

A woman approaches a microphone. She clears her throat. "The winner of the most walleyes is the Coffee Crew."

I jump up and down, shrieking with happiness. Grandpa stands up, unsteady in the boat, and pulls me into a hug. I lean over and hug Walt and then Juan.

The lady on the microphone comes on again. "Second place is Abram Contracting with ten walleyes. Third place is Feed and Seed with nine walleyes."

As Grandpa and I hug once again, I look back at Jake's boat. They look stunned. There is so much heat in Jake's eyes they are nearly sunburning my skin.

"Now get back out there for the rest of the contest," the microphone lady says.

We pull out of the dam, and I make sure to blow Jake a kiss on our way to open water.

# CHAPTER 15

I wake up from a long nap and can hear the band warming up just down the street. The time on my phone says that Robby should be here any minute if he isn't already downstairs. I've never missed Robby this much. He's my other half, and I have so much to fill him in on.

Robby was nearly three years old when I was born. The difference in our ages was great enough that we didn't fight much but not too great that we didn't connect. Robby has been my one constant in life. Although we wouldn't say it out loud to each other, we're each other's best friends. I know I'm his, and he is definitely mine.

In the mirror, I note that my skin is the tannest it has ever been. I push on my skin and watch it turn white for a moment before it goes back to olive. I've never spent so much time in the sun. I go through the closet and decide on a black halter dress. Then I put on the cowgirl boots I found several days ago in the closet. I think my grandparents tried to gift them to me as a teenager, and I probably stuck my nose up at them, but now I can smell the leather and recognize how beautiful they are. They go perfectly with my dress. I look like a real Wheaton girl.

The excitement gets louder as I go downstairs. The minute I see Robby, I run into the kitchen, tackle him from behind, and wrap my arms around him. He turns and pulls me into an embrace. It's hard to recognize that Robby and I are biologically related. He got the Bergland height and is over a foot taller than me. He also got my mom's dark hair and dark eyes but my dad's paler skin with freckles. I got my mom's short stature, olive skin, and curly hair but ended up with my dad's blond hair and blue eyes. My brother and I couldn't look less alike if we tried.

"You've only been gone a month, but you look so different." Robby puts his hand under his chin and takes me in. He extends his arm and squeezes my right shoulder. "Look at this. You have muscles. You've never had muscles."

I swat his hand away. "Okay, that's enough. I've been doing a lot of manual labor here."

"And fishing," Grandpa chimes in over his newspaper.

"And fishing," I add with a chuckle.

Grandma enters the room with Annie and grabs Robby into a hug. "When did you get here? I didn't hear you come in."

"I arrived a few minutes ago, Grandma Sis. I flew into Minneapolis and rented a car."

Grandma's eyes well up with tears. "I've been so lonesome for you, Robby."

Annie points to the door. "Now you three get going. The band has already been playing for an hour. Sis and I are going to work on our knitting."

Grandpa kisses Grandma Sis on the cheek as I take in Robby's outfit. "Are you going to wear that?" His polo is obnoxiously pink. Even though it's a hot summer day, he's wearing dark-wash jeans that hit him at his ankles and a pair of loafers with no socks. "I mean, you look like you just arrived from Chicago."

Robby examines his outfit. "I did just arrive from Chicago. And you look straight-up country in those boots."

"I fit in, and you look straight-up city." I do a little spin as Grandpa chuckles.

Grandpa walks to the door and motions for us to follow. "Let's go, you two."

Two full town blocks are cordoned off. The classic rock cover band is so loud that the bass vibrates under my feet as I walk. People stand around tables, drinking. Many have already taken to the dance floor. Nearly all of Wheaton has come alive.

Robby puts his arm around me and talks into my ear. "This place is a trip."

"You have no idea," I say. He walks away when Walt waves him over from a table.

When I see Jenna serving drinks at the bar, I pull Robby over. "That's Jenna Abram." I point toward Jenna. "The youngest of the three."

We get to the bar, and Jenna's face lights up when she sees us. She waves at me and then stares at Robby. She pours us both a beer in a plastic cup. "Who's your friend, Camilla?"

Jenna and Robby don't take their eyes off each other.

I sip my beer and observe them. "This is Robby, my brother. Has he changed that much?"

Jenna smiles and puts her hand out to shake Robby's. "It's been a while. It's so great to see you, Robby." She can't look away from him, which is reminiscent of all my girlfriends in life. They all tell me how hot my brother is. I don't get it. He's Robby.

"You too, Jenna. It looks like we've both grown up a bit." Robby won't take his eyes off her either, which is making me blush. "Will you get any free time tonight?"

Jenna looks at her watch. "I'm off in two hours. In the meantime, I'll keep the beers flowing. But let's meet up later for sure."

Robby and I grab our beers and head closer to the dance floor. I know what he's going to say before he even says it. Either that's the type of bond we've always had or Robby is just that predictable.

"Jenna grew up nicely." He goes to hold his hands out to make sure I know exactly what he's talking about, but I swat him before he has a chance.

"Don't be gross, Robby."

We laugh.

"Plus, you're only here for a few days. Don't go breaking hearts."

He gives me the side smirk that I've noticed girls always respond to. "Fine, but no need for you to fetch the beers tonight. I'll get beers for both of us." He finishes his cheap beer in a plastic cup. Then he tips mine up, so I drink faster, but most of it dribbles down my face. He walks back to the bar with our two cups.

Grandpa is off in the distance, but I know he will leave shortly. The sun has set. He hates being away from Grandma Sis for long, and it has already been a long day. Dax is off talking to a few of his friends. There is Jake just beyond him. Jake sees me and tips his head in acknowledgement. He says something to his friend and then starts walking toward me.

Everything around him seems to fade as he gets closer. His aqua polo hugs his skin. He's so tall, and with every step, he gets bigger.

"Hey there, City Girl. Or should I call you cheater?"

So it was true. He saw Dax give me a signal. He stands close. I roll my eyes and shake my head. He didn't shave, the evening scruff having taken over.

"How about you don't call me at all?" My comeback doesn't appear to affect him.

He nods toward the bar. "Is that your boyfriend from Chicago?"

I look back to see Robby and Jenna engaged in a conversation. Robby's back is to me, but I can see Jenna laughing and leaning into whatever it is he's saying.

"You mean that guy flirting with your sister?"

Jake's eyebrows raise when he realizes I'm right.

"That's my brother, Robby. He flew in for a few days."

Recognition comes over Jake's face. "Well, in that case, here you go."

My hand grazes his as he hands me a plastic cup of beer.

I take a drink and then pull it away from my lips. "Did you poison it?"

"You think I would do something to your beer?"

I shrug. "I wouldn't put it past you."

Jake's mouth opens to say something. Then he closes it and looks beyond me. I turn to see Robby approaching with his hands full.

"Robby," I say, "I don't know if you remember Jake Abram, the oldest." I nod at Jake. "This is him."

Robby gives Jake an awkward elbow bump, as he doesn't have a hand free to shake. He's a few inches shorter than Jake and with a much slenderer build. "Great to see you, Jake. I get at least a daily text from Cam about you." Robby holds out a beer for me. "I brought you a beer, Cam, but it looks like you already have one."

Jake coughs. "I can only imagine what she says about me."

My skin feels warm. I'm not sure if it's from Jake looking at me, Robby glancing at me with a confused expression, or the fact that I spent too long in the sun today.

I continue to stare ahead as Dax approaches us. He smiles as he gets closer and turns his attention to my brother. "Robby, is that you, man?"

They pull each other into a man hug.

I have many memories of Dax and Robby playing together. Dax is two years older than Robby's twenty-seven, if I remember correctly.

As Robby and Dax catch up, I throw a gentle elbow into Jake's side. "See, everyone likes everyone more than they like you."

When Jake smiles, I'm surprised that he doesn't seem annoyed like he usually does when looking at me.

"If you'll excuse me, I'm going to explore," I say. I walk around, finding no trace of Grandpa or his friends. Probably he had one beer and then left to get home to Grandma Sis.

I get lost in the crowd, cross over to Main Street's other side, and stare into the dark store windows. I can smell the flowers outside of the flower shop. The morning bread and doughnuts still linger in the air outside of the bakery. I pass the Main Street Bank, where my grandma worked so many years ago. Away from the blocked-off streets, the music is still so loud.

I keep walking until I see my reflection in the window of the old Wheaton Thrift Store. This was always my favorite store in town. Dark wood outlines the store, setting it apart from the others. I put my hands on the glass to look inside, finding it empty. I'll never forget my fourth birthday, when my parents brought me here and said I could pick out one thing—anything I wanted. I ended up leaving the store with a blue-and-yellow Big Wheel. I spent hours driving it around at the cottage.

A reflection appears behind me, and I don't need to study it to know who it is.

"Why are you so far away from the street dance?" he asks.

"I'm dreaming." I don't turn to face him. Jake is everywhere.

The streetlight shines behind him, making his hair look golden in the reflection. "About what?"

I look back at him. "About this store. What if it was mine? I could hang art from my various designs, have brochures and swatches for people to look through. My own little store."

The song turns slow. A woman on stage belts out one of my grandparents' favorites. The cover of Dusty Springfield's "You Don't Have to Say You Love Me" comes through the speakers.

Jake holds his hand out to me. "Dance with me?"

I hesitate but then put my hand in his. His hand smothers mine with its size. I look around. "Here?"

"Why not?"

"With you?"

"Am I really that bad?" He doesn't smile and doesn't seem to be joking. He stares at me blankly, waiting.

I shrug. Jake takes my right hand and holds it, and I slide my left down his arm as his other hand tightens around my waist. My arm feels the hardness of his muscles through his shirt. When he holds me against his body, my head can feel the music's vibrations through his shirt. He spins me, and I laugh out of shock as he pulls me back in.

"Tell me more about this dream of yours," he says into my hair. His heart beats against my ear.

"In this dream, I stay here. At least for a while. I see Sunny and Sis every day, and I become wildly successful and own my own business. And this thrift store, it's my home base."

The song ends.

Jake slides his hands to my shoulders. "You should do it."

"It's called a dream for a reason. It won't happen."

He rubs my bare arms. "That's up to you."

Thunder rumbles in the sky. I feel a drop, and then, without any warning, warm rain pours down from the sky. Jake grabs my hand, and we run to the overhang in front of the thrift store, but it's no use, as the sideways rain pelts us. Jake lets go of me, and I hold my hands out and spin as the rain splashes on my face.

I look to the skies and laugh at how hard the rain is coming down, about how we received no warning, and about the commotion of all the people running for cover. It reminds me of the monsoon rains in Cambodia. The rain would come out of nowhere and never lasted long, but everything seemed cleansed and new again afterward. The rain splashes off the street, and puddles begin to form.

Water drips from Jake as he combs his hair back with his hand. "It sounds like you have a lot to say about me to Robby, City Girl."

I laugh. "I hope you never see my phone. I warn you, they aren't nice things."

"That's most surprising." Jake opens his mouth and lets the rain in. "Because Robby just told me that you told him you were going to marry me someday."

I grab Jake's shirt in disbelief and make a mental note to kill Robby later. With his shirt balled in my fist, I say, "He didn't."

Jake puts his hands back on my shoulders and laughs. "Oh, he did." He smooths back my wet hair from my face, and even though the rain is warm, I start to shiver.

"I was eight. What do eight-year-olds know, anyway?"

The clouds part, and as fast as the rain came, it tapers off until nothing more falls from the sky. The band climbs back up to the stage and begins tuning their instruments. Everyone who took cover heads back to the dance area.

"Not much," Jake says as he takes his hand off my wet hair.

"If you don't see Robby again, you'll know why. I've killed him."

Jake wraps me in his arms, and we're both soaked to the bone. His chest rumbles as he laughs. "You remind me of another pesky sister that I never really wanted."

I freeze. I don't know what I wanted him to say, but it wasn't that.

He releases me, then turns and walks toward the dance area. He speaks as he glances at me over his shoulder. "I'm going to go find my friends, but maybe I'll see you tomorrow."

My thoughts are conflicted as I continue standing under the overhang, body shivering, dress heavy. Jake is infuriating on even the best days. He thinks he knows everything and always starts arguments. He orders me around and is oddly secretive about his life. He lives in Wheaton and probably always will. So why do I feel gutted that he just compared me to a pesky sister?

# CHAPTER 16

I lie awake in bed, hearing the thumping of the band that started again after the five-minute downpour, and I feel like it's never going to stop. A towel is wrapped around my wet hair. My dry pajamas keep me warm.

The bedroom door opens. Robby tiptoes to his bed and then trips and laughs.

"Seriously, Robby."

He shushes me but laughs louder than my whisper.

"Robby, you're going to wake Grandma and Grandpa."

I see the silhouette of him taking his pants and shirt off. He hangs them off the back of the chair before jumping into the other twin bed. This was always our room when we would visit. We would lie awake in bed, look out the window, and talk about life.

"Where did you disappear to, Robby?"

He has his head on his folded arms as he looks up at the ceiling. I pull the blanket up to me and curl into a ball and face him.

"Jenna and I climbed the water tower."

I can barely see the outline of his face, yet I can hear his smile when he talks.

"Oh no," I whisper loudly. "Robby, I like Jenna. And the Abrams are like family. Don't mess around with her."

"In case you've forgotten, I'm still dating Lilly, so it's not like that." Robby's face turns serious. "And you should talk. I saw you and that Abram boy."

"Jake?" I quickly cover my mouth, as I spoke the name loudly enough to fear waking my grandparents.

Robby laughs quietly. "You can't keep anything from me, Cam. You're still crushing on him. I can tell."

I get out of my bed and sit on the edge of Robby's. This way, we can quit screaming across the room. "You've never been more wrong."

"He's still too old for you. But I suppose I get the appeal."

"Ten years older. And there is no appeal. And I'm leaving." I'm grateful for the darkness, so Robby can't see my red face.

"You don't have to." Robby pulls me down, and we lie side by side, staring at the ceiling. "You literally have nothing grounding you anywhere. You should stay longer."

I elbow him in his side. "Um, not likely."

Robby laughs. "That's right. You never stay anywhere long. I call it the Emily effect."

I go to sit up, but Robby pulls me down and links his arm around mine. I rest my head against his. Robby should have become a therapist instead of an investment banker. He has a theory that dates back to being twelve years old and moving from the Netherlands to Portugal for my dad's job. Emily was my best friend from the moment we arrived in the Netherlands, which happened to be right after spending time in Wheaton and attending Jake's high school graduation.

Emily had moved to the Netherlands at the same time. Her family was from England, and her mom had a government job there. We were inseparable. Every weekend, we had a sleepover and would take turns between our two homes. We lived two houses away, walked to and from school every day, did our homework together, and told each other all of our secrets. At that age, there weren't many, but they were ours.

After four years, my dad got assigned to a job in Portugal, and her family was sent to Finland. It was devastating. We cried together for six months leading up to the departure, and then I cried every day for six months after. Robby says something changed in me after that. His theory is that Emily is why I move around so much and don't allow myself to get close to people. I find the view maddening.

"It's not the Emily effect."

"Whatever you say, Camilla. But our upbringing had two vastly different effects on us. It made me want to place roots somewhere, and it made you never let anyone get too close."

"Okay, Dr. Robby."

"Regardless, Jake's a player. So stay clear of that one."

"He's a total player," I admit. "And he's already playing someone, so I'm safe."

"Good, we agree," Robby says through a yawn.

I get up but not before giving him a smack on his stomach.

Back in bed, I turn on my side and face the wall. Robby is wrong. I've had many friends since Emily. In Portugal, I always hung out with Sophia and Estella. Sure, I was the third wheel and didn't get very close to them, but we still hung out. I hung out with some cool people when I started college in Savannah. I wanted to get to know people better, but I wanted to study abroad. Twice. I met friends everywhere I went, though.

I think back to the man from the Netherlands I met after my freshman year of college when I spent the summer at an Israeli kibbutz. Anders and I met on day one of orientation and had the same schedule to work in the fields. After a week of working together, he pulled me aside after the communal dinner and told me that he liked me. We spent that entire summer hanging out. He was so straightforward in his feelings toward me. I never had to guess how he felt. Of course, the relationship ended when Anders asked me to go to the Netherlands with him.

Robby is wrong.

*****

I don't feel well rested when my eyes pop open the next morning, but I have pies to make with my grandma, and I have anxiety over what kind of day she'll have today. I pray that it's a day where she has clarity.

Grandpa watches Grandma Sis lay out all of her pie ingredients.

"Hi, Grandma and Grandpa."

Grandpa's face lights up when he sees me. "Oh, good. You're here. Sis is feeling anxious about getting all the pies baked in time for the festival."

I pat his hand. "I'm here, Grandpa. You take a break." I squeeze my grandma's shoulder, take the knife out of her hand, and give her the dough. "How are you feeling today, Grandma Sis?"

She looks at me and shakes her head, and her eyes get clearer again. "I'm nervous we won't have enough time."

"Don't worry. We have more than enough time. You start rolling the dough and let me get out the marinating apples."

While Grandma rolls the dough, I put the tea-kettle on. Black tea, as always. I'm thinking today will be best if I try to keep the routine as normal as possible.

When it's ready, I hand Grandma her cup. She dips the teabag in the water. She blows on it methodically and then puts it to her lips. I place the apples on the dough. Grandma cuts slices of her homemade dough to place on top of the pie.

"Camilla, it's wonderful having you and Robby here. I know it's temporary, but every day, Sunny and I wake up excited for the day."

"We love being here, Grandma."

She places piece by piece of the dough over the pie. "When Sunny and I were raising your dad and your uncle, we knew we were raising independent men who weren't going to stay here. Watching you all be successful in Chicago and Larry and his family be successful in Florida makes us so proud. But we get lonesome."

I wonder what life would have been like had my dad not moved to Chicago for college and then found a job that didn't allow him to be grounded in one location. He and my mom tell the story that they met on the first day of his government job. The rest is history.

\*\*\*\*\*

Grandpa Sunny and Robby help us bring our pies to our display table. The festival is a few short blocks away, and the crowd is already thick. There are so many young kids here enjoying the few carnival rides. Booths are set up for various contests throughout the day, like the best pie and the best pickles, and then there are also knitting and sewing contests.

A brass band of four plays in a shady spot on the grass. The grass is still damp from last night's rainstorm. The low hum of the tuba vibrates in my chest. I stop at a few tables to admire the beautiful homemade jewelry made by some members of Wheaton's large Native American population. I run my hands across the beaded turquoise earrings, take out money, and buy a couple of pairs. I also admire the necklaces, but when Grandma tugs at my arm, I decide I'll have to come back and shop later.

Grandma and I stand in our booth. Grandpa is next to us with Walt and Robby. Annie comes over and hugs me and Grandma in turn. Walt takes Annie's hand and whispers in her ear, and Annie covers her mouth as she laughs. I still can't believe that I missed the signs before. It's now obvious to me that they're together. Robby continues to check his phone. I elbow him sharply. Entering the pie contest means a lot to Grandma and Grandpa, so it means a lot to me and should mean a lot to him.

I lean over to my grandma. "I've never seen better-looking pies."

She pats my forearm with a slightly trembling hand.

The judge reaches our table and takes a bite of our pie. She then moves onto the next. Now all we do is wait. I pass the time by thinking about the apple tree that helped us make these pies. Hopefully, it produces well this year because the cellar will need plenty of replenishing. We ended up making many more pies than usual because we wanted to present the best one for this competition.

When the judging starts, we all move to the front. Grandma looks agitated. I motion to Grandpa to come and take her hand as well. They start with pickles and then move onto the best pie. They announce the third-place winner and then the second, and our names aren't mentioned. They get to first place, and I shriek as the judge names Sis Bergland. We all clap. Grandpa walks us up to the podium for our blue ribbons.

As the ribbons get pinned on our shirts, Grandma Sis looks at me and smiles. She pulls me into a hug. "We did it, Mom. We did it."

"Grandma," I whisper. "It's me, Camilla. Your granddaughter."

Grandma Sis laughs. "Quit being so silly, Mom. I don't have grandchildren."

Warm tears bloom for me as her eyes descend into blankness. I pull her into another hug, wanting nothing more than to get her home before her confusion gets worse.

"I love you so much."

Her soft and wrinkly cheek rubs against my own. I had about three good hours with my grandma today, and I know I need to be happy with that. But instead, I feel a deep sadness and resentment that this disease is robbing us of all this time. I have to actively work to stay in the present because when I look back, I get sad about how much has changed, and when I look forward, the runway never seems long enough.

Grandma and Grandpa go home for their midday nap.

Robby and I head out to the cottage.

"Grandma was so confused earlier," I tell my brother.

"I know." He puts his hand on my shoulder. "I feel so helpless."

"Me too," I admit.

We ride in silence for a bit longer before Robby turns to me. "I can't wait to see the cottage and all the work you and the dreamboat Jake Abram have been working on."

I punch him in the arm without taking my eyes off the road. "He's not a dreamboat, and if it makes you feel better, we do all the work while arguing. I'm not even exaggerating."

Robby laughs as we turn down the driveway. "I know you better than anyone, Cam, and I'm not convinced that you aren't crushing as hard as you were as an eight-year-old."

"Next subject." I punch Robby again as he continues to laugh at me.

# CHAPTER 17

As we take a right down the gravel road, voices echo out at Jake's place. I'm intrigued to see how things are going at the party, but we keep driving to the cottage.

"We put on a new roof," I tell Robby when we pull up. "And then we had to get rid of rotten wood, which meant we went down to the studs and insulated, drywalled, painted, and the floors are nearly complete."

As we approach the cottage, Robby looks unimpressed by the improvements to the exterior, but when we enter, his jaw drops.

"There's still more to do," I say. "I haven't turned the water back on, but Jake did order a new water pump. I need to get the septic system working, and there is still outside painting and lawn work to do, but my goal is to be done by the end of summer."

Robby doesn't speak at first. I can tell he's in disbelief about how much work has been done. His big eyes take in all the changes.

"And Jake's been helping you with all this for free?" he asks finally.

"Not for free. We'll be paying him for materials. And I'm helping decorate his space. Grandpa knows what I'm doing out here and gave his blessing, but it would overwhelm Grandma, so we haven't told her yet."

I follow Robby out of the cottage.

"We have apple pie in the back seat," he says, "so we better get going to Jake's."

We go to the car and grab the pies, along with the bag I brought for Kylie. Side by side, my brother and I walk along the rows of corn on our way to Jake's place. The corn is now half as tall as me, providing more shade on the gravel road.

Robby's arm brushes against mine as we walk. "The cottage looks great, Cam. I'm proud of you. I'm actually blown away at how beautiful it's becoming."

I exhale. I hadn't realized how much I wanted Robby's approval.

There are so many cars here. The one that stands out is Tiffeny's obnoxious candy-apple red sports car. Front and center.

I'm convinced that there are nearly as many people here as were at the festival. We grab our pies to take inside. People are on the lawn, where a net has been hung. Many swimsuit-clad coeds play volleyball. People float on rafts in the lake. Others paddle around on paddleboards and kayaks. I follow Robby into Jake's house, where a large group congregates. We place the apple pies on his kitchen island.

I pull Robby close to me. "You are not allowed to leave my side to find Jenna. Promise me."

Robby laughs as he hands me a knife to cut the pie. "Why would I go look for Jenna. I told you, it was just nice to catch up with her. Nothing else."

We go outside. Coolers line the entire side of Jake's house. Robby grabs us both a drink. He has always had confidence around large groups of people. I've always hated crowds. I like connecting with people on an individual basis. I spot Jake on the water trampoline several yards from the dock. I wrap my arm around Robby's as his eyes scan every direction, clearly looking for Jenna.

Small hands wrap around my waist, and I turn to see Kylie. "I was hoping you would be here, Kylie."

"I was hoping you'd be here too, Camilla."

I sit in the grass and pull her into a hug. "I brought a bag of some goodies that I think you'll like." I open the bag for her, and she inspects it. "I know this doesn't seem exciting, but this is really great product for us curly-haired girls."

Dax comes over to sit with us in the grass.

I motion all around us. "This is quite the crowd."

"I know." Dax looks at Kylie. "And Kylie has had so much fun. Her grandma should be here any moment to take her home for the night."

"Dad," Kylie protests. "But Camilla brought me a bag of goodies."

"That's true, Dax. Do you mind if Kylie and I go through some of it?"

"Dax!" A man I recognize as always being with Jake approaches us. He turns to me. "Hi, we haven't met. I'm Malik."

Malik is tall, his handshake firm.

"It's nice to meet you. I'm Camilla."

"Yes, the infamous fishing tournament winner," Dax says. He goes to the coolers and grabs himself a drink.

When Malik laughs, I recognize him as the other member of Jake and Dax's fishing team.

Now it's my turn to laugh. "All's fair in fishing. Right, Malik?"

He grins, and I like him already. "Do you want to dip our toes in the water?"

Kylie holds my hand as Jake, Dax, and Jenna's mom approaches.

"I'm here to take you home, Kylie," Mrs. Abram says with a warm smile.

"But Camilla has goodies for me," Kylie protests again.

I greet Mrs. Abram and then turn to Kylie. "I'm free all day tomorrow if your grandma and dad say we can spend time together."

"Grandma?" Kylie looks up at a smiling Mrs. Abram.

"If it's all right with you, Camilla, I know Kylie would love to see you tomorrow."

I say my goodbyes to a waving Kylie. Then Malik and I walk to the beach area and sit in the chairs near the water. Jake and Tiffeny are the only two on the water trampoline, and from here, it looks like they're arguing.

"Are you from Wheaton?" I ask Malik.

"No," he says with a chuckle. "I'm from Oklahoma. Jake and I were teammates at Stanford. Jake was my quarterback."

"Did you play professionally too?"

"I played arena ball, but it never amounted to much. Jake asked if I wanted to move here and work for his company, so I decided to give it a go."

"You're pretty far from Oklahoma."

"I am, but I love it here. I didn't think I would, but here I am three years later. I'm Jake's chief financial officer, and he's still my quarterback."

I notice Jake observing me as Tiffeny talks to him.

A woman I recognize from the fundraiser pulls up a chair next to Malik. "You must be Camilla," she says. "I'm Carrie."

Carrie wears black linen pants, a lightweight long-sleeved shirt, and a wide-brimmed hat.

"It's great to meet you," I say. "I'm sorry I didn't get to meet you the night of the fundraiser. But I was happy to be there."

"Thank you for coming. Sunny and Sis are special to me." Carrie adjusts her hat. "Jake has told us a lot about you."

"I'm not going to lie. That scares me. Jake isn't my biggest fan."

Malik puts his hand on my chair. "Jake can be hard to get to know, but once he decides to let you in, he's yours for life."

"Good to know," I say skeptically. "Honestly, I wish I knew him better. I'm supposed to be designing his place, which would be a lot easier if I knew anything about him."

Malik bounces up from his chair. "Come with me. I'll show you some things."

Carrie and I both get up and follow Malik inside.

Malik goes upstairs and opens the door to Jake's bedroom. He heads into Jake's closet. Carrie and I are engrossed in conversation about how she works at the bank and owns the former thrift store, now vacant. I almost tell her that it's my favorite store, but Malik starts showing us things.

"I'd give you the story of how I know this stuff is in here, but I don't want to bore you to death." Malik pulls out a box hidden by clothes, and it's full of books. Next, he grabs a few large frames that face away from us and turns them around. There are pictures and newspaper clippings depicting Jake in his Oakland Rockets uniform. The pictures are beautiful. It's hard to reconcile the football player in the frame with the Jake I know.

"You're the designer, Camilla, but these pictures have been stuck away in here since he built this place. They should be displayed somewhere."

I sit on the floor and start looking through the books. "And these?"

"I wanted to show you all of his books. I've never known anyone who reads as much as Jake."

It's all starting to make sense. Jake's tattoo, the fact that he knew I was quoting Confucius. Jake is deeper than I realized, and I hate to admit it.

I hear voices down the stairs, and they're drawing closer. Malik pulls the door shut and turns off the closet light, hiding us. We all go silent.

"What's your problem, Jake?" a high-pitched squeal rings out. Tiffeny.

"I don't have a problem," Jake says. "I'm hosting people here and trying to have fun. Now isn't the right time to discuss this."

"But, Jake, I'm tired of you not committing. I don't want to waste my time anymore."

We all exchange glances. Malik rolls his eyes.

"Then don't waste your time."

I take a step back and trip, tumbling against the closet wall with a thump. I try not to laugh. Carrie presses her finger to her lips to stifle her own laughter.

"What was that noise?" Tiffeny says.

"I didn't hear anything. Look, Tiffeny. We'll talk. But today, I need to be the host, okay?"

"Fine. But tomorrow, we talk."

"Go back to the party. I'll be right down."

Footsteps draw near, the door swings open, and when the closet light switches on, it nearly blinds me.

Jake hides his amusement when he sees us. "This is not the group I expected in my closet."

"Sorry, man." Malik walks out and puts his hand on Jake's shoulders. "The women wanted a tour of your closet."

"No, we didn't!" Carrie and I say at the same time.

"Out of my room." Jake points to the door.

He doesn't have to ask me twice. Carrie laces her arm under mine as we scurry down the stairs. I decide that I like Jake's friends a lot. They're fun and nice, and they gave me some great ideas for Jake's place.

When we get downstairs, I make a beeline for Jenna. "I heard that you and Robby hung out at the dance last night."

"Yes." Her face turns red. "Hung out. That's it. It's great to see him again."

Jenna avoids looking at me by taking a drink. I grab her arm, and we head back outside, where the night is starting to get dark and the sky is lit up the most beautiful shade of pink. The party thins as the night goes on. Several cars have left. No one plays volleyball anymore. There's just a handful of people still hanging out now that the sun has set. Jake and Tiffeny engage in what looks like another heated conversation. Then she and a friend of hers leave.

Jake starts a fire. I pull up a chair, excited for the warmth, as the night has gotten chilly in a hurry. Robby pulls up a chair next to me, followed by Jenna.

"Where's Dax?" I ask my brother.

"He told me he was going to enjoy Kylie being with his parents tonight." He smiles. "I think he ended up overserving himself."

Jake pulls up a chair. The four of us sit and look at the fire against the blackness of the lake.

Robby starts to laugh. "Do you guys remember when we were kids, that one night when we took a canoe out to Diamond Island in the pitch dark? You were there, Jake. Dax, Liam, and David were there too."

Jenna clears her throat. "Why wasn't I invited?"

"You must have been sleeping, and Cam would have been too young."

Jake grunts. "I remember. The five of us almost sank the thing. We stole some beers from the cottage and paddled out to the island. We sat under the stars and drank every single one of them."

"Yeah," Robby cuts in. "And we would have gotten away with it except the next day your dad went out to the island to fish, and our beer cans were still there."

"That's right." Jake leans back, his hands behind his head, and smiles at the sky.

Robby sits up. "We should canoe out to Diamond Island."

Jake shrugs. "It is the best place to see the stars."

Jenna pops up. "I'm game."

Robby looks at me. "Cam, are you in?"

"You mean now?" I ask.

"Why not?"

My options are canoeing to Diamond Island or sitting by the fire alone. "I guess, but I don't want to get wet."

Jake jumps up and grabs a small cooler. We all follow him to the canoe. Jenna and I sit on the bottom as Jake and Robby push off the beach. Robby gets in first. Jake gives us one final push before hopping in. The canoe wobbles at first but then settles. Diamond Island isn't far, but it's eerie boating through the water in complete darkness. The only sound is the oars hitting the water.

The outline of the island comes into view. Robby gives Jake a look, and I turn to see the response. Jake puts his hand on the side of the canoe, and at the same time, he and Robby give it a shake. Jenna screams, and I brace for the impact of the water. In a flash, the canoe is upside down. As Jenna and I cling to it, Robby and Jake can't seem to catch their breath from laughter.

"Are you kidding me right now?" Jenna shrieks.

The water is so cold that my teeth immediately begin to chatter. My feet touch the sandy bottom. We all turn the canoe over and haul it the rest of the way to the beach at Diamond Island. As I drip in the sand, I hear the zipper of the cooler.

Robby hands me a beer. Then he grabs Jenna's arm. "I want to show you where we hung out as kids."

They hurry off in the darkness, leaving me alone with Jake. I think about what a terrible job of staying by my side Robby has done today. I sit on the sandy beach, too cold to drink my beer. My skin pebbles with goose bumps. A laughing Jake sits next to me.

"You look cold," he says. "I'd offer to warm you up, but my clothes are as wet as yours."

"Why do I always end up wet when I'm with you?" I ask through a shiver.

Jake slides closer, wraps his arm around me, and rubs my arms. His body blocks the cool evening wind. My teeth stop chattering as my body begins to warm.

"I wasn't lying," he says. "Diamond Island is the best place to see the stars."

I look up to find a sky lit with stars as far as my eyes can see. It takes my breath away.

Jake points out at the lake. "And just on the other side of the lake is where you conspired with my brother to win the fishing competition."

I push Jake's arm off me. "Blame your brother. I had nothing to do with it."

"I know that, Camilla." He picks up a pebble and throws it into the water. "I'm just giving you a hard time."

I sip my beer, immediately regretting it because it returns the chill to me. "Why do I never see you drink?"

He continues to chuck pebbles into the water. "I don't drink." His gaze cuts to mine.

I lie back on the sand to get a better view of the stars. I'm tempted to bury myself in search of warmth. I smile as I realize something. Jake lies down next to me. I sit up and lean back on my elbows and can see the red outline of his scar. I run my fingers across it and feel the unevenness of his skin where it comes together. Jake inhales sharply, but he doesn't stop me.

"Shark attack? Farm accident? Bad breakup? Or will you confirm that it was football?"

Jake puts his hand behind my hip and pulls me toward him. His fingertips graze my skin as my wet dress goes up. One of his fingers slides under the seam of my bikini bottom. I bite my lip from the sensation of his touch. He puts his hand behind my head and pulls me closer. I open my eyes to look into his, and our lips draw close. We pause for a moment, chest to chest. I can feel his heart racing beneath his skin.

Jake watches as I lick my lips.

"You'd get this close to me just to avoid answering a question?" I ask.

I can feel his warm breath on my lips.

"You are wise, Camilla."

Branches break behind us. Laughter follows. I jolt away from Jake, and he backs up too.

"I wanted to show Jenna the other side of the island," Robby says. "I think the stars are brighter over there."

As I stand and brush the sand off me, I avoid looking at Jake. It was like he put me in a trance, the world stood still around me, and all I could focus on was him. I shiver as I get in the canoe, ready for the short ride back.

# CHAPTER 18

We pull the canoe up to the shore, and Robby and Jenna run inside before I have a chance to grab his arm and plan our escape. Jake takes a hose and douses the fire until the last ember stops glowing. I look to his house and back at Jake. I don't realize that I'm holding my breath until I breathe out. After a few minutes, I know for sure that Robby and Jenna aren't coming back.

"You may be stuck sleeping here." Jake gestures toward his house.

I look at the lake, peek in the direction of my family's cottage, and then at Jake. He seems as unenthusiastic as I feel.

He reads my mind. "You're not driving, City Girl."

I don't tell him this, but I'm also not so desperate that I'll sleep on a half-finished, dusty floor at my cottage. "You didn't drink. You could drive me."

Jake glances at the dark driveway. "My truck is blocked. You're out of options."

I sigh and follow him inside. It's dark when we enter, but I can see a few shapes on the floor. A half-dozen or so people have passed out on the furniture, leaving nowhere for me to sleep. Jake looks toward a closed door and then goes to the other end of the house, where the door is also closed.

"If I had to guess, Robby is in one of the bedrooms with Jenna, and Dax is most likely in the other room. You know where my room is. Take your pick."

Robby has a girlfriend back in Chicago, I think, and nearly say out loud. I look around, unsure of what to do. Jake holds his hand out to me, and after a brief hesitation, I take it.

"Trust me, City Girl. I'm safer than Dax."

I'm not fully convinced that this is true.

He opens the door to his bedroom, and I look around at where I'll sleep. He goes into his closet and comes out with a T-shirt. He throws it in my direction. It hits the floor before I have a chance to catch it. I haven't even returned the first shirt of his that I wore.

"I'm guessing you don't want to sleep in a wet swimsuit and dress."

I hold the shirt up, another red Stanford shirt, this one with big white letters. I know I have no other options.

"I do have your clean bibs, if you'd rather sleep in those."

As I enter the bathroom, he calls after me.

"There are unopened toothbrushes in the bottom left drawer. Help yourself."

I peek around the bathroom door and hear Jake in his closet. "Is it okay if I use your shower? I'm full of sand."

Jake reappears from the closet with a towel. He places it on the counter. "Here you go." He leaves the bathroom without so much as glancing in my direction.

There is a clawfoot tub and, next to it, a walk-in shower all in stone. I turn on the spigot and step inside. The warm water hugs and comforts my cold skin. I scrub Jake's shampoo into my sandy hair. The sand falls from my hair and body and pools at my feet as I move out of the way and watch it go down the drain. I grab a bottle of body wash and scrub my skin. It's a combination of sandalwood and citrus, the way Jake smells.

After my shower, I pat my hair as dry as possible. Since I don't have a brush, my curls will be loose and wild. I pull on the Stanford shirt. In the bedroom, I find Jake wearing nothing more than a pair of shorts. He looks at me as I bite my bottom lip.

I tug at the shirt that doesn't feel long enough. "Shorts, please."

Jake returns to his closet. "I'm going to take a shower too," he says from inside.

He tosses me a pair of shorts on his way back through to the bathroom. Soon, I hear the shower through the closed bathroom door. I glance at Jake's nightstand, where F. Scott Fitzgerald's *The Great Gatsby* sits. I've never pretended to be anything but nosy, so even though I know I shouldn't, I open the drawer of his nightstand. Condoms. So many condoms. Not everything about Jake surprises me.

After a few minutes, he comes out again, still wearing nothing but shorts. Now he has his wet hair brushed back.

"Where are you sleeping?" I ask him.

"I'm sleeping in my comfortable bed. You're welcome to sleep in it as well."

"I'll sleep on the floor," I say quickly.

He sits on the edge of the bed and looks at me, annoyed. "My bed is a California king. I promise I won't go near you."

I sit on the other edge, knowing that I'll get better sleep on the bed than on the floor. My butt hangs off the side as I try to be as far away from Jake as possible. He lies down facing me and pulls the blanket up to his waist. I get under the covers and pull them over me as I stay as close to the edge of the bed as possible. I make myself so small that if this were two twin beds pushed together, I would easily slip through the crack.

Jake scowls as he tucks a hand under his pillow. "You're the only woman I've had in my bed that didn't want me to touch her."

I grab an extra pillow and throw it at him. "Are you sure?"

"Oh, I'm sure." He picks at a loose string on his blanket. "Relax, Camilla. I promise you're safe with me."

"According to the stash you keep in your nightstand, everyone is safe with you." The words pour out of me before I can stop myself.

Jake laughs. "You looked in my closet, so I guess I'm not surprised you looked in my nightstand too. One can never be too safe. Don't worry. I would never use those with you."

"Ugh, really, Jake?" I'm not sure if I should be offended or grateful, but perhaps I'm both.

Jake is right. This bed is huge, and there's so much space between us that I begin to relax as we both lie on our sides, looking at each other.

"I mean," he says slowly, "unless you wanted to. But I have something else in mind."

He holds my gaze as my mouth hangs open. Then he laughs.

He rubs at his scar. "Yes, football. The injury was a huge bummer. I was having my best season, and everyone was talking about going to the Super Bowl. Instead, I broke my humerus near my elbow. The bone basically shattered. And yeah, I tried to rehab, but it was no use." He stares down at his scar as if he's seeing it for the first time. "I didn't see the rush coming. None of us did. I stepped back to throw, and the pocket collapsed, and as I extended my arm, I was hammered by a three-hundred-pound defensive lineman."

My arm aches sympathetically. "I'm sorry. That must have been awful."

"Then it healed wrong, and I needed surgery to rebreak and set the bone. And now I'm a Wheaton loser."

"I never said that." I prop myself up on my elbow.

Jake's skin looks warm after a day of sunshine, and I wonder if he shaves his chest because I don't see one hair. "You didn't need to. I could see it all over your face."

"You don't know my face very well then. I never thought that. I think you're projecting how you feel about yourself."

He doesn't break my gaze. His hand caresses his blanket, and he seems to concede. "Maybe you're right."

"I usually am."

Jake smiles and throws the pillow back at me. Then he rolls onto his back and rests his head on his folded arms. "I'm thirty-four years old and live in the same town where I was born and raised."

I roll onto my back, too, thinking about how I'm twenty-four years old and don't even know where I consider home. Jake and I aren't that different. He wants to create a home here and feel safe. If I dig deep, I probably want to create a home somewhere too. I just don't know where.

His low voice takes me out of my head. "I need to get serious about the rest of my life."

I prop myself up on my elbow again. "Like getting serious with Tiffeny?"

"No, no," Jake blurts. "That's not what I mean. I mean fixing past mistakes, being better to people in general."

"Who are these people?"

Jake props himself up as well. "Like you. I suppose I haven't been very nice. That isn't fair."

189

"Don't worry about me. I can take care of myself." I pull the blanket up until it reaches my chin.

"That's clear." He moves his hand in my direction and then pulls it back.

I study his features. His sandy-blond hair tries to cover his one eye, but he moves it away with a flick of his head. His turquoise eyes are bright, his lips full and pink.

"You know more about me than I do about you, Camilla."

"But I still know so little," I say through a yawn.

He switches off the lamp on his nightstand, plunging us into darkness. He turns away from me, and I stare at his back until he speaks again.

"You're like my little sister, Camilla," he says. "It's crazy. Or maybe you're like the younger version of myself. Experiencing everything ten years after me. But we're eerily similar."

*Little sister. Again?* I shudder at the thought as I close my eyes.

\*\*\*\*\*

The next morning, the sun wakes me. Somehow, in a bed the size of Jake's, we have gravitated to the center, our faces inches apart. His eyes open almost at the same time as mine. Neither of us moves. My knee grazes his under the covers. The freckles on the bridge of his nose are barely visible against his tan skin. His eyes contrast with his white comforter. He looks so young with his hair falling over one of his eyes again. Without thinking, I reach out and tuck his hair back. He takes my hand in his and, for a brief moment, holds it.

I see the room get lighter before I hear the door to Jake's room slide open. As if we're doing something we aren't supposed to be doing—and maybe we are—we jump away from each other and sit up on opposite sides of the bed.

"I'm sorry." Jenna laughs through her hands, covering her face. "Robby needed to get to town. And, well, he assumed you'd taken the car back last night. I came in here to find your keys, Jake, so I could drive him back."

"What's wrong with your car?" Jake says, his voice gravelly as he shakes off sleep.

"It's boxed in. Your truck isn't."

"It was boxed in last night."

"Well, it isn't now. Can I have your keys?"

The blood rushes to my head as I stand up too quickly. It takes me a moment to orient myself to the floor. "I was just leaving. Robby and I can drive back together."

Jenna doesn't try to hide her amusement as she looks at me, then Jake, and once again back at me. "Okay, I'll let Robby know." She slips out of the room and closes the door.

Jake glances at me and then falls back on the bed and groans, hands over his eyes. "I need a lock on my door."

*A lock wouldn't have made this morning any less awkward*, I think. "I'm going to grab my clothes and get going." As I hurry into the bathroom, I have to keep a hand on the shorts Jake gave me so that they don't fall off.

"You can wear those clothes home," he hollers through the bathroom door.

"I appreciate it," I say. "But I haven't returned your other clothes yet and I don't want you to think I'm a clothing thief."

I throw on my suit, which is still damp from last night's swim at Diamond Island. There is nothing more uncomfortable than putting on a cold, wet suit. I pull my dress over it, stand in front of the mirror, and brush my teeth. My hair is wild, my curls sprouting in every direction. I leave the Stanford shirt and shorts folded on the bathroom counter. I'm ready to make my exit downstairs.

The bed is empty, but then I hear movement in the closet. Jake comes out wearing a T-shirt to go with the shorts he wore to bed. This is how he looks in the morning—rested and bright, ready for the day. It hardly feels fair.

"Thanks for letting me crash here." I walk toward the door. "It won't happen again."

I hear Jake start to say something, but I'm out of his room, running down the steps two at a time before he has a chance to speak.

Now that the sun is up, I can see the people who crashed on the floor last night. They remain unmoving. I hurry to the room where Jenna and Robby slept, knock, and wait by the door.

Robby emerges, rubbing his eyes, and follows me out of Jake's place. Neither of us says a word as we walk, arm to arm, down the gravel road toward the cottage where my car is parked. Robby is my best friend, but there's one topic that has always been off limits for me. He'll speak to me about girls, and I've given him plenty of advice, but I've always avoided the guy talk. The one time I tried, Robby feigned throwing up in his mouth.

We get right in the car instead of heading into the cottage.

I pull onto the road and look at Robby. "Are you really not going to speak to me?"

"I'm trying to keep the visuals of you and Jake out of my head."

"First of all, I blame you because you ditched me. After Diamond Island, you disappeared, and I wasn't going to drive back to town after having a drink." I open the window and let the fresh morning breeze come in. "And second of all, my choice was to sleep in Jake's bed or in my car. I made a choice."

Robby looks at me for the first time today. "Okay, as long as that's all that happened. Sleep."

I pass a tractor on the road and groan. "You should talk. You ran off with Jenna the moment we got to the party yesterday."

"That's different." Robby laughs. "I'm older. Plus, I slept on a mattress on the floor, and we stayed up talking. That's it."

"And Lilly?" I ask as I slug his arm.

"And Lilly nothing."

We reach town, the bright orange Wheaton History Museum to our left, trucks starting to gather at the café.

"I decided to come back for the week of the Fourth of July," Robby declares.

I glance at my brother and then back at the road. Robby loves Sunny and Sis as we all do, but he's a once-a-year-visit kind of guy. He has never been able to tear himself away from whatever city he's living in for any longer than that. He went to college in Chicago, then moved to Philadelphia to attend Wharton, then moved back to Chicago and got a fancy investment banking job.

We pull into my grandparents' house at the same time as Annie arrives. It's earlier than her usual eight-thirty arrival time.

"Sunny called," Annie says as we get out of our car. "Sis is having a rough morning."

Robby and I follow Annie into the house.

Grandpa meets us in the kitchen. "Sis finally laid down. She's been very confused and upset this morning. I'm going to lay with her. I'm sorry for calling you so early, Annie."

After Grandpa is gone, Robby puts his head down and runs his hands through his hair. He looks up at us and rests his face in his hands. "Has she started acting out yet? I guess what I'm asking is, can Grandpa still handle this, and can you?"

Annie wipes her eyes, the tears of a woman who has known my grandparents for nearly seventy-five years. She's more than a friend. She's their family.

"I've only witnessed one angry episode, and she came out of it quickly. But we may get to a point where neither of us will be able to keep her safe, and the Wheaton Nursing Home isn't equipped to deal with Alzheimer's."

The tears start to flow freely down my cheeks too. Robby looks up and pinches the bridge of his nose. We all realize that this situation isn't going to get better.

# CHAPTER 19

Coffee today with the men is much like the others. The local farmers are here when we arrive. They have already been working in the fields for hours, and this is their first break. According to the farmers, the corn is doing well so far, but Wheaton needs a lot more rain, and there hasn't been a drought as bad as this in at least two decades.

The conversation is always predictable at the Main Street Café—the weather, farming, who's catching fish, and where. Then the mood turns somber when someone asks, "Did you hear the sad news?" Usually, everyone has already heard. It's almost always that someone has died, and then everyone shifts to discussing the person's age and condition. Other than me and a few of the farmers, the youngest person here is probably seventy-five years old. I can only hope that my grandparents will be here to have many more of these conversations before they eventually become the topic. I'm not ready to lose them, and I never will be.

Walt hooks his thumbs through his camouflage suspenders. I try to treat all of my grandpa's friends the same, but Walt is my favorite, and he knows it.

He leans toward me and snaps his suspenders back in place. "Sunny says the cottage is coming along. What's left on the project?"

I light up, happy to be discussing something other than farming, fish, and death. "The floors are so close to being done. Jake's going to see if he can find some cheap throwaway cabinets to fancy up the bathroom and kitchen. Then it'll be almost ready... well, except for the outside. That will need to be painted."

Walt glances over at Grandpa, who's arguing with Juan and Lawson about some fish tale from half a century ago. When Walt notices that no one is paying attention to us, he says, "It's great what you're doing for your grandparents. It's all Sunny talks about—his Cammy coming to town and fixing up the cottage."

This surprises me. Grandpa has been so silent about the project that I've sometimes wondered if he wasn't in favor of it. The whole thing gives me anxiety because I'm doing all this work to bring happiness and some semblance of normalcy to his life. My assumption has been that he has focused more on how the cottage will be maintained once I'm done. If I stayed, I could take care of it. It's not the first time the thought has come to my mind, but it is the first time I don't immediately feel compelled to push it away.

"Thanks for saying that, Walt. I've enjoyed every minute of it, and I hope everyone is happy when it's all over."

"They will be, kiddo." Walt pats my hand.

I drive out to Jake's house because today is the day everything will arrive. I've informed him that he's not allowed back to his place until I give him the okay. My intention is to surprise him with all the new accoutrements I have ordered to decorate his house. Not everything will be a surprise, as a carpenter has already come to build the most beautiful bookshelves to frame his fireplace. But there is plenty more arriving today that he will not have seen. So after he works all day, he plans to head to the cottage and finish the floors. Meanwhile, I will spend the day setting everything up in his house.

Robby has been back in Chicago for a few days, but he still plans to return for the long Fourth of July weekend. A few days have passed since the night of Wheaton Days, where I slept in Jake's bed, but it's a topic we don't bring up. Our relationship went right back to normal, with Jake being a curmudgeon and me giving it back to him.

I empty my back seat of all the things I've brought for Jake's place. The furniture should be arriving soon. I can't wait to see it, as I feel like it might be just what Jake needs. Like me, he clearly still doesn't quite feel like Wheaton is home. My goal is to dress up his house to where he finally feels like this is where he belongs.

I hear the sound of the truck approach and run outside to greet them. The two deliverymen haul in the furniture, shelves, and accessories. At the same time, the local woodworker brings in the table I had custom-made. I lay out rugs, arrange furniture, and hang pictures that I had blown up and framed, some of them in black-and-white.

I smile as I take my gag gift up to Jake's bedroom. The pile of photos Jenna gave me included a framed one of him holding me on my first birthday and his eleventh birthday. I wear only a diaper and have blue frosting all over my belly and hair. Both of us wear matching birthday hats. He looks annoyed to be holding me.

I place the framed picture on his nightstand. His bed is made, but I see something sticking out under the comforter. I fold a corner down, and on the pillow is the Stanford shirt I wore when I slept over. That was more than a week ago. I pick it up and smell a combination of Jake and me.

I run downstairs when I hear my phone ring. It's Jake.

"I'm still at the cottage," he says. "When can I come home?"

A quick assessment tells me that I'm very close to being done. "Soon. But don't come in. You have to call first."

I can practically see his eyes roll through the phone.

"I'll call you when I pull in." He hangs up before I have a chance to respond.

I run around like a crazy lady, making everything perfect. I'm so nervous that he won't like something. What if I've gotten his taste all wrong? I suppose I could return some furniture. I find myself hoping desperately that it won't come to that.

I place my real gift—my favorite book by Minnesota author Sinclair Lewis—on Jake's bookshelf. It's a first edition, a beautiful copy. I picked it up during a stop in Lewis's hometown on my way in from Chicago. I write Jake a note and place it in the book.

I step back to admire my work. I haven't done much, really, apart from ordering the built-ins, adding some new lights and furniture, and decorating. My degree in interior design wasn't really necessary, but the space still looks great.

A car door slams outside, and then my phone rings.

"Hi, Jake," I say. "I'll meet you outside." I run through the door, nervous energy keeping me going.

Jake walks toward me, carrying a bag that smells really good.

"Be easy on me," I say. "I'm nervous."

He laughs as he shakes his head. "I'll be easy on you, but you'll know if I hate it."

My heart races again at the thought that he may hate this. I stare as Jake walks through the door. The first room, the mudroom, is underwhelming, as all I did was install shelves for his fishing poles and gear, along with a beautiful framed poster of Lake Traverse. Everything is organized, from life jackets to fishing poles to shoes. Jake doesn't say anything as he opens the door to the rest of his place.

I watch him look around. He runs his hand against the distressed dark leather sectional in his living room. He removes his work boots and crosses the area rug that ties together two mustard-colored chairs. He examines the books and pictures on the new bookshelves on either side of the fireplace. Here, he finds the beautiful leatherbound books that Malik first showed me in Jake's closet—books from a few Minnesota writers like F. Scott Fitzgerald and Maud Hart Lovelace. A few mint-condition early editions of Hemingway, Kerouac, Huncke, and Ginsberg join them. Jake's collection is enviable. It contains so many of my favorite authors, including Dickens, Solzhenitsyn, and too many works by Kierkegaard to count.

Next, he moves to the open dining room space. His hand glides across the table I've had made from polished wood taken from his grandparents' original cottage. The table is more beautiful than I ever could have hoped for—so beautiful that I'm sure I didn't pay the woodworker enough. Ten beautiful chairs surround it, and it's big enough that more chairs could fit if needed. I couldn't believe it when I first stumbled across this wood in his woodpile and in his shed. All of it. In piles. Strewn across the ground.

Jake looks at me as he spreads his fingers wide across the wood. "Where did you get this table?"

I can't tell by his reaction if he likes it, but it's beautiful, and he's crazy if he doesn't think so. "I had it made. All the wood is from your grandparents' cottage."

Jake enters the kitchen. The island now features four rustic stools that give him options on where to eat his meals. He looks at the new wine rack in the corner of the kitchen and holds up a bottle. He studies the label and then picks up another. I bought all the wine before I realized that Jake didn't drink. I contemplated not putting it out, but I couldn't return the wine holder, and anyway, it aesthetically adds to the space.

"I'm so sorry, Jake. I ordered this when we first made our deal. I can take it out of here if you don't want it."

"That's not necessary. I like having wine around for when I entertain. Where did you get this?"

"Napa Valley. I ordered a bunch of my favorites. I'm so sorry. I didn't—"

"Don't apologize." He places the bottle back in the rack.

He moves to a gallery wall I created, a wall full of photos of Jake's grandparents and parents when they were younger. Pictures of his childhood. Dax, Jenna, and Jake as kids. In another corner, I have arrayed the prints of Jake playing football.

We stand back in the kitchen as Jake continues to look around. With the subtle hues and pops of accent colors, I was going for a rustic-chic look. I want him to feel at home. I want him to picture having a wife and kids to share this space with him someday. But Jake reacts to none of it.

I put my hand on his arm. "Say something. Please. I'm dying to know what you think."

His chest swells, and it looks like he holds his breath before he exhales. "You're good at this."

"Yeah?"

"I'm speechless." He leans in, puts his arms around me, lifts me off the floor, and holds me as my feet dangle.

I wrap my arms around his neck, hold on tight, and feel weightless. I bury my face in his neck for a moment before pulling away. As he holds me off the floor, our height difference is less apparent, if only for a moment.

"You really like it?"

"I love it. Everything. You blew me away. And I know I need to continue soaking in all the details." He holds me at eye level. "Should I ask how much you spent on my credit card?"

"Let's not ruin our evening." I laugh. "I have all the receipts, though."

He kisses my forehead and places me back on the floor. "Should we open one of these bottles of wine for you?"

"You don't have to. Again, I'm sorry."

"Enough. There's no reason that someone shouldn't enjoy better wine than Wheaton has to offer." He winks.

When he goes to the kitchen, he skips the wine and starts with the bag he brought in with him, pulling out the food it contains and spreading it across the island.

"What?" I say. "You got me dinner too?"

"I went to the tavern. I hope you like burgers."

Surprise ripples through me. *This is what it feels like to get along with Jake*, I think. I'm cautious, but I like feeling like his friend. "I do."

He looks through the different wines in the rack and holds up a Caymus Cabernet Sauvignon. I give my approval. He opens the bottle and pours me a drink. Then he gets himself a can of sparkling water.

"To my new place." He holds up his can and stares into my eyes. "Beautiful."

After we enjoy our burgers, Jake leads me outside. We sit on Adirondack chairs and watch as the sun draws low over the South Dakota hills. Given Jake's admonishment from last time, I don't pull out my phone and snap a picture. I want to see tonight's sunset through my eyes and not a screen. Inch by inch, the orange ball of fire disappears behind the rolling hills. When it's finally gone, the sky lights up in pink and orange hues that contrast beautifully with the deep blue of dusk.

I don't know how long we've been sitting here, but I turn to Jake, who is watching me watch the sunset. I grin. "Why are you looking at me?"

Jake runs a finger through his hair and smiles. "I thought I was the only one who enjoyed a sunset this much." He crosses his hands in his lap and leans back in his chair. "Sometimes I look at the setting sun and think of all that happens between sunsets. A lot of life is lived."

"Or not lived," I add.

"True." Jake turns to me. "Tell me something about yourself?"

I pause. I think back to all the places my life has brought me, never feeling grounded in one place. I don't open up about this to many people, but I feel safe with Jake in this moment.

I bite my lip. "I'm trying to figure out where to go next."

"I thought you were contemplating staying."

"Not contemplating as much as dreaming." I lean back in my chair. "It's hard being here and seeing Sunny and Sis so old."

"Is that the reason you haven't been back to Wheaton in so long?"

I shut my eyes and purse my lips. "I don't think it's that odd for teenagers not to want to visit their grandparents." I try to hide my defensiveness, but his words cut me.

"That's not what I meant, Camilla." He sits up in his chair. "I was at Stanford when my mom called and said that if I wanted to say goodbye to Grandpa Abram, I needed to come now. They bought my ticket and everything, but I didn't come, and he died a few weeks later."

My chest feels heavy. "Why didn't you come?"

"Who knows why twenty-something-year-olds do anything. If I think about it hard enough, I probably didn't come home because I wanted to remember Grandpa Oscar as healthy and vibrant."

I can relate to that. I know that to spend time with Sunny and Sis is to love them, and I know that loving them means I'll have to lose them. I avoid being close to people because I don't want to feel pain in the loss. I lack the bravery to put myself out there and be vulnerable. I always have.

"Camilla, can I ask you something?"

I nod.

"Why'd you come to Wheaton? Why now?"

*I'm lonely*, I want to say. *I'm tired of the flights, learning a new language, where to get the best takeout. I'm tired of having to learn new names. I'm tired of always needing to figure out the time difference to call home or call my grandparents. I'm so tired of having only one person, Robby, to call anytime I have big life news. Growing up and starting a career scares me. But mostly, I'm tired of getting scared when someone gets too close, pulling away abruptly, and then hurting them. I'm so tired.*

Instead, I say, "Because I was the one member of the Bergland family who wasn't anchored to any person or place."

The pink in the sky fades away into the deeper blue. I need to get back to my grandparents' house, as I'm exhausted after the long day.

"And as quickly as you came, you'll leave?" Jake's gaze looks searching, like he's trying to solve a puzzle.

"Jake," I say hesitantly. "You said you don't know a lot about me, so here's something you should know. For better or worse, leaving is what I do best."

# CHAPTER 20

It's so late. I want to be sleeping, but instead, I've been staring at the flower wallpaper. I watch as Robby tiptoes into the bedroom, thinking I can't hear him. He arrived back in Wheaton yesterday. He managed to have tea with Grandma and me and coffee with the men, but he hasn't been around much besides that, and he seems to be spending a lot of time with Jenna. He's mentioned Lilly several times to me, the woman he met at Wharton, who followed him to Chicago, but he doesn't seem that excited about her. He flops onto his bed, and I don't say anything as he pulls the blanket up and turns to face the wall.

The next morning, I wake up to Robby standing above my bed, staring at me.

"What are you doing, Robby? You look like a crazy person."

He laughs and throws a pillow at my head. "It's the Fourth of July. Wake up."

"So what? I'm tired." I moan into my pillow, my eyes narrowed to slits. I feel like I barely slept last night.

"I promised Jenna and Dax I would pick up a few things to run to Jake's," he says. "It sounds like it'll be a big crowd. Should you and I drive separately?"

I stretch over to the nightstand and look at my phone. "Yes. I want to spend a little time with Grandma and Grandpa first and then run things to the cottage so I can sleep out there tonight. I'll meet you there at some point."

Robby never wakes up before me. I make a note to ask him if something is going on with Jenna because something about him isn't adding up to me.

Meanwhile, I'm excited because most of the cottage furniture arrived a couple of days ago, and today I'm bringing out the new bedding. The floors are done, and I can't spend enough time there because it has become the perfect space. The new water pump is installed, so we have running water now, but the shower isn't salvageable. Jake has been looking for a replacement option.

I hug my grandpa as he reads the paper on the sunporch. Then I find Grandma sitting in the kitchen. "Good morning, Grandma Sis. Are you ready for tea?" I lean down to kiss her on the cheek.

She stares out the window as if deep in thought. "Tea would be great, Camilla."

I put the kettle on and pour us both a cup. "Today's the Fourth of July, Grandma. Do you like to watch the fireworks?"

"Heavens, no, dear. They start much too late for this old lady."

In Grandma's eyes, I see my eyes. Dark blue, almost gray. Sometimes I wonder if her fate will be mine. Will I eventually forget everyone in my life and what they mean to me? Am I going to wake up someday and not know who I am? And if so, is all of this memory-making between now and then essentially pointless? I shake the ideas out of my head.

My grandma grins and leans into me. "Camilla, if I tell you something, can you promise to keep a secret?"

I wrinkle my forehead and clap my hands in excitement.

"I have a boyfriend," she says. "His name is Tom, and he works across the street at the gas station."

I pull back, trying to hide my surprise. I've met Tom. He can't be more than twenty-five years old, and I know my grandma is confused. My chest still feels heavy. "Grandma, why do you say he's your boyfriend?"

"He and I have been dating for several months now."

"Does Grandpa know?"

Grandma Sis playfully swats my hand. "Of course he knows, dear. Sunny and I have no secrets."

Grandpa Sunny walks in, and I can only imagine how shocked I look because he sees it too. "What are you two discussing?"

My grandma looks at him and puts up her finger. "I told Camilla about Tom."

Grandpa's body slumps. His face distorts, his eyes weary. "Sis, we've talked about this. Tom is the grandson of our friends, the Larsons. You and I are married. I'm your husband, Sunny. You don't have a boyfriend."

Her irritation grows. "You can't tell me what is true and what isn't, Sunny Bergland."

I take my grandpa's arm. His skin is soft and wrinkled. I can't imagine what he's feeling right now, but disagreeing with Grandma when she isn't in her right mind won't help even a little.

"Grandpa," I whisper into his ear. "Let me handle this one. Please leave me with Grandma for a moment and go sit in the living room."

With glistening eyes, he leaves.

I sit my grandma back down and pull my chair right next to her. "Tell me more about your boyfriend, Grandma."

As Grandma tells me about her boyfriend, Annie walks in, sits at the table, and doesn't say anything. Grandma's demeanor shifts. The tension she's been holding escapes as her lips turn up in a smile. I really feel for Grandpa in this moment. I can't imagine loving someone for most of my life and then having them not remember that I'm the one they love.

After we talk for a while, Annie heads home, and my grandparents go upstairs for a nap. I don't dare leave, which turns out to be a good thing because Grandma is in another spell when they wake up. This time, she's saying that her sister is trying to steal their house. The whole day is like this. My grandpa does his best, but I can see that this is killing him.

As the sun gets lower in the sky and the heat of the July Fourth day becomes bearable, my grandparents fall asleep for the night. Annie comes and sits in the living room. When she pulls me into her arms, I release the tears I've been holding in all day. My chest shakes as the sobs escape.

"I know that today was hard, but she has good days too." Annie squeezes my hand as she speaks the words into my ear. "You're young, and it's a holiday. You need to get out of this house and be a kid. There's no point in you being here while they sleep."

I know she's right. I look at my phone, which I haven't done all day, and have several missed calls and text messages. Most of them are from Robby, wondering where I am, but I also have a few from Dax and a couple from Jake. The first one from Jake asks if I'm coming to his party, and the second one is him asking if I'm okay.

I don't know if I'll be able to pull myself together enough, but I'm going to try. I drive to the cottage first to drop off a few things. I look forward to sleeping here tonight and to waking up to the sound of the birds and the lake crashing onto the rocks. The cottage feels like a place where bad things can never happen.

The noise of the party echoes from up the gravel road as I make my way toward Jake's. Music playing and people splashing in the water mesh with the sound of Jet Skis and boats and laughter. I look around the place for someone familiar. I'm starting to recognize some of the faces I've seen at Jake's or around town. Malik is here talking to a group of guys. Carrie talks to Tiffeny and another woman I often see with Tiffeny.

"There you are, Cam." I whip around to see Robby come toward me in his swim trunks. "Where have you been? You haven't responded to my texts."

I give him my best smile. It takes all the energy I have to fake it with him. "I'm sorry, Robby. I decided to spend the day with Grandma and Grandpa and didn't have my phone with me. What did I miss?"

"You've missed hours of fun." He laughs. "There was a cool boat parade, and we've been swimming, playing games—you know, typical Fourth of July activities."

Jenna approaches, hair dripping wet, a sundress pulled over her swimsuit. "Camilla, wow, Jake's place looks great. You did amazing." She pulls me into a hug, and I can smell sunblock and the lake all over her.

"Thanks. I think so too. And he seems to really like it."

"Are you kidding? Jake loves it. He says you nailed his inner essence."

"I didn't think Jake had an inner essence." I open one of the coolers and grab myself a drink.

I notice that Jake's new wine rack is empty, and I blush at the reminder that I gifted wine to someone who doesn't drink. Not for the first time, I wonder if there's a story behind why he doesn't drink.

"Camilla, I've been trying to get ahold of you." Dax pulls me into a hug. His skin is warm and damp and full of the smell of sunblock. "I'm glad you're here. I was hoping you would come."

I hold the glass to my lips. "Yeah, I had a few things to do first."

"Jake's place looks great." Dax puts his hand on my back as he walks me out the door. "And I'm supposed to tell you that Kylie is sad she missed you. My parents just took her back to town."

"Tell her I'm sorry I missed her, too, and that she and I will have to hang out soon."

I've been thinking a lot about how the Fourth of July always feels like the crescendo of summer. From here on out, it will only be the dog days. The days will get shorter, and we'll march toward the end, where the climate changes and everyone leaves. I remind myself that there is a lot of summer left and that it's up to me where I go at the end of it.

I feel like eyes are burning into my back. Jake is watching me. I smile and give a pensive wave. He returns the wave but not the smile. He has joined Malik's circle of friends—just a few men standing around talking with drinks in their hands.

Jake says something to Malik before coming over to Dax and me. "Hey, City Girl, I wasn't sure if you were going to make it. Glad you got here in time for the fireworks."

I look up to the sky. A sliver of sun peeks out from behind the hills. "Where's the best place to watch?"

"The lake," Dax and Jake say at the same time, causing me to chuckle.

"It's a consensus then. Everyone watches from the lake."

After the sun disappears behind the hills, everyone starts working their way to the water. Some get on Jet Skis. Others have already taken to boats anchored just beyond the shore. A few people lay blankets in the grass and lean back, waiting for the fireworks to start.

Dax turns to me. "I'm going to go inside and grab a drink. Can I get you anything?"

I shake my head.

Jake takes my hand and pulls me toward the water. "Are you up for an adventure?"

I look down at Jake's hand in mine and then toward his house. "Umm…sure?"

"You can trust me."

Warm sand massages my feet as we grab a double kayak and put it in the water.

"We're going to row toward your cottage," he says.

I take the seat in front—carefully, as I have a summer dress on and no suit underneath it.

Light from Jake's house leads the way as we paddle in silence. A boat pulls out from the dock and goes full throttle as it races out to the middle of the lake. Residual waves reach us. Our kayak makes it over the first one without incident, but the second one reaches us with enough force that we begin to wobble. I scream and try to correct the kayak, but it's too late. Jake and I end up in the water, yet somehow the kayak stays upright.

We're both fully clothed and soaking wet as we grab the side of the kayak. When Jake looks at me, it takes a moment to recover, but then I laugh. This whole day is one I would like to forget. Grandma Sis is losing her mind, and now I'm in the lake, in the dark, fully clothed with my dress weighing me down as I push a kayak with Jake. It almost makes sense that this is where the night has led me.

"I'm surprised you're not more upset, to be honest," Jake says.

I laugh harder as we trudge closer to the shore near the cottage. "It's the perfect ending to this messed-up day."

We reach a sandy bottom and push the kayak the rest of the way to the shore. I walk out to where the dock stops in the water. I'm still laughing, the first time I've felt any measure of happiness all day. Water drips off Jake's shirt, and my dress is caked to my body. Jake puts his hands around my waist and lifts me onto the edge of the dock. Then he leans against it as we look to the sky, where the fireworks have just begun.

"They're really something, aren't they?" he says.

"So beautiful." And they are. I've never seen fireworks better than this. The bright colors shine against the dark lake and rolling hills. The fireworks illuminate the lake in shades of red, white, and blue.

"So beautiful." Jake rests with his back between my legs as my feet dangle over the water.

The finale comes with one boom after another. The fireworks start small and grow until the whole sky is alight with magnificent color. Deep, thunderous bangs vibrate through me. Then everything goes dark. Voices echo from various cottages along the lake. Some people begin lighting their own fireworks, but nothing like the show we just witnessed.

Jake turns to me, still standing between my dangling legs. He's almost the same height as me as I sit on the dock. He brushes my hair off my shoulder. "Where were you today?"

I take a long breath. "Grandma Sis had a rough day. I didn't want to leave her or my grandpa."

His hands rest on my damp upper legs. Casual touch. Like this is our new normal. "Are you okay?"

I can barely see his features because the moon isn't bright enough tonight. The more I look at him, the more his face comes into focus. He's the first person who's asked me if I'm okay. The tears well up in my eyes. I'm aware of the weight of his hands caressing my thighs. His face is so close, water dripping from his hair.

"I'm sad," I admit.

"I'm sorry you're sad." He studies me. "I've been meaning to thank you for spending so much time with Kylie. She told me her auntie Camilla has been giving her dad tutorials on doing hair. And I know you spent six hours on her braids the other day."

"It's no big deal." I smile, thinking of the precocious five-year-old who has found her way into my heart. "I love spending time with her. And as I told her, us curly-haired girls need to stick together."

Jake leans in. He's so much bigger than me that it feels like he surrounds me from all sides. "It is a big deal, though. There's been such an emptiness in all of us, but especially Dax and Kylie, ever since Zari died. But they're both smiling and laughing again. There's this light around you that causes people to feel like there's hope. That maybe things will get better." He pauses. "So it isn't nothing. It means more than you—"

His mouth opens like he's about to continue, but instead, his lips crash into mine. I almost fall back, but his arms surround me, holding me upright. At first, I'm motionless, eyes wide with shock. But then I wrap my arms around him and kiss him back. His lips are full and warm with a hint of coconut ChapStick. My hands find his hair. I tug and grab and pull, my senses awakened. I kiss him harder when my mind tries to wander. I'm kissing Jake Abram, the person I obsessed over as a kid. I've perhaps daydreamed once or twice about this, maybe even as recently as this summer.

He lives up to the fantasy.

I've had many first kisses—awkward ones, sloppy ones, fast ones, and I-can't-wait-until-they-end ones. My most common first kiss is the one where I simultaneously make my grocery list. This is my first I-never-want-this-to-end one. Jake wraps his hand around my head and pulls me deeper into him as our kiss intensifies. His hands feel needy as they grab my hips, under my arms, and then finally wrap around my shoulders as he struggles to get closer.

His lips are so soft, and I burn for more of him as his tongue flicks mine. I want it to last longer, so much longer, but instead, he pulls away. We struggle for air, and I'm left empty.

We don't speak or even look at each other. Jake rests his head on my lap and wraps his arms around me. I run my hands through his hair and then reach down to his back and rub my nails in a downward motion beneath his damp shirt. His skin is smooth and cool. I touch my lips, which are still warm from his kiss. His breathing is heavy against my lap.

Jake lifts his head off me and unwraps his arms from my body. "I should go back to the party."

I stand up and make my way down the dock as Jake wades to the shore. The yard is dark, the crickets and cicadas screaming. My wet dress hangs off me, the straps refusing to stay on my shoulders. We reach the cottage's door, where I turn to see Jake's turquoise eyes again.

We stand and look at each other, neither certain what to say.

"Do you want to come in?" I blurt out, part nervousness, part desire.

"Yes," he says.

I go to open the door, but he puts his hand out to stop me.

"Which is why I need to go."

I wrinkle my forehead and stare at him. I reach out to touch him, but he pulls away.

"I'll see you later." He leans forward and kisses my forehead before walking off in the dark.

# CHAPTER 21

I wake up earlier than I was hoping for my first night sleeping at the cottage. The bedroom I'm in doesn't have window coverings, so the sun wakes me a little after five in the morning. Once I open my eyes and stare out at the lake from the bedroom window, there is no going back to sleep. I thought Lake Traverse was most beautiful at night, but seeing it at dawn is a sight to behold.

A large family of geese swims by—first, two adults, followed by a litter of fuzzy babies. A fish jumps in the distance, and through the open windows, I can hear the waves collide into the rocks on the shoreline. The mourning doves are up with the sun. The male calls out to the female, a beautiful sound that reminds me of my childhood. I'm living in a pinkish wonderland as the sun calls out to all the creatures that another day is upon us.

As I roll onto my side and stare at the lake, my mind goes to Jake. That kiss. What was I thinking, inviting him inside? What if he would have said yes? It might have been fun. Actually, it probably would have been, but I don't need to wake up with that kind of regret. It doesn't matter, anyway. He didn't say yes.

He kissed me and then flat out said no to coming inside. Message received.

I get dressed and ready for the day, hoping that Robby will show up, but he doesn't. After the day my grandma had yesterday, I'm worried about my grandparents and want nothing more than to head to town and have tea with Grandma before Annie arrives. I drive down to Jake's. Several cars are still parked there, but the place is quiet. The grass glistens with morning dew, and the mourning doves continue to call out. I know that Robby must have stayed here with Jenna last night, but he won't answer my texts.

I tiptoe through the front door into Jake's house. The couch and rug are full of passed-out people. I creep in further and find that the main-floor bedroom doors are closed. I don't know if I want to wait for Robby to get up. When I left Grandma and Grandpa's yesterday, I noticed that his rental car was still parked there, so he must have gotten a ride to the party. Anyway, I suppose my big brother can find a ride back.

I turn to leave, and just as my hand reaches for the doorknob, movement catches my eye from above. I look up to see Tiffeny leaving Jake's bedroom. She's wearing yesterday's clothes. When she gets a few steps down, Jake emerges from the room in shorts and nothing else. Tiffeny pauses, and when our eyes meet, she pulls Jake closer to her. His body stiffens, but she wraps him into a side hug. I'm positive that life halts for a moment. Everything goes still except for the pounding of my heart. I turn to open the door and kick a glass bottle in the process. The sound vibrates through the house.

My feet slosh against the dew-covered grass as I dash to my car. The faster I can get out of here, the sooner I can start trying to forget that last night ever happened. Maybe I'll be able to get the image of Tiffeny walking out of Jake's room permanently out of my head. I reach my car door just as Jake calls out to me.

"Camilla, wait."

He hurries across the lawn in my direction. I keep facing the car, not wanting to look at him.

"Come on, Camilla. Look at me."

I turn around and lean against my car door. "Is Robby here?"

"I think so." Jake smooths his hair back, trying to tame it.

I point to the house as words flow out of me. "So she's why you didn't come in last night?"

He sighs. "First of all, this isn't what it looks like. Second of all, I didn't come in because it would have been the wrong thing to do."

I put my hand on the door, signaling that I would rather be anywhere than here. "You shouldn't have kissed me."

Jake laughs as he wraps his arms around himself and rubs his bare arms. "You didn't seem to mind as you kissed me back."

"It was instinct." Anger overwhelms me. I take deep breaths as heat floods my face.

"Was inviting me inside instinct too?"

"You came on to me." I feel trapped between my car and Jake. I place my hand on his chest and try to put space between us.

"You're making a bigger deal out of this than it needs to be," Jake says as he reaches his hand for my shoulder.

I brush it off and open my car door.

He leans against the open window. "Camilla, it doesn't have to be like this."

I crank the window closed. "You're right. Don't kiss me again. I find you repulsive."

Before he can respond, I throw my car into reverse and take off. This is why I don't let my guard down. I'm impenetrable. I don't let people hurt me, and Jake is the last person I'll ever give that power to.

*****

Robby has been back in Chicago for a couple of days, the sun has been hiding under perpetual clouds, and Jake hasn't been able to get away from his job to help me finish the cottage—or so he says. I'm glad that he hasn't been available. I don't feel ready to face him. I've stayed in town with Sunny and Sis, watching TV, going to coffee, and baking with my grandma. There's an ease in the predictability of it.

Today, though, the sun showed up, and Jake texted that he has time to paint with me if I would like to get started. As much as I don't want to see him, we have to get the exterior painted, and doing it alone would take a long time. My car's air conditioner, even on high, is no match for the sun today. It's a humid heat. Painting outdoors will be brutal.

When I pull up to the cottage, Jake is already there unloading buckets of paint from the back of his truck. Beige. A safe color. He glances at me but doesn't say a word. I follow suit. At times, I like silence. However, this silence feels intentional, heavy, and directed at me. It's not the peaceful kind of silence where I feel comfortable in someone's presence without words.

"Where do you want me to start?" I ask, hands on my hips.

Jake gives me the once-over. "Let's start with all the trim. Once we're done with that, we'll start rolling."

I grab a paintbrush and wait for him to open the cans. I do the lower trim while he does everything requiring a ladder. We work without speaking. Music plays in the background, and there is no breeze or reprieve from the heat. Jake never once glances in my direction. I quit trying to catch his gaze and return to painting around the windows.

I don't know how long we've been trimming, but we save the cottage's south side for last. I wipe the sweat dripping from my brow and sit in the chair for a break. Jake climbs off the ladder and sits in the chair next to me. I hand him a bottle of water.

"Thanks for helping," I say, staring straight ahead at the cottage.

"It's not a problem," he says, picking away dry paint from his jeans.

Tires roll against the gravel. It's Grandpa's car. He gets out with Walt, Juan, and Lawson. I run over to them and grab the pie out of my grandpa's hands.

"Sis made that," Grandpa says. "And the men thought we'd watch you paint as we have coffee time."

I wrap my free arm around him. "Thank you! Pie and coffee sounds great." What also sounds great is not having to be alone in silence with Jake.

"Hey there, Jake," Grandpa says as he gives a wave. "You two get back to painting, and I'll put the coffee on and bring out plates for the pie."

When I grab the paintbrush, my hand is sore. We're almost done trimming, and then the rolling can begin. There are still several hours of sunlight if my body can hold up.

The men pull up chairs facing us, and each takes up a cup of coffee.

"You guys make a great team," Lawson says. Even though it must be close to a hundred degrees, he still wears a tracksuit.

"We can't thank you enough, Jake," Grandpa says. "You're doing so much for our family."

Jake takes a break from painting to glance at me. "It's not a big deal, I assure you."

Walt stands next to me, inspecting my work. "Well, Jake, you must have a sweet spot for Camilla to be helping her."

We look at each other, but neither says a word.

Walt returns to his chair. "Do you guys remember ten years ago or so when Wheaton was put on the map?"

The men all start laughing.

"There was a national story that not enough women lived in Wheaton," Walt says, "so busloads of women showed up to meet the local townsmen."

"Even you couldn't find a woman out of those busloads," Lawson says, slapping his leg.

Jake's mouth turns up in a smile for the first time today.

Walt lets out a noise. "I could have ended up with one of those women if I wanted. There were plenty interested in me."

"Oh, Walt," Grandpa says, "it sounds like you're telling a fish tale now."

"I was a lady's man in my day," Walt insists.

"Everyone in town knows that you're beholden to Annie," Juan says.

Jake and I stop painting and look at Walt.

"Oh, why'd I bring this up, anyway," Walt huffs as he hands his cup to Lawson. "I'd like another cup of coffee, please."

"So did any of these women stay in Wheaton and marry the local men?" I ask.

"Thank you for bringing us back, Camilla," Walt says. He waves away Juan as he tries to say something. "Two women stayed and married farmers. After a while, the news trucks left, and our town returned to normal. Jake, too bad you were away in California. You may have found yourself a prospect."

Jake clears his throat. "I'm good."

Juan stands and inspects the painting. "Aren't you courting that Tiffeny gal?"

225

"That's been over for a while." Jake looks at me and then back at the cottage. He's a closed book.

We get back to painting for a while. Then suddenly, Lawson cries out from the cottage. Jake and I drop our brushes and rush inside, where Lawson lies on the floor, his leg bent at an angle, the rug wrinkled up on the floor, seemingly the source of his fall.

Jake rushes to his side and turn Lawson onto his back. "Where does it hurt?"

"Ope," Lawson moans. "It's my ankle."

Jake pulls up Lawson's pants leg. "It's already swelling up." His eyes find mine. "Camilla, do you have ice?"

Grandpa, Walt, and Juan find their way inside.

"Oh, dear," Grandpa says when he sees Lawson on the floor.

"I'm going to call my dad and tell him we'll be at the hospital in fifteen minutes," Jake says. "Sunny, you drive Walt and Juan back and meet us there. Give Georgia a call and let her know what happened. Camilla, do you have any wrap? I want to immobilize the ankle as much as possible."

We all follow Jake's orders. I find a wrap in a bathroom drawer that hasn't been opened in years. Then I come back into the living room as Jake gets off the phone with his dad. I hand it to him, and he puts it around Lawson, keeping his shoe on the whole time.

"Lawson, Camilla and I are going to help you up, and I don't want you to put any weight on your ankle. We're going to put you in the back seat of Camilla's car. My truck is too tall."

Jake and I pull Lawson to an upright position. Jake stays on Lawson's right, where his ankle is injured. I do my best to help, but Jake practically carries him. He puts him in the back, then gets in the passenger seat, knees in his chest.

"Your car is miniature," he says, never looking at me.

"My car is a normal size," I say as I back up to turn it around. "You're a giant."

We pull into the hospital parking lot, where the staff is already waiting with a wheelchair. We help Lawson into the chair, and they take him. Grandpa, Walt, and Juan join us as we wait in the waiting room. Lawson's wife, Georgia, is back with him. Jake stands against the wall, quiet, just as he's been all day.

After a time, Dr. Abram comes out to the waiting room. "Lawson is doing great."

Everyone lets out a breath.

"His ankle is fractured, but it's the good kind of fracture. It won't require surgery. I'm going to cast it up and give him crutches, but he'll be in a walking cast. As soon as he's comfortable, he can put weight on it."

Grandpa shakes Dr. Abram's hand. We all go back and visit Lawson, who's in good spirits.

After a few hours, Lawson is finally able to leave the hospital. We all follow him out.

"Can I get a ride back to the lake?" Jake asks as we walk back into the waiting room.

Dr. Abram approaches us as we get to the door. "I'm glad you were there, Jake. I don't think the other men would have been able to carry him."

Jake looks tired as he puts his hand on his dad's shoulder. "What type of fracture is it?"

"It was a lateral malleolus. Honestly, it's probably the best he could have had, but your quick thinking kept him comfortable, so thank you."

We drive to the lake in silence. I'm shaken from Lawson's fall, and I can barely process how much worse it could have been. Jake's dad was right. I don't know what we would have done if Jake hadn't been there.

I drive down the driveway, the corn sprouting to the blue sky. "How did you know what to do?" I barely recognize my voice after not speaking for so long.

"It was nothing." Jake never glances in my direction.

"It wasn't nothing." I turn to him. "Your dad is right."

"I played sports. I know all about orthopedic injuries." He finally looks at me. "And I started my college as a premed student before switching to business."

"You're full of surprises," I say as we reach the cottage and I turn off the ignition. Coffee cups are everywhere, along with open paint cans and stiff paintbrushes that never got rinsed.

"Yes, I'm not the simpleton you think I am," Jake answers.

"What are you talking about?"

"I saw the book you left for me. I don't know why I didn't see it sooner. *Main Street.*"

I laugh. "You're mad because I bought you a book I thought you'd like? *Main Street* is by one of my favorite Minnesota authors. I thought you would enjoy adding it to your collection, especially because so many were written by Minnesotans. I even wrote you a note. It was a thank-you for letting me decorate your space."

Jake starts cleaning the paintbrushes with a hose. "I'm not mad. But I'm curious. Am I Kennicott in this story?"

"You're so full of yourself." I chuckle. "It isn't a story about you. Or about Wheaton. I think it's a beautifully written story, and I thought you would too."

Dusk settles. The paint supplies are as put away as they can be, and my body aches. Jake looks agitated. I know the feeling. I've been on edge as well. I don't know if it's the heat, the fact that for the first time in my life I don't know if I want to leave a place, or if it's about all of the things I'm not saying, even to myself. But something is in the air.

"Quit making everything a fight," I say.

"We are oil and water," he says as he bends over to grab the last paintbrush.

I move closer to Jake. "I'm just glad you didn't come in. I was clearly caught up in the moment and lonely because of my day with Sis. What a disaster that would have been."

Jake glares at me. "Oh, City Girl, you keep telling yourself that."

"Trust me, Jake, I would have regretted it. Remember, oil and water."

He throws a paintbrush across the lawn and looks at me, stone-faced, maybe even hurt. "Well, luckily one of us had our wits about us."

He walks to his truck, leaving his supplies behind. He doesn't look in my direction as his tires squeal and he drives away. I try to regulate my breathing, unsure of what we're even fighting about anymore. Is this about the kiss or the rejection? About the book I left him? I doubt it's about Tiffeny because I get the distinct impression that he was never hers to begin with. We spend so much time talking around our feelings that I'm left perplexed at what this could actually be about.

# CHAPTER 22

The cottage is so near completion that I can almost imagine what it will look like. I'm back in my painting bib overalls, not quite sure how long it will take now that I'm painting alone, but I decide to start today, anyway, unsure if Jake will show up.

I wanted to paint yesterday, but my body needed to rest. Every muscle hurt from painting and then carrying Lawson. But today, I'm back at it. I open a can of paint and pour it into the tray. My grandparents plan to come out later, so at least I won't be alone all day. I start on the west side, and the painting goes slowly. I roll as high as I can but then need the ladder for the rest. At this pace, I may be painting all week.

When a car door slams, I expect to see my grandparents, but instead, it's Jake. He approaches with paint supplies in hand.

"I wasn't sure if you'd show up," I say.

"I wasn't sure if I was going to," he says as he bends down and grabs a roller.

"You just can't stay away from me, huh?" I laugh as I continue painting.

Jake throws his shirt off and starts working on the high spots.

"I want you to know that I didn't give you the book to insult you."

Jake chuckles, a sound I haven't heard come out of him in a while. "It wasn't about the book."

"Then what was it about?" I ask, never breaking my paint rhythm. "I mean, things have never been great between us, but they're the worst they've ever been."

Jake steals a glance at me over his shoulder before starting to paint. "I've been having big feelings."

"You want to talk about it?" Feelings are usually the point where I like to stop the conversation. My own feelings make me uncomfortable at times. Add other people's feelings, and I tread lightly. "You said things are over with Tiffeny. Are your feelings about that?"

He stops for a moment and looks at me. "This has nothing to do with Tiffeny."

"If you say so."

We paint alongside each other, me focusing on the bottom, Jake focused on the top. We're back to silence but not the uncomfortable silence from before—instead, we share a concentration-on-painting type of silence. Jake's shirt hangs out of his back pocket. His muscles flex as he reaches high above his head.

We both turn our heads as we hear the car pull up and see my grandparents. I go greet them at the car. I grab Grandma's arm and help her walk to the cottage.

"Grandma, there's so much I want to show you."

Jake greets my grandparents before we all walk inside.

Grandma looks into the bedrooms. Her eyes are wide and glistening, her hands folded over her chest. "Camilla, it's so beautiful. Everything is how it should be." She pats my arm. "Is this what you've been doing all summer?"

I look at Jake and smile. "Yeah. Well, Jake has done most of it."

Grandma goes over to hug Jake. "We owe you so much."

I get my grandparents some iced tea. They sit near us in the shade and watch us paint.

"The boys and I have been having coffee out here and watching them work," Grandpa says as if this is news to Grandma.

Grandma nods but doesn't say anything. She's rarely a woman of few words, but I can tell she doesn't know what to say.

Now that there are two of us working together, we make so much progress with the painting that we're nearing the finish line far sooner than I would have guessed. Grandpa walks to the dock and looks around the yard, but Grandma continues to watch us paint. I'm so close to Jake that I can smell the sweat on his shirtless body. Our painting is a game of long glances and quick looks down when we're caught. Every time I look at my grandma, she's smiling as she watches us work.

"Jake, even when you were younger, you'd never wear a shirt," Grandma says. "Your Grandma Eleanor and I would sit around and say, 'That boy needs to put a shirt on, or he'll get sunburned,' but you never listened."

Jake's chest shakes as he laughs.

"Eleanor would hose you off outside at the end of the day," Grandma continues. "You'd be covered in dirt. You'd strip out of those shorts, and we'd laugh because your butt was so white compared to your tan torso. We'd joke that the cows might mistake it for the moon."

I drop the roller so I can cover my mouth with both hands as I laugh.

Jake looks at me with a mischievous smile. "You think that's funny, City Girl?"

I bend over with laughter. "I'm picturing it right now." I close my eyes. "Yep, I can see it."

Jake takes his paintbrush and paints me from my neck to where my bibs cover my bikini. I jump back. Then I lunge forward and poke him in his hard stomach. The best sound is my grandma laughing behind us.

"I didn't mean to embarrass you, Jake. You were just a boy. But this one over here..." Grandma points her finger at me. "We had to force Camilla to wear clothes. Even as an eight-year-old, she'd try to take her clothes off and run around the yard in front of Robby and her cousins. Eleanor and I would say, 'No one is going to be able to tame that girl.'"

Heat rushes to my face, as now it's Jake's turn to laugh.

"So you liked to run around naked, huh, Camilla?"

I bend over and grab a roller. "At least I had even tan lines."

Jake chuckles. When he turns to talk to my grandma, I run a roller full of paint from his neck to the waist of his jeans. His mouth hangs open as he tries to get out of the path of destruction. "You did not just paint my back."

"Oh, come on, Jake. You know me better than that. Of course, I painted your back."

Grandma's eyes shine, every one of her teeth visible through her smile. "And our little Camilla was so smitten with you, Jake. She'd follow you everywhere and tell us that you were her boyfriend."

We stare at each other. I flick paint in Jake's direction, my face turning bright red.

"So Camilla had a crush on me, did she?" He smirks as if to remind me that he already knew this bit of information.

Grandma Sis pulls her straw hat up a bit. "Oh, heavens, yes. She said she'd marry you someday."

I've never seen Jake with a bigger smile. Now two people have admitted this to him. I'm mortified. Grandpa returns. As he takes Grandma's hand, I suck in a deep breath and decide that today has seen enough excitement. Jake walks them to the car. I watch as he kisses Grandma Sis on the cheek and helps her into the passenger seat. Grandma Sis makes every space she's in happier, even if she does share all of my secrets.

"I had the best day watching you two paint," Grandpa Sunny says. "Thank you for what you're doing out here."

We wave my smiling grandparents away.

Jake walks back to me, shaking his head and smiling. "I love your grandma."

"She's the best. She has much better days when she lives in the past, so we have to let her continue to do that."

"I love hearing her stories. It brings me back to simpler times, and it makes me feel so close to my grandparents." Jake looks deep in thought, but then he grins. "And you must have been hard up for me, City Girl."

"A very long time ago," I practically yell.

Jake and I paint side by side for a couple more hours and nearly get the entire first coat on. But we're losing light, and I'm losing visibility of what we've painted and what we haven't, so we call it quits. The clouds have rolled in, and it looks like it may storm.

I look down at myself. I'm covered in paint and sweat. I stretch out in a lawn chair, looking at the lake and feeling unable to move. "Will you grab me a bottle of water?" I yell back to Jake.

Jake goes into the cottage and returns with a bottle. I undo my bib straps, pull them down to my torso, and put the cold bottle on my chest, forehead, and then stomach, trying to cool myself.

Jake takes the lawn chair next to me and laughs. "Your grandma's stories remind me of the picture of us on my nightstand."

I sit up and put my hands on my knees. "I forgot I did that."

"You'll be happy to know it's still there." He takes a drink of his water, nearly draining it in one sip.

"It was a joke, in case that wasn't clear," I say. "You don't have to keep it."

"I like it."

I lie back again and shut my eyes.

"Have you had many serious boyfriends, Camilla?"

"Why are you asking me that?"

"I'm curious is all." He picks at dried paint on his torso.

"Relationships, blah," I spew out. "How long were you with Tiffeny?"

"I was never with Tiffeny." He sits up further and leans toward me. "I mean, we hooked up for a few months, but it was over before the Fourth. She came up to my room and asked if she could crash, so I let her. Nothing happened. I feel like I owe you that."

Knowing that he didn't spend the night with Tiffeny after kissing me, I find the sudden relief that washes over me surprising. "Any serious relationships for you?"

Jake looks at the lake. "I mean, yes and no. It's complicated."

The paint is now crusty and clumping into balls on my skin. It pulls on my skin and becomes tighter. We're teetering on the edge of deep conversation, and

I don't want to ruin the lightness, so I walk to the lakefront and look back. I can't see Jake because it's so dark.

"Are you still here?" I call out.

"Yes." His voice echoes through the darkness.

If I can't see him, he can't see me. I peel off my bib overalls the rest of the way and then remove my bikini and run into the water, squealing.

"What are you doing?" he hollers after me.

"I'm reliving my eight-year-old life of nakedness. Are you joining me?"

Jake's shadow appears as he strides to the lake. I swim farther into the water. I can barely make him out but can tell he's standing there, thinking.

"Sis was right about your inability to keep your clothes on."

I hear the noise of a zipper and see the shadow of Jake bend down. Next comes the sound of him splashing into the water. I swim out to where I'm deep enough to be covered even while I stand. He follows.

He gets out to where I can finally make out his features. He turns so his back is nearly touching me. "Will you clean my back?"

I splash water and scrub the paint off his back the best I can. His skin is so warm under the water.

When I'm done, he spins back toward me. "My turn to get you."

He scrubs at my neck and stops short of where the water hits me, right at my collarbone. His warm hands rub my skin on my chest and then move to scrape my arms. I reach down into the water and splash water in his face.

I laugh as I swim away. He comes right up and grabs me, spreading his fingers as they grip my waist. I put my hands on him to balance myself and keep myself submerged from the neck down.

"You're different from most women I know," he says as his grip tightens. "Most can't wait to talk about themselves, but you share so little."

My feet float above the bottom of the lake because Jake's hands are firmly on my hips.

"You haven't exactly been forthcoming yourself." I push his hands away and start swimming toward shallower water. "I mean, we work alongside each other all the time, fixing up my family's cottage, and we barely speak."

He wades along beside me until we reach a point where the water only comes to his waist. "I don't trust easily," he admits.

I'm thankful for the cloud cover over the bright moon because the water barely reaches my chest. "Why not?"

"Why don't you?"

I think back to what Robby coined as the Emily effect. It seems so silly that I would allow the loss of a childhood friend to prevent me from getting close to people in life. But when I dig deep, I realize that I do tend to wall up. And it isn't only because of the loss of friendships. It's because I've never stayed in one place long enough to feel safe. It's because I don't feel like I have a home. It's because I've had to leave every home I've had and every relationship I've made in those places. It's because Sis is forgetting everyone and everything, and I fear the same for myself. Saying goodbye is easier when there's distance.

My body tightens as Jake wades toward me. His hands go to my shoulders and rub them.

"I'll tell you something if you share something," he says.

I can just make out his features in the darkness. "I don't have anything to share," I lie. "What you see is what you get with me."

His hands return to my hips. I fall toward him as I lose my balance. I wrap my arms around his shoulders to catch myself. For a split second, my body presses into his. Skin on skin. Jake leans and licks his lips. His face gets closer to mine, and it's about to happen. Again.

"We can't do this," I say, displacing as much water as possible to splash him.

He releases me. "Do what?" He furrows his brow.

"Kiss, or whatever this is." I point to the two of us. "I told you to never kiss me again, remember?"

His expression goes blank. He splashes his chest with water and tries to remove more paint. "Camilla, I don't know what handbook you got your rules from, but you got into the lake naked, and then you rubbed your breasts against me."

My body prickles with heat. "That's what you think of me? I got into the lake because I don't have a shower that works. And I didn't rub up against you. I lost my balance."

Jake comes closer. "You can see why I'd be confused, right? I must have read the situation wrong."

"You want to talk about confused?" I yell. "How about sharing a pretty great kiss and then getting rejected? How about then finding out that you spent the night with someone else?"

"I didn't spend the night with someone else," Jake says as he follows me to shallower water. "And are you kidding me, Camilla? I wanted to come in. That kiss was—"

He stops talking, backlit by the light outside the cottage, the water barely to his waist. "I never would have forgiven myself. You're young. Too young. Hell, you were only twelve years old when I started playing in the NFL. Plus, I have a lot of loose ends to tie off in my life."

"Perfect!" I squeal. "Believe it or not, I can live with that. But what I won't do is continue to put myself in a situation where we end up here. I'm too young? Fine. But you're too messy. Let's stop putting ourselves in this situation."

The dull moon seems to light the water around him. "You get to leave Wheaton at the end of the summer, but I'll still live here and need to see Sunny and Sis. I'd have to live with the fact that I slept with their granddaughter, who is only twenty-four years old. No thank you."

"I get it," I bellow. "But remember who made the first move. Because it wasn't me."

"You got me there, but I'm being the responsible one." He has his hands on his bare hips.

"If you're so responsible, then just leave."

He looks at me, surprised. Then as he walks out of the water, I mostly look away but glance up as he reaches the grass. His body is a work of art. His muscles flex as he walks, and I allow my eyes to travel down to his perfectly muscular butt.

"My grandma was right," I yell. "Your butt is as white as the moon."

Jake grabs his clothes and walks into the darkness.

# CHAPTER 23

I wake up the next day as mad as I was when I went to bed. I have this desire to get to know Jake better, but I also want to look the other way and never turn back. He's maddening, yet he's also my friend. But he's only my friend in bits and pieces, and that isn't actually a friend at all. I can't stand thinking about him. I try to shake him from my mind. Some things aren't meant for me, and that's okay.

My phone beeps, and I check the text.

*I forgot to mention that I'm heading out of town for a bit. I'm hoping you can finish the paint job without me. I'll finish the inside work when I'm back.*

He never mentioned that he had anywhere to go, but what a convenient thing, seeing that neither one of us wants to see the other. I need a break from him as well, so this works out for both of us. I reply,

*K.*

The three dots indicating that he is writing a reply appear and then disappear. I stare at my phone for a few minutes, but Jake never responds. I'm exhausted from the mental back-and-forth, and I look forward to not having to deal with him for a few days.

I'm up now, so there's no point in trying to get back to sleep. I get dressed and head to town in time to have coffee with my best guys. I call and wake up Robby on my way to town. He tells me that Jenna is coming to Chicago for the weekend to visit and look into potential jobs.

I pull up at my grandparents' house just as Grandpa is shuffling out the door. "Cammy, you're here. I wasn't expecting you."

I reach my arm out to help him balance. "I wanted to have coffee with you and the men. Is Grandma doing okay?"

He nods. "Oh yes. Sis is doing just fine. She and Annie are knitting mittens today."

Grandpa and I walk down Main Street. I observe the "For Rent" sign again on the old thrift store and remind myself that I need to call Carrie.

"Seeing the cottage and watching you paint," Grandpa says, "it's been great for your grandma."

I rub my free hand on my grandpa's arm and notice the sunspots. "Keep coming out and watching. I love getting to hear her old stories."

We arrive at the café. "You have no idea how much your grandma loves having you here."

I feel the tears prick at my eyes. "I love being here too, Grandpa."

We enter the café, where the men await us at our usual table.

Walt's eyes light up as he sees me. He pulls another chair over to the table. "Camilla, you're here."

I pat Walt on his hand and then greet Juan and Lawson. Today, Lawson's tracksuit is navy blue. All of us have signed his cast.

"I've been so busy out at the cottage," I say, "but I've missed you guys."

We talk a lot about how tall the corn has gotten, how cloudy it's been, and how much we need a big rainfall.

Walt leans in. "Camilla, do you have a boyfriend?"

I laugh as everyone looks on. "Not at the moment, no."

Lawson puts his hand on his chin and looks deep in thought. "You're a looker, just like your grandma Sis. We could help find you someone."

I bite my lip and can't hide my amusement. I'm curious about who they would choose for me. "Do you have anyone in mind?"

Juan puts his hand out. "You're an independent kind of girl, so you need a man who's also independent."

Lawson nods. "Someone who can get you in touch with the nature side of you."

I take a sip of coffee.

Walt looks to the others. "Next coffee, we'll have a list of some of the eligible fellas. I have a couple in mind."

Grandpa looks at his watch. "I have to get Camilla home, as we have a call with her brother soon."

We both stand. Everyone waves and says they hope to see me soon.

Only after we get outside in the muggy weather do I release my laugh.

"I'm sorry, Cammy," Grandpa says. "They can be a bit much."

"It's fine, Grandpa." I smile. "I like that I have you guys looking out for me."

"Well, that's sweet of you. Most kids your age would find our meddling annoying."

We walk down Main Street in silence as a couple of trucks drive by.

"I've been lucky to get to live my life in the same place," Grandpa says after a time. "It may seem boring to some, but this town, these people, especially Sis…I always have people looking out for me. It's my favorite thing about Wheaton."

I wrap my arm around him tighter. "Did you and Grandma ever think of moving?"

"Not once."

We reach their front yard.

"But from an early age, we knew that Larry and your dad had their eyes set on something different. And that's okay. Sis and I always told them that they'll always have a home with us in Wheaton wherever they end up in life. And that goes for you too, Cammy."

"Could you ever imagine me in Wheaton, Grandpa?" I ask slowly.

He stops walking and turns to me. "Any place in this world would be lucky to have you, including Wheaton." He winks at me. "And you have the ability to make friends easily. There isn't a place you wouldn't fit in."

\*\*\*\*\*

Tonight, as I sit in the cottage and start some new job applications, I feel alone. The clouds have broken, and it's going to be a beautiful sunset, but the beauty feels like a waste, given that I'm unable to enjoy it with anyone. I think about my earlier conversation with Grandpa. Home. I've never felt that anywhere. I feel bad thinking it. My parents gave Robby and me everything. It was exciting for me to get to live in so many places, but I feel like it may be time to give that lifestyle up.

Guilt overruns me. My parents paid for a private education and probably thought I would end up doing business design for some sort of firm or corporation. Those possibilities wouldn't exist if I stayed here.

I think of how inexpensively I could live in Wheaton. If Grandpa and Grandma let me, I could stay at the cottage—I mean, if they were willing to heat it. I could network and get to know people here and in the surrounding towns and find myself some work. Until I landed a design job, I could see if there were any openings at restaurants and bars. Living here could be so easy.

I look at my phone and decide to text Robby. He's probably out with his coworkers at the latest hip bar in Chicago, but I still try him.

*Do you think it's crazy that a part of me wonders if I should stay in Wheaton? At least for a while.*

Before I have a chance to put my phone down, he responds.

*No.*

*No I shouldn't stay, or no it doesn't sound crazy?*

As I wait for Robby's reply, I realize that it's too quiet in the cottage. The wind is calm, the birds have gone to sleep for the night, and my mind daydreams about what life would be like here. It's not the worst idea I've ever had, and I wouldn't have to stay any longer than I wanted to. I could live on so little, and perhaps the lake and Wheaton would be the inspiration I need to be a designer.

My phone beeps again. I expect it to be Robby's response, but instead, it's a text from Jake.

*Hi from the world's biggest jerk. I'm sorry.*

Unexpected. I pause before responding. I'm convinced that Jake and I are the same person, which is why we rub each other in a bad way.

*Thanks. I guess I can be a jerk sometimes too. But let's agree that you're a jerk more.*

*I can agree with that. I need to say this. The kiss was my fault. I mean, fault assumes regret, and I don't regret it. I always want to kiss you. The way you were looking at me the next day, though, like I was the most disgusting person you've ever seen. It broke me. I don't want to hurt you.*

I throw my phone down on the bed and jump up and scream into my hands. There is safety in being able to react without witnesses. It's easier to be brave when I don't have to look into Jake's eyes.

*Not disgusted. Disappointed.*

I wait for what seems like forever, but it's really only a few minutes.

*I know. I'm sorry. And I need you to know this. I can try, but I can't promise that I won't want to kiss you every time you lick your lips or look at me with those blue eyes...or let's be honest, grace me with your presence.*

I change the subject. This conversation is going in an unexpected direction. I'm not ready for that. We start texting about whether we like small towns or large cities better. We agree that both have positive things and have a lot to offer and that regardless of where we live, it's important to travel. I tell him about my favorite small town I ever visited, a place called Flisa in Norway.

I ask him the best place he's ever traveled to, and he tells me all about Vietnam. He shares how much he loved the history and climate, exploring Halong Bay and lighting a lantern in Hoi An. I tell him about Cambodia and Barcelona. I also mention the few months I spent in Botswana in a study-abroad program when my family lived overseas. I did community planning, and the local village women taught me how to braid hair, which is why I know how to do Kylie's hair so well.

Jake: *I finished the book, by the way. I loved it. I can see why it's one of your favorites. It's about so much more than a small town.*

Me: *Exactly! It's about narrow-mindedness, mediocrity, and conformity, but it's also about doing good wherever you go. Being bold. Being the change.*

Jake: *I think I met my match in my love of books!*

Jake and I spend hours texting back and forth. He seems curious about what it was like to travel so much for most of my life. I explain that mostly I like the adventure. I love experiencing a new place for the first time, and I've loved getting to meet people from all walks of life, all with their own stories and life experiences.

When he asks about my past dating life, I'm honest that I've never fully fallen for anyone. Although I feel bad, it's easy for me to walk away from relationships when things get too serious or when it's time to move to a new place. As I type the words, worry spreads through me. Perhaps there's something wrong with me that it's been easy to move through life without feeling the need to get close to someone.

Jake opens up about his life as well. He shares that he couldn't wait to get out of Wheaton to go to college. When he got to Stanford, he focused heavily on academics, too, because he knew how short a football career could be. He started in premed before moving to business because it was a broad enough major that would allow him to go in different directions.

He shares that when he got drafted into the NFL, the entire town of Wheaton had a watch party. It made Jake feel guilty that he'd been in such a hurry to leave this great community. When he was injured, he was sure that his life would never have a purpose again. He tells me that he doesn't drink because he saw it potentially becoming a problem. He said it started as fun, and then it became fun with problems, and finally, it only caused problems. He explains that alcohol was never an addiction for him, but it added no value to his life. So he quit.

We discuss the grossest food we've ever had while traveling. Mine was a silkworm in Cambodia, and Jake's was blood pudding in Vietnam. Jake has me rolling with laughter when he tells me about a night when he and a few teammates on the Oakland Rockets wanted to get a drink in a bar, so they all went in disguise. He texts me a picture of himself with big glasses and a black mullet wig. I text him some pictures of my favorite travels.

Just as with Grandma Sis, the past feels safer, so neither of us discusses the future. It's easier to share what my experiences have been and much scarier to admit that some of these experiences have made me a terrified twenty-four-year-old, worried by how my past life will contribute to an unfulfilling future.

I could talk to Jake all night, but my eyes can barely stay open. I look at the time, and it's three in the morning.

Me: *I need to get to bed. When will you be back?*

Jake: *Hopefully in a few days. Sweet dreams, City Girl.*

# CHAPTER 24

Days have passed, and I have finished painting the cottage. My grandparents have come out every day to drink iced tea on the lawn and watch me work. Jake has been gone almost two weeks, and we haven't communicated since the first night he left. I almost texted him a few times, but each time, I would erase my message. I hoped that he would reach out to me again, but he hasn't. I still have no idea when he's coming back, though, and there's an emptiness in Wheaton without him here. Next week is the last week of July. We have nearly come to the last full month of summer.

The heat is stifling. There is so much humidity in the air that I feel like I'm walking through a rainforest. My hair sticks to my neck as I tie it up on my head. The cottage doesn't have an air conditioner, and even opening every window doesn't help because there's no breeze. My clothes cling to me. Everything feels sticky. I decide to drive to town to get a reprieve from the heat.

I stop at the Main Street café, knowing that I'll find Grandpa and his friends. As I enter, lively conversation is happening everywhere. The farmers talk about the rain that is supposed to come tonight. Grandpa's back is turned to me, and I put a hand on his shoulder.

"Hi, Grandpa. Hi, guys." I pull up a chair as everyone greets me.

My grandpa lights up. "I wasn't sure if we'd see you this morning, Cammy. I'm glad you drove in."

"Yeah, me too. It was so hot out at the cottage, but it's not much better here." I fan my face with the napkin on the table.

Walt also fans his face and leans back in his chair. "They say there's a storm front coming through tonight, Camilla. You should stay in town. Storms hit the lake differently than in town."

"Yeah?" I look at my grandpa.

He nods. "It's up to you, Cammy, but I think Walt is right. We've had some bad storms on Lake Traverse."

Juan leans in like he's about to tell us all a secret. "Do you guys remember the storm of 1997? It took out so many cottages on the South Dakota side of the lake."

Everyone nods.

"How about the Armistice Day storm of 1965?" Lawson says. "Remember the Deal family that was stuck out on the lake that day?"

"That's right," the men say at the same time.

"The farmers need the rain," Juan says. "But they don't need hail."

"You've got that right," a voice chimes in from the next table.

Even though it's well over a hundred degrees today, Lawson wears another tracksuit, this time bright green. He has already graduated from a cast to a boot. I can tell that the air is humid because Juan's usually straight hair is almost as curly as mine. Everyone in the café looks miserable as they fan their faces and lean back in their chairs.

I blow on my coffee and observe the four gentlemen staring at me. "I have a few things to do at the cottage, but then I'll come into town later."

Walt pulls at his pants as he straightens his suspenders. "Do you and that Abram boy have more projects to do yet? I saw him driving down Main Street today. Looked to be headed to the lake."

"Do you mean Dax?" I ask.

"No, I'm sure it was Jake."

I had no idea Jake was back, and I'm not sure how to feel about this. "Jake and I are nearly done at the cottage. He found some secondhand cupboards and countertops. He's going to put in a new shower in the bathroom, and then I think the last step is taking down a few trees."

Everyone stands up, so I guzzle the rest of my lukewarm coffee.

Grandpa leans on my chair. "Just be careful, Cammy," he says as I rise to stand beside him. "Lake Traverse doesn't answer to no one."

"I will. I think I'll head out to the cottage now and then come back to town once I clean the place up."

My tires squeal as I hurry out of town. These country roads turn and wind, and it's not uncommon for a deer to jump out, but I'm anxious to see if Walt is right that Jake is back in town. I turn down the gravel road, and the corn that was no more than speckles of green when I arrived for the summer is now taller than me. I turn right toward my cottage and let out a breath when I see Jake's white truck parked in the driveway. I cover my face from the smile because I don't know what's going on with Jake. All I know is that he's starting to feel like a real friend and that Wheaton isn't the same without him here.

He's in the yard, shirtless as usual, cleaning up paint supplies. When I slam the car door shut, he turns in my direction. I walk to him, and his lips turn up in a smile.

I give him a small wave. "You're back."

"Hey, City Girl. I'm back."

"How was your trip?"

He comes closer and stops in front of me. I fight the urge to hug him. I'm also nervous that our interaction will end how it always does, in a standoff and us yelling at each other.

"Productive."

"I thought you'd be back sooner."

"Everything took longer than expected." His smile is broad and genuine. "But I'm home now."

"I see that." I laugh. "And you seem happy to be home."

"So happy."

He pulls me into a hug, and my feet lift off the ground. He wraps his arms around my waist. I throw my arms around his neck and hold him close. Just as I go to breathe him in, the embrace is over. He places his hands on my shoulders and kisses my cheek.

I sweep my hair out of my face and wipe the sweat off my forehead. I look at the cottage. "Well, did you inspect the paint job?"

Jake heads over to the cottage, and I follow. "If you ever need a job, I'd hire you as one of my painters."

I raise my eyebrows. "It's not bad, right?"

He glances back at the cottage and then looks at me and smiles. "It's not bad."

I bite the inside of my cheek. "What's next out here?"

His eyes scan the property, and then he looks toward the lake. "I've been out here a few hours installing the shower, so that can be used now. I can do the cupboards and countertop anytime. The yard should be cleaned up of trees, but then we're done."

My heart sinks. I don't want it to be over—not ready to inch toward the end of summer and the end of my excuse to see Jake so frequently. "I bet you're happy not to have to see me around for much longer."

He pokes me in the forehead. "We'll have to find noncottage-related reasons to see each other."

My heart pings with hope. "Yeah?"

"Until you leave, that is." He avoids my gaze as he picks up more supplies in the yard.

"Yeah," I say. "Until I leave."

I help him haul supplies to his truck and then clean up the rest of the space by throwing old supplies into the garbage and recycling. My skin is wet from the humidity. I take my hair out of my ponytail and then put it back in, higher and more off my neck.

Jake's golden back glistens with sweat. He bends over to pick up the remaining paintbrushes, and as he stands, he blows the hair out of his face and then sweeps it back. "I don't like the color of the sky."

I follow his line of sight and look up.

"You shouldn't sleep out here tonight, Camilla."

The air is still. "Grandpa told me the same thing. Will you stay out here?" His place is a lot bigger than the cottage, so perhaps he will.

"I'm not sure yet. I have a family dinner at my parents', and if the weather looks bad, I'll crash there."

I remember storms out here as a child. We would huddle around the window and watch the waves crash and the lightning light up the sky.

"Town is safer?" I ask.

"Yeah. The wind off the lake can be relentless. The trees take the brunt of it, but I wouldn't chance it."

"I have a few things to do here, and then I'll be right behind you."

"Speaking of family dinner," Jake says, interrupting my thought, "I need to go home and shower before I head to my parents' house. You're welcome to join me at dinner. I know Kylie especially would love to see you."

"I have too much to clean up before heading to town," I say. "But thanks for coming by and finishing the shower. I can't wait to use it."

He pauses as he reaches his truck. "Don't be out here much longer, Camilla. I mean it. The sky doesn't look good."

"I'll shower and most likely beat you to town."

Jake opens his door. "You better."

"Say hi to the family, and thanks again."

Jake gets in his truck and rolls the window down. "In case it isn't obvious, I'm really happy to see you, Camilla."

My heart grows in my chest, but I try to play it cool. I lean against Jake's open window. "In case it isn't obvious to you, I'm really happy you're back in Wheaton."

I hit his truck with the palm of my hand. Jake smiles as he rolls up his window and drives away. After he leaves, I spend some time putting away the life jackets from the boat. Then I drag the kayak farther away from the water. I get a few items to the shed and then organize the space so everything will fit. I arrange lawn chairs behind the cottage where the wind doesn't reach.

The heat lightning captivates me as it ripples through the sky in waves. I hope the farmers get the rain they've been hoping for. I've officially become a Wheaton girl, thinking about the weather. Thunder rolls in the distance, the vibrations echoing off the hills. The lake sleeps, with not a ripple to be seen.

The sweat drips off my skin. I go into the cottage and peel my clothes off. They stick to me and are hard to remove. The new shower is in place. I figure that the old shower's remains are most likely in the dumpster outside. I get in and let the tepid water cool me. Salt drips down my face and makes its way to my lips. I'm so happy I can finally shower out here.

Once I'm cooled off, I step out of the bathroom and throw on Jake's Stanford shirt and a pair of shorts. I lose all track of time as I pick up the cottage. I put together a bag to bring to town. The breeze comes through the window, and I look outside. The leaves of the trees blow in the wind. There is finally relief from the oppressive stillness.

I go room to room, shutting all the windows. As I go to close the large living room window, the wind stops again, and I've never felt such calm anticipation in my life. The birds must know the storm is coming because they can't be heard anywhere. The sky is now green. I go into the bedroom and throw together the remainder of the items I wanted to bring to town.

By the time I come back out, the sky has turned black. The lights in the cottage flicker and then go off. As I search for my cell phone, my heart races. I find it on the counter, dead.

Waves start to crash against the shore. The wind invades the cottage as the walls begin to shake. I have no idea what time it is, but I know I've missed my opportunity to drive into town.

# CHAPTER 25

The lightning provides glimpses of what's going on outside. The waves have white caps and are dangerously close to the cottage, but I can't hear them over the wind. Between lightning strikes, I sit on the couch in the darkness. Rain pelts the roof, and because of the wind, it feels like it's hitting the cottage sideways. Thunder rattles the windows. The wind sounds so violent that for a moment, I fear the cottage is going to blow over.

I run to the back bedroom when I see the living room window distend in my direction. It's going to take one more gust of wind to shatter the glass. I contemplate running outside and getting in the car, but there's no way I could drive through this storm, even if I could make it to the car through this wind.

I shut my eyes, put my hands over my ears, and try to sing myself a song. No matter how loud I sing, all I can hear is the wind, which sounds more like a train off in the distance. There is a loud bang in the living room, and I put my head between my knees. I hear more loud noises and then, unless I'm delirious, I hear my name.

"Camilla, where are you?" A door slams, and Jake's voice rings out.

I lift my head as the lightning glows through the cottage. "I'm in here!" I scream over the howling wind.

I stand up just as Jake appears in the doorway. My body collides with his, and I wrap my arms around his torso. He pulls me further into him as his arms envelop me.

"What are you doing here?" I scream over the wind.

"I told you to go to town," Jake yells. His arms shake as he holds me.

He walks me back toward the wall, and we sit next to each other on the floor.

"I was going to, but the storm came up so fast. I was stuck."

He shivers under my touch. "You never listen. I drove to Sunny and Sis's, and when I didn't see your car, I came here." He trembles as he talks. "I told them I would look after you."

I pull my knees to my chest and can hear Jake's teeth chattering between the bursts of thunder.

"You need to get out of your wet clothes," I tell him.

The whites of his eyes illuminate with the next strike of lightning. I pull at the bottom of his shirt and lift it over him. His skin is cool and damp.

"Your shorts."

Jake pauses, but then he shimmies himself out of his soaking wet shorts. I grab the comforter off the bed and wrap us in it. He continues to shiver, so I rub my hands over his arms and then his chest and stomach. I feel every muscle in his abdomen. Touching him makes it hard for me to breathe. The storm doesn't care that we're stranded here on the floor, hoping the cottage doesn't blow down. The wind whips all around us as a reminder that we aren't going anywhere anytime soon.

We both jump as we hear the loudest bang of the evening. It shakes the cottage. For a moment, I think this is it.

"What was that?" I ask as I bury myself into Jake's chest.

"Let me check." I watch the silhouette of him as he peeks through the bedroom door and walks into the living room.

I wait for what feels like forever. As Jake finally returns to the bedroom, a bolt of lightning illuminates the space.

"What was that noise?" I ask.

He reaches up to the bed, grabs two pillows, and lays them on the floor. I reach for his face because the room is once again pitch-black, the lightning so unpredictable. My fingers graze his lips, and then I rest them near his eyes. Jake puts his hand behind my head and helps me lie back on the pillow. He tucks me into our shared blanket.

"I think we're on the floor for the night," he says as he lies next to me. I pull my body into him as he continues to shiver. The lightning is bright and unyielding. It's like a strobe light pours in through the windows.

His hand travels up beneath my shirt. His eyes find mine, and for the first time since I've known him, he looks scared. His hand moves to my side. He never breaks his stare as he pauses when he reaches the underwire of my bra. I hold my breath. The heat from his hand envelops me as it explores my neck and then my shoulder until he spreads his fingers across my stomach. In one swift motion, he lifts my shirt over my head.

"I figured you could help warm me up with some skin-to-skin contact," he breathes into my ear.

"That's only fair." I say as I press against him.

I exhale and spread my hand across his chest and then down to his stomach. His skin is still clammy and wet as I try to warm every inch of him. I spread my fingers, and my hand feels so tiny in comparison to his body. While my body is all soft, Jake's is hard. I pull myself closer to him as my hand explores his back. No part of him feels cold anymore.

My hand moves to his face, brushes his wet hair, and then I run it over his eyes, his long eyelashes between my fingers. I feel back along his jaw before I rest my fingers over his open lips. My fingers tremble as his lips part.

His hands roam until he draws lines on my face with his finger and then squeezes the back of my neck. The storm continues to rage outside, but my own storm is erupting inside me. Our lips are so close, and my breathing is in sync with his, our chests touching as we breathe in and out together. The storm refuses to lessen outside, yet I feel like the sound of my heart is louder than the wind and thunder.

"I like you so much," Jake murmurs against my lips.

"I like you too."

He lays a kiss on my lips. It's quicker than a beat of my heart—his lips soft and perfect.

"In case the cottage topples onto us tonight, I have a confession to make." He cups my face in his hand. "I think about you. All the time."

I pull the hair at the base of his neck to get my body closer to his, the storm nothing more than background music. Everything fades into nothing, and all I see is Jake. With the next crash of thunder, our lips collide. We hold our breath as we make contact. Nothing but everything will ever do as it relates to Jake, and I've known it since our first kiss. We breathe air into each other as if it's our only hope to survive the night.

It's a frantic type of touching. The lightning provides a sporadic light show. I look into Jake's eyes as he rolls me on my back and presses his weight onto me. Next comes the thunder as I grab him and pull him closer, and he falls onto me. I'm sure that if I'm crushed by the weight of him, this would be the best way to die. I dig my fingers into Jake's hair. He loops his fingers in my underwear, and I do the same to his. We move desperately as the storm swirls around us.

Without taking his lips off mine, he pauses and speaks into my mouth. "Are you okay?"

I go to answer, but the sound that comes out surprises us both. I start laughing. My hand goes over my mouth, but once I start, I can't stop. Jake looks stunned, but only for a moment, and then he props himself up on his elbow and laughs into my neck. It's the most glorious sound. I don't know what's gotten into us.

"I'm sorry," I say. I plant kisses along his neck and then move to his chest. His skin tastes like summer.

He kisses my neck and then chest as he continues to laugh. "I have to be honest. Your laughter doesn't give me great confidence."

I grab his head, and his eyes flick up. "You make me nervous," I confess. "I mean, you're Jake Abram."

"You make me nervous too."

We both stop laughing.

He plants kisses along my face and then pauses. "You're Camilla Bergland."

"But, Jake…" I bite my lip, embarrassed about what I'm going to confess. "I followed you around. I was obsessed with you. I told my family I was going to marry you someday."

I try to cover my face with my hands, but Jake takes them both in his hand. "And now I'm obsessed with you," he says.

The laughter has gone out of me. I trace my fingers over his arms as he continues to hover over me. He kisses my lips and caresses my face.

"This means something to me," he says.

Jake's hair tries to hide his face, and I brush it back with my fingertips. "Me too."

I'm overcome with an all-consuming affection as I wiggle myself closer to Jake. It isn't that he was nice to me when I was an annoying child or the fact that he grew up to be beautiful. But there are strong feelings—a longing for someone I've known in one way or another for my whole life. Someone who once meant something to me. A person who captivates me, both the good and bad parts of him. There are so few people whom I've known to some extent throughout my life, but Jake is one of those people.

We are in sync. Here for each other. Tender, affection, and sometimes belly laughs that this is happening. As Jake's body slides over mine, he trembles. Sex is right there, on the horizon. We both know it, but we also savor every touch, kiss, and caress. The friction of my thighs against his groin causes him to moan into my hair. He seeks permission, and all I see are his turquoise eyes beating into mine as I take the first press.

It's gentle, testing, and for a moment, Jake's eyes roll back in his head as I take more of him, and I cry out when I have all of him. Jake pulls my leg over his shoulder, and I nearly lose it in that moment.

First sex has always been awkward and left me wanting, but Jake Abram knows what he's doing. He glides over me with measured control, and presses his forehead into mine as I grab the ass I've spent the summer admiring.

"I've thought of this so many times this summer, you have no idea," Jake confesses as his tongue swirls around one of my breasts, while his hand cups my other.

"Me too," I admit as I arch my back in response to Jake's rolling hips.

Jake's kisses move away from my chest, up my neck, to my earlobe, until his lips find mine once again.

"But this is so much better," Jake says, his voice rugged, and his motions become more frantic.

"Jake," I plead but find myself unable to finish what I had wanted to say. Instead, I give in completely, and it's not a delicate thing sweeping over me. Instead, I scream out into the thunderous night. The pleasure is so intense that my leg shakes, and I nearly kick Jake in the face. But instead, he grips me beneath the knee, places his forehead on mine, and with one swift motion, he loses control before all of his weight falls on me.

Jake's crushing me, and when he realizes it, he moves to his elbows, caging me in. He kisses me so softly, and his fingers twirl the end of one of my curls. And then he grows against me as I open my mouth to receive more of him. I reach down and take him in my hand, and when he groans, I know I'm causing this.

"I don't think I'll ever be able to get enough of you, Camilla," he breathes into my mouth as he continues to grow in my hand, ready for round two.

With a swift motion, he pulls me on top of him, and he feels like a giant underneath me.

"How long do I have you for?" he asks, hands kneading my hips.

"For as long as I'm in Wheaton," I say, leaning in to kiss him once again.

\*\*\*\*\*

The sun shines through the windows, and every light in the cottage comes on at once. The hum of the fridge can be heard again. I lie on my side, Jake pressed against my backside, his arm wrapped around mine, fingers intertwined. His other hand starts rubbing my back, so I know he's up too. Kisses on my shoulder make my skin pebble. He nuzzles his scruffy face into my neck. I sit up and turn to him, the blanket pulled up to my chin. He smiles as I move the hair out of his face. Neither of us bothered to put clothes back on last night.

"We survived," he says, smiling into my hand.

"Close call." I remove his grip on me and look for something to put on. Our clothes are scattered all over the room.

He moans and sits up on his elbow, also searching the room for his clothes. I grab his shirt. It's still soaking wet.

"Either I'm going to have to stay naked or perhaps you'll let me borrow the shirt you took from me."

"I vote for naked." I laugh but throw the Stanford shirt to Jake.

He puts it on and wraps a sheet around his bottom half, as his shorts are still drenched. I wrap myself in the blanket and go to the other room to put on my clothes. Now that the lights are on and the sun is up, everything feels different. All I can think about is last night. Jake and me. A few times. My childhood crush. The boy I told Robby I would marry someday. The man who has driven me crazy all summer. My skin turns crimson just thinking about it.

Outside glows with the promise of a new day. Now as the sun comes up from behind the cottage, Jake and I can assess the damage.

"I'm going to take a look outside," he says.

Last night, the lake looked like an ocean, its waves swelling and crashing. Today, there's nothing more than a walleye chop. I smile as Jake inspects outside, the sheet hanging to his feet.

When he returns to the cottage, I bite my lip. "So how bad is it?" I ask.

"Well, the loud bang we heard was a tree falling on the cottage. Come outside with me."

I feel like I can't catch my breath. He reaches his hand out and I take it. The humidity has been zapped from the air. The chill that hangs over us pierces into me as well. A large tree in the front of the cottage has fallen. Other branches have come down as well, but everything else looks intact.

"Was it a tornado?" I ask.

He looks up at the sky. "We don't get tornadoes up here. It was a straight wind. It could have been so much worse."

Save for the tree, everything else seems fine. From the sounds last night, I never would have guessed.

"I'll see if there's any roof damage," Jake says. "You'll have firewood for a long time once we clean the yard and cut up the fallen tree."

I lean on the doorway of the bedroom I usually sleep in, the one that looks at the lake. It hadn't felt safe to sleep here last night because of the storm. I open the window and let the cool breeze enter the room. I hear footsteps and turn back to see Jake leaning on the doorway.

"We could start the cleanup outside, go to my place, and I'll cook breakfast. Or we could lie in bed all day. We have so many options." He breaks into a half-smile.

Part of me wants to jump into his arms and have a repeat of last night, and another part of me wants to talk all day. I only slept for two hours last night. We talked for hours, and between talking, we got to know each other in every other way possible. I've never met someone for whom these multiple truths could exist simultaneously, where I'm as wildly attracted to their mind as I am to their body.

Jake stands in wait of my answer. I go to him and step onto the bed so I can pull his shirt off over his head.

"Looks like you've made your decision, City Girl."

"I have."

I kiss his chest and neck. He grabs my legs and wraps them around him. We fall back on the bed.

"Wise choice," he says as we get under the covers. "Which family member should we tell first?"

"You mean about us?" Unable to hide my surprise, I shoot up and look at him. "No need to share."

He laughs, pulls me back down, and kisses my forehead. "Dax will take it the worst," he says. "Kylie will be the most excited. Jenna will claim she knew all along."

And here I thought that last night was just a distraction to weather the storm. Jake continues to be full of surprises.

# CHAPTER 26

As a child, this part of the summer in Wheaton always made me melancholy. Mornings this far north in Minnesota this time of year are chilly enough to need a sweatshirt. By the afternoon, if the sun comes out, it's hot enough to swim and be outdoors, but then the evenings turn brisk again.

I know some people who live for sweatshirt weather, but for me, it has always signaled a pivot to a less carefree time. As a child, I always knew that my family would be packing up our stuff and flying to whatever home we had at the moment. I knew we would soon be saying goodbye to Grandpa Sunny and Grandma Sis, and Labor Day would be here, and school would start back up again, and I would get a pit in my stomach at the thought of having to meet new people in a new city.

I can't help but feel melancholy once more as I wake up and feel the cool breeze through the cottage windows. Just as it had been for me as a child, I don't know what's next for me. It's not the coolness that makes me sad. It's the leaving. And unless I make some decisions, I only have a month left in this place.

The past few days have been *interesting*, a word that my Minnesota relatives use in an all-encompassing way, one that describes something that we don't quite understand or have the appropriate name for. Yes, this new thing with Jake and the past few days have been interesting.

Before I head to town to visit my grandparents, I check my email. Two entry-level design jobs have shown up in my inbox. Chicago. Suddenly, I realize that I can't delay in making decisions on what's next.

During my drive to town, I call Carrie, wanting to talk about the vacant thrift store on Main Street. The call goes directly to voice mail, and I don't leave a message. I think my decision is made, though I don't know how long I'll stay. I just know that I'm not ready to leave yet.

As I pull up to my grandparents' house, my phone vibrates against my leg. It's a text from Jake.

*I'm going to work on the cupboards today. Do you want to see if Sunny and Sis are free to come over for an early walleye dinner? Say, 4:00?*

I give his text a thumbs-up.

Grandma sits at the table in the kitchen, looking out the window. "Oh, there you are, Camilla. Are you ready for tea?"

I go to the stove to put the kettle on. Grandma has been good about waiting for someone to turn on the burner since her near-miss fire. I hand her a cup and join her at the table.

"Jake is wondering if you and Grandpa want to have walleye dinner at his place tonight around four."

Grandma moves the cup to her lips and backs off when the tea is too hot. "That would be lovely, Camilla, but he doesn't need to go to the trouble."

"He insists, Grandma."

I hear the shuffle of my grandpa, and then he appears in the doorway.

"Who insists?" he asks.

I stand up and offer him my chair. "Jake invited you and Grandma to his place for walleye dinner tonight."

Grandpa puts his thumbs through the loop of his pants. "I guess we should assume the boy has caught some fish. Probably not as much as the boys and I caught at the dam yesterday."

I laugh about how being invited to eat fish at someone's home has some element of competition for my grandpa. "Does that mean you'll come?"

My grandparents agree.

"I'm going to help Jake out at the cottage today," I tell them. "We're hopefully going to finish the cupboards."

On my way to the cottage, I call Robby. He never responded to my text from over a week ago. "Good, you picked up," I say into the phone.

"Sorry. I've been swamped and trying to get caught up before I head to Wheaton again at the end of the month."

"I'm glad you aren't ignoring me. I want to continue our conversation about me staying. You said no. Did you mean that no, I shouldn't stay, or no, it's not crazy?"

"Did I never respond?" Robby breathes into the phone. "I thought I did. My no was that I don't think it's crazy. What are your options? Stay in Wheaton or move in with Mom and Dad? Go back to Savannah? I love you, Cam, but you aren't moving in with me."

"You don't think it seems crazy? I mean, staying in a town this size, living at the cottage."

"Candidly speaking, Cam, it's a lot less crazy than the other times you called me to tell me where you were headed next. Wheaton makes sense."

I sigh at the truth of it.

Robby laughs. "Remember when you told me after only being at Savannah College for two weeks that you were going to apply to study abroad? Or what about when you told me you wanted to spend the summer in Israel on a kibbutz? Yeah, Wheaton doesn't sound that provocative to me."

I had thought that my contemplating staying would be bigger news for Robby, but people in my life have always expected the unexpected as it relates to me. "Don't come to any conclusions yet. This isn't well thought out at all, and it may not even work out."

I say my goodbyes to my brother just as I pull into the cottage. Jake is walking out, dusty from the day.

"I came to help with the cupboards."

Jake takes his cap off and wipes his brow. "Your timing is perfect. I'm done for the day. How about

I drive you to my place instead?" He stops when he reaches me, hand on my face, and his lips brush against mine.

I've been trying to maintain my space as far as Jake is concerned. I'm doing everything in my power to maintain my individuality without giving him the brush-off. This hasn't been easy, given how close my cottage is to his house and how we see each other every day for projects. He seems to be an all-or-nothing kind of guy because he always asks me to stay.

At Jake's, he showers as I make a tomato-cucumber salad. The tomatoes and cucumbers are from his garden, as is the red onion I slice next.

"Camilla cooking in my kitchen," Jake says from the balcony. He runs his hand through his wet hair as he comes down the stairs. "Who would have thought it?" He wraps his arms around me as I finish making the salad.

I turn to face him and loop my fingers through the buckle of his jeans. "Not me. I was determined not to like you."

He laughs against my head. "My parents are also coming to dinner. They're going to drive Sunny and Sis."

*Jake's parents*, I think, panicked. I know them, of course, and have seen them a few times this summer, but dinner feels very much like a big step—like I'm meeting the parents. "Oh, okay."

Jake puts his hands on my hips, lifts me onto the island, and kisses me in that all-consuming, intoxicating way of his. I lock my legs around him. What starts as a kiss, as it always does, quickly becomes a hunger.

I speak into it. "This would be a hard position to explain when our family shows up."

Jake sighs and pulls away. "You're right, but it gives me an idea for later."

He winks, and I blush.

When my grandparents arrive, they are followed closely by Jake's parents. I help my grandparents get situated in chairs and grab them a drink. Then I greet Jake's parents.

"Hi, Dr. Abram. Lucy." I give them both a hug.

"You have to stop calling me Dr. Abram, Camilla," Jake's dad says to me through a smile. "I'm George."

I'm amazed at how much Jenna looks like her mom. George and Lucy sit by my grandparents while I help Jake with the final food preparation. Jake puts the last of the walleye on a serving plate, pulls the salad out of the fridge, and pours the beans into a bowl. I grab the plate of watermelon and bring it to the table.

Jake calls everyone over. "The food is ready."

George puts his hand over the table. "This table is beautiful, Jake. Where'd you get it?"

Jake points to me as he starts dishing up food. "Camilla had it made. It's wood from the original cottage."

George looks up at me, surprised, and Lucy smiles.

BETWEEN SUNSETS

"I recognized the wood right away," George says. "Jake doesn't invite his old parents over much, so I appreciate your good influence on him."

Lucy looks around the place. "Honestly, Camilla, you did a beautiful job. It looks professional."

I put a fork in the fish and then pass the plate. "Thanks. It's what I went to school for, so I'm glad it wasn't a total bust. Now I just need to get a job somewhere."

Lucy's eyes are kind as she smiles. "Well, I'm sure that will happen. You've transformed this place. It's so classy, but it's also so *Jake*."

Jake snorts. "Thanks, Mom. Clearly, *Jake* and *classy* aren't used in the same sentence very often."

Lucy's face reddens. "That isn't what I meant."

We all continue to chat as we enjoy our dinner. Jake's fish is cooked to perfection. I squeeze lemon on top. There is nothing better than Lake Traverse walleye. Grandpa Sunny asks Jake so many questions about where he's been catching fish these days. I enjoy sitting back and watching my grandparents converse with the Abrams. They have a sweet relationship based on mutual respect and a lifetime of knowing each other.

Grandma brought an apple pie that I helped her make. I serve everyone a plate, along with some coffee.

"Camilla, is Jake your beau?" Grandma asks, looking mischievously from Jake to me.

Jake draws a breath to answer, but I practically yell, "No, Grandma Sis. We've become friends from

279

all the time we spend together on the cottage, but that's it." My face reddens as I avoid looking at Jake or anyone else at the table.

Grandma puts a forkful of pie in her mouth, and her face contorts from the tartness. "Eleanor and I always used to say we needed to marry a Bergland to an Abram."

Grandpa puts his arm around her and changes the subject. "This is the best apple pie you've made, Sis."

Lucy clears her throat. "I agree. It's wonderful, Sis. What a treat for us."

Jake stays quiet through dessert, and when everyone is done, I start clearing the plates. My grandparents and Jake's parents say goodbye. Now it's just Jake and me. I load the dishwasher as Jake goes upstairs. He comes down with a sweatshirt and pulls it over me.

"You looked cold." His lips press to my forehead, and neither of us moves for a moment. He takes my hand and leads me over to the sectional. He picks up a photo album.

He sits next to me, and our legs brush up against each other. "My mom brought this today. She said you and I might enjoy it."

I run my finger along the jagged edge of the photo album. I pull my legs under me and cuddle into Jake's side. The album is full of pictures from our childhood. The first pictures are of Jake, Dax, and Jenna. Then the Bergland family is introduced—

mostly Robby and my cousins, Liam and David. I enter the album later, after I'm born.

I usually celebrated my mid-August birthday at the cottage, so there are pictures of Jake and me on every birthday for many years. The progression is obvious. In the photo of when I turn five and he turns fifteen, he seems less willing to be part of the annual birthday picture. My sixth birthday is the last one of Jake and me together. I stand in my swimsuit, which is on backward, holding up six fingers. My hair is so blond that it's nearly white, my curls darting in every direction. Sixteen-year-old Jake has his elbows on the top of my head as he rests his grouchy face in his hands.

I pass my thumb over the picture and look at Jake. He watches me study the photo. I wrap my arm around him and run my fingers through his hair.

"You were over it, Jake."

He gives me a long stare before looking back at the album. There are so many pictures, and I don't know if I remember all of these moments or if they've been retold so many times that I just think I remember them. Either way, there are pictures of me naked and running around the yard. There are several pictures of Jake pulling me in a wagon. There are pictures of Jenna and me putting on performances for the two sets of grandparents. I rest my head on Jake's shoulder and breathe him in.

"You're a lot younger than me." Jake speaks the words as if seeing these pictures is forcing him to acknowledge the facts all over again.

I pinch his stomach. "So you like to bring up."

He shakes his head and, in one swoop, has me lying on the couch with him between my legs. He props himself on his elbows to avoid putting weight on me. "Our age difference doesn't bother you?"

"Not having things to talk about bothers me. Not so much age." I lift my head to kiss him. "And anyway, I'll be twenty-five in a little over a week."

"Oh, you mean the same day I'll turn thirty-five?" He laughs as he shakes his head. "I was thinking about having a bit of a get-together here. We should have a joint birthday party."

"Jake…" I pause. "I'll celebrate with you, but a joint party feels a little serious."

He presses his weight into me. "So I'm really not your beau then?"

"Ahh," I say. My body tenses. "Is that what has you looking so pensive? I've told you I don't really do relationships. Nor do I prescribe to culturally normative definitions of such things."

Jake cups my face in his hands. He kisses my nose and then my cheek and then my other cheek. "Camilla, you know I love—"

"Jake." I pull him closer and speak into our kiss. "I love spending time with you too. I do." I don't care to know what he was going to say. I want to be in this moment and not think about feelings and where this is going. That's a mistake I've made too many times. For now, it's us, and that's enough.

Jake pulls away for a moment, his expression a mixture of confusion and contemplation, so I do what feels natural. I part his lips with mine and pull him in deeply until our tongues dance. He wraps his arms around my legs and picks me up. I drape my arms around his neck as he carries me upstairs to his bedroom.

He lays me on the bed and helps me undress. My body craves his. I pull his shirt over his head and kiss his stomach from his belly button up until I've come to my knees, face-to-face with him. I experience déjà vu—like I've been here before. And I have, just never with Jake. I know how to make him feel good with my body, but I haven't mastered how to make him feel good with my words.

He flips me over. I place my hands on his forearms.

"You don't seem ten years younger than me," he says into our kiss.

I want to agree, but I realize that Jake is nearly a thirty-five-year-old man who seems ready to settle down and fully embrace his adulthood. I still have half of my twenties in front of me. I fear this isn't going to end well.

# CHAPTER 27

I wake up before Jake and watch him for a few minutes. He looks so peaceful and young when he sleeps. Fully on his back, his chest peeks out from the covers. He's dead to the world. A heaviness consumes me as I prop myself up on my elbow and watch his chest go up and down. The summer continues to tick away, each sunset bringing me closer to decisions and absolutes. I tiptoe out of the room, not wanting to disturb his slumber.

There's something peaceful yet lonely about early mornings at the lake. The morning dew clings to the grass, a mourning dove calls out, and a chill in the air signals that the birds will soon fly south. Autumn is a time for melancholy, and although it's still summer, the signs are clear—it's right around the corner, and I won't be able to stop it.

*****

I'm much too early for coffee with the men or tea with Grandma, so I sit in my car in my grandparents' driveway and stare at the house. I figure that Robby is up for the day, so I send him a text.

*Robby, I'm freaking out. Don't call me. Please. I can't talk to you, but I think I messed up. You won't even believe what I did.*

I don't have to wait long before the dots appear on my phone, and I can see that Robby is composing a message.

*Let me guess. You finally hooked up with Jake.*

I pick up my phone, fingers trembling, and call Robby. "What do you know? Who said something? How can you know this?"

Robby laughs. "So am I right?"

"I mean, you aren't wrong," I confess.

Robby makes puking sounds into the phone. "Spare me the details, please. I will throw up if you share the specifics. But seriously, Cam, what's the issue here?"

"The problem is that I'm contemplating staying in Wheaton. How am I going to stay now that I've gone and messed this up?"

"Wait, wait, let me get this straight. You're nervous because you're staying? Doesn't staying make a relationship with Jake feasible? You know, as opposed to you leaving?"

I go to answer, but Robby cuts me off.

"Or are you saying you only wanted this to be a fling, and now that you're staying…"

He quits speaking. He gets me. With every other guy I dated, there was a natural ending. The

285

summer of backpacking through Europe was over. My time at the kibbutz was coming to an end. My family was moving cities or countries. I was leaving Savannah to study abroad. I've always had an out. But Jake appears invested. And he, more than anyone before him, is someone I don't want to hurt.

"Honestly, I don't know what I want." I sigh into the phone. "I didn't plan for anything to happen. Why couldn't I come to Wheaton and not find ways to complicate my life?"

Robby laughs. "You may not have planned it, but I also bet zero people will be surprised if they see the two of you together. How do you feel about him, Cam?"

How do I feel about Jake? How do I say out loud what I barely let myself think about? I care about Jake so much. I've known him almost longer than I've known anyone, even though until this summer, I really didn't know him at all. I'm wildly attracted to him, but I'm surprised at how sensitive and thoughtful he is too. We got off to a terrible start, but he's busted his butt helping me with the cottage. And we have so much in common. Besides our stubbornness, we love reading, traveling, and learning about other cultures. I want him to be happy and have good things in his life.

"It's hard to explain," I concede. "But I really like the guy."

"Of course you do, Cam. So quit holding back and go for it."

This has been enough talking about feelings for one day. "Grandpa is waving me inside," I lie. "So I have to go. We'll talk later."

"Fine, Cam, but don't mess this up. You two make more sense than I was willing to admit, and—"

I hang up before he can finish his sentence.

*****

A while later, Grandpa and I join the men at the café. Lawson still has a boot on his leg, but he's getting around so well that he should be able to take it off soon. The café isn't as busy this morning, as many farmers are tending to their fields and not having their morning coffee.

"Camilla," Walt says as he stabs a fork in his egg. "Back to finding you a boyfriend. I think I have the perfect Wheaton guy for you."

I had forgotten about this matter.

"Jake Abram," Walt says, looking to the others. "Am I right, guys?"

Juan nearly gags as he slaps his hand on the table. "Yes! Why didn't I think of that before? Jake would be perfect for you."

"Let's give Cammy her privacy, gentlemen," Grandpa interjects.

No one seems to hear him.

Lawson tucks a napkin into his collar before he bites into his jelly doughnut. "You two seem to have a lot of chemistry," he says, his mouth full. "When you guys drove me to town after my fall, I saw the way he looked at you."

"Okay," Grandpa says. "Let's let Camilla think about this, and we can talk about something else."

I can't escape Jake anywhere, so it seems. Of course, Grandpa's friends are right. We do have chemistry. In hindsight, we always have. We're perfect for each other, they say, but it scares me how much Jake seems to like me.

As I'm in town, Jake texts to let me know that he's hanging out with a special girl today whose only request is to see me, so I drive back out to the lake and go to the cottage first. I inspect the work. The kitchen cupboards are almost complete. Everything looks so beautiful. I can't wait to have family out here for Labor Day weekend.

A car door slams. Soon after, Jake and Kylie stroll into the cottage. She's holding a beautiful bouquet of flowers. Her smile stretches from ear to ear as he hands them to me.

"Kylie and I saw these and thought of you." Jake pulls me into a kiss.

"They're beautiful, but you didn't have to."

"We wanted to." He opens a cupboard, pulls out a vase, and puts the flowers in water.

"It was actually Uncle Jake's idea," Kylie admits. "He thought the yellow looks like your hair, and the blue like your eyes, and the red like your—"

"Okay, Kylie." Jake swoops her into his arms. "I need Camilla to think I'm cool, so we can't give away everything I said."

Kylie laughs as she scrunches up her face and nuzzles into Jake's neck.

"I'm so happy to see you both," I say. "But don't you have a day job, Jake?"

"I'm the boss and have people to cover for me. I couldn't think of anything better than spending the day with you and Kylie."

Kylie plays on an iPad as Jake and I work side by side on the cupboards. We exchange few words, a lot of long glances, and plenty of closeness as I stand on a chair and hold things in place for Jake to drill.

"I will never be able to repay you for all the help you've given me, Jake," I tell him as he takes a measurement.

He puts down the tape measure and looks at me. "Speaking of payment, I hope you know I don't want your money. I had ulterior motives."

I poke him in the back. "So you did want to buy the cottage from my family."

Jake wraps his arms around me and kisses my neck. "No. But I did think if I made it nice and winterized it, maybe you'd stay in Wheaton."

I go to respond, but Kylie beats me to it. "Uncle Jake, I'm bored."

"I don't have much longer, Kylie, but I have to finish up this one piece."

"It's fine," I tell him.

"No, I need to finish this."

I look to Kylie, who's now standing with her hands on her hips. "Then why don't I take Kylie on an adventure? When we get back, maybe we can go on a boat ride or do something fun."

Jake looks relieved, and I'm more than happy to get out of work to spend time with Kylie. We don't waste any time in leaving.

As we make our way up the road, Kylie puts her hand in mine. We stroll in silence until we reach the point by Jake's house, where I search in the sand for flat rocks to skip.

"Uncle Jake likes you," Kylie says as she finds a flat rock and cleans it in the water.

I slip off my shoes and stand in the water. "I like him too. He's been a good friend to me."

Kylie laughs. "That's not what I mean. He likes you in a romantic way." She holds her shirt out and gathers rocks in it.

I shake my head and grin. "What do you know about romance, Kylie? You're five."

"My dad and mom liked each other in a romantic way. They'd kiss and stuff."

"I see."

I sit in the sand. Kylie sits next to me. We've both pulled our knees to our chest as we gaze out over the water.

"You must miss her so much," I say.

"I do. So does Daddy." Kylie throws a pebble into the water and then another.

"I've heard your mommy was great."

"Yeah, but I have Auntie Jenna, Uncle Jake, and two grandmas and grandpas. And I have you."

"That's right, you do." I put my arm around her.

Kylie runs her hand in the sand, molding it to the shape of her little fingers.

Footsteps cause us both to jump.

"Well, ladies," comes Jake's voice, "we have a change of plans. Your dad just called, Kylie, and he'll be here in two hours to pick you up. So I say we make a pizza and some popcorn and find a movie to watch until he shows up."

"Yes!" Kylie screams as she jumps up and hugs Jake's leg.

Twenty minutes later, we're sitting on Jake's couch, the sun still high in the sky, watching a cartoon princess try to save a village from evil intruders. We each have our own bowl of popcorn. Kylie sits between Jake and me. Jake reaches behind her and puts his hand on my shoulder. When I glance in his direction, he smiles knowingly, like I'm in on whatever it is that runs through his mind. I'm not.

Just after the movie ends, Dax arrives and picks up a sleepy Kylie. "Thanks for spending time with her today," he says. "She can't get enough of Uncle Jake and Auntie Camilla."

I give both Dax and Kylie a hug as he holds her in his arms. "We had fun, didn't we, Kylie?"

She smiles, never lifting her head from her father's shoulder.

After they leave, I start bringing popcorn bowls and pizza plates to the sink. Jake leans in and kisses me—coconut ChapStick, soft lips—and my heart flutters just like it does every time. I pull his shirt over his head with urgency, and my hands explore every inch of him. I glance at his tattoo. *You can't get away from yourself by moving from one place to another.*

Jake pulls my shirt over me, and I work to unbutton his pants. His kisses cause the skin of my neck to pebble. He lifts me onto the counter. In this position, I have the best view of him. He's beautiful. And he feels like he could be mine if I want him to be. Everything between us is so frantic—like if we don't get closer to each other at this moment, then we never will.

Chemistry is a funny thing. Although how I feel toward him is new for me, I sense that this gravitational pull won't last forever. Maybe it won't even last for long. It starts as an indefatigable desire, and then it fades to occasional yearning, and then only friendship remains, and then at some point, we don't even like each other. And then if I'm anything like Grandma Sis, I'll grow up, get Alzheimer's, and won't even remember Jake by the end. I won't remember this moment and how it felt, and I'll spend my days apologizing for things I have no control over.

My phone starts buzzing on the counter. I pull Jake closer, press my body into his, and try to tune out the ringing. But my phone starts buzzing again.

Jake pants against my neck. "I think someone is trying to reach you."

"They can leave a message." I pull him to me and devour his lips.

When my phone starts buzzing again, I groan and give up. The screen says I missed three calls from Annie.

"I better take this." I hop off the counter and pull on my clothes. "Annie, is everything all right?"

"I'm so sorry to bother you, Camilla," she starts. "But Sis had an episode, and Sunny had no choice but to call an ambulance. She's fine, but I still thought you should know."

"I'll be right there." I hang up and look at Jake as he puts his shirt on and smooths out his hair. "I need to go to the hospital."

"Let me drive you." He buttons his jeans.

"No, no. Annie said Sis is fine. You stay here. I'll take care of it." I grab my purse from the counter and head toward the door.

"Camilla." Jake reaches out, takes my hand in his, and spins me back to him. "You aren't alone in this world, you know? I said I'd drive you."

"Jake," I say, preferring the simplicity of relying only on myself. Then I sigh because I know he's right. "Fine. If you insist."

Jake opens the passenger door for me. I hop in, and we drive to town mostly in silence, his hand over mine. My mind races about what kind of episode Grandma Sis had this time and how odd it feels that I'm sharing such an intimate moment with Jake.

The hospital is eerily silent when we arrive. A long, empty corridor leads to a few rooms, one of them likely housing Sis. A light flickers overhead as I take a seat in the waiting room, hands folded between my legs. Annie comes out of an exam room first and then Grandpa. I stand up, wanting to rush to him, but my feet are like heavy weights against the floor. Dr. Abram joins us next. He looks at Jake first, then me.

"What's going on?" I ask evenly, trying to hide the panic I feel. "Is Grandma all right?"

"She's much better," Dr. Abram says.

"A nurse is in with her now." Grandpa Sunny wraps his hand around my wrist and gives it a squeeze. "We'll be able to go home for the night."

Annie puts her hand on his shoulder. "I'll go make sure Sis has her things. Why don't you pull the car around, Sunny?"

Grandpa nods, takes his keys out of his pockets, and jingles them as he steps through the door and into the darkened parking lot.

When Jake takes my hand, I involuntarily shake him off and put my hands to my face. "How bad is it, really, Dr. Abram?"

I don't know what it is about the best doctors, but compassion oozes from their eyes. I almost feel like Dr. Abram can feel my pain—almost like he's as sad as I am. "She's so much better, Camilla. But she became very irritated tonight, and Sunny couldn't control her. She was threatening to take the car, and she's beyond the point of being able to drive. Sunny called the ambulance." Dr. Abram looks toward the hallway and then back at me. "Physically, Sis is doing pretty well. Her blood sugar was low, so you guys will need to stay on top of that. But these episodes are going to be more frequent and severe in the coming weeks and months. You may need to start talking as a family about the nursing home. Wheaton has a great memory care unit. It may be the best thing for her. And for Sunny."

"Thank you," I say, remembering how he had asked me to drop the formalities, "George."

"Of course," he says. "Now if you'll excuse me, I need to get back to another patient." He strides down the hallway and enters a room.

"Can I be with you tonight?" Jake's voice brings me back to reality, and tears threaten to escape.

"I need to be with Sunny and Sis."

He caresses my face. "I know you do, Camilla. I can stay with you there."

Footsteps echo down the hallway as Annie and Grandma emerge from a room. Grandma sees me right away.

"No, Jake," I say. "You go home. I'll call you tomorrow. I promise."

I don't know all of his looks yet, but the expression that spreads across his face makes it seem like my words hurt him, even though that's not what I intended.

"Fine," he says. "But I'm here for you. If you'll let me be." He cups my cheek and gives a sad smile. Then he goes to greet Grandma and wish her well.

I've always preferred to experience sadness alone. Sharing my pain with someone else feels like too much to take on at the moment. So I let Jake leave. And then I wrap my arms around my grandma, wanting never to let her go.

# CHAPTER 28

The birthday I share with Jake is tomorrow, but today is the party. I'm happy that our birthdays fall on a Sunday this year. They say that Sundays are a Leo's favorite day. I'm not sure if that's accurate, but I like the positive sign. In hindsight, all the traits that annoyed me about him are the same traits most common for a Leo. We're oddly similar, and it's taken me almost all summer to realize it.

Now that I know him, I see all the positive sides as well. He's passionate about people and pursuits, he's generous and helpful, and he's a great listener. On the negative side, the wall he's built around himself is layered, much like mine. And we share a strong stubborn streak.

I drive to town early to check on my grandparents. Annie's car is already in the driveway. From their spot at the kitchen table, Annie and my grandma smile as I walk through the door.

Grandma gets up and pours me a cup from the teakettle.

"You're here early today," I say to Annie.

"I thought I'd come and spend the day with Sis," Annie says. "She and Sunny told me that you and Jake Abram are having a party at the lake today."

Word travels fast in Wheaton. "Yes, but it's nothing big. We happen to have the same birthday, so Jake thought it would be fun to celebrate. It's really his party."

I sit down at the table and blow on my tea.

Grandma puts her hand over mine. "You kids have a fun time, and don't worry about us old people."

After tea, I meet Jenna at the store, where we pick up a few things for the party. I resist the urge to ask her if anything is going on with Robby. He is adamant that they are only friends. Instead, we focus on picking up some food and drinks for the party.

Once we have everything we need, I drive back to the cottage, knowing that I need to talk to my parents about everything happening here. I want my grandparents to see everyone, and I need the family to understand how little time we have before Grandma Sis is lost to us forever. I reach out to my dad and Uncle Larry first, sending them an email asking if they still plan on coming to Wheaton for the long Labor Day weekend. Both families had said that they couldn't wait to visit. We have been planning to make it a little family reunion.

In this confirmation email, I tell them about how Grandma has good days and bad days, about my project to fix up the cottage, and about how I can't wait until we can all be together. I let them know that there is plenty of room at the cottage or in town at the grandparents' house for all of us to fit. I send a separate email to Robby, Liam, and David, who also plan to attend.

After writing to my family, I head down to Jake's place. I know he says that this is a birthday party for the two of us, but as guests start arriving, I realize that I don't even know half of these people. These are Jake's friends. Jake pulls me outside and puts his arm around my waist as he introduces me to everyone.

When I see Malik and Carrie, I make a beeline to them. "Hi, guys."

Carrie hugs me first. "Hey, Camilla. It's so great to see you."

Malik looks past our hug and toward the food arrayed on the picnic tables. "You guys have quite the spread here."

"Well, the spread is courtesy of Jake." I turn to Carrie. "Not to talk shop at a party, but I'd love to sit down with you and discuss the thrift store."

Carrie smiles as she adjusts her headscarf. "Yes, let's connect. I saw I missed a call from an out-of-town number, but no one left a message. I was wondering if that was you. Let's grab a coffee on Monday if you're free."

"I'd love that." I give her another hug. Things are coming together. Staying in Wheaton is becoming more of a reality. And more of a necessity.

Dax and I make eye contact. He heads my way as Carrie and Malik slip inside the house. "Joint birthday party, huh? Sounds serious."

I relax when I see Dax smiling. "This is not my party. I can't help that Jake and I share the same birthday."

"Well, Jake is introducing this as a joint party with his girlfriend Camilla. Kylie will be thrilled."

"His girlfriend, huh? That sounds official."

"And a first for Jake." Dax waves at a guy who walks past us. "I knew Jake was in for it after I saw the way he looked at you at the street dance."

I hide my surprise. The street dance seems like so long ago. Was that this summer? I thought Jake hated me then. Perhaps I was wrong.

Kylie shows up with Dax's parents and runs to me when she sees me. "Happy birthday, Camilla!" She wraps her arms around me.

"Let me look at you." I kneel and look at her hair. "Did your dad do your hair?"

"He did!"

Kylie does a spin for me. I find Dax's eyes and give him a thumbs-up.

The water is full of people floating on inner tubes, escaping the heat of the day. Jake is in host mode, but every time we make eye contact, he waves me over to him, and he acts like we're very much a couple.

Tiffeny and a friend arrive. I'm not sure who the friend is, but she's always with Tiffeny, and every time I see them, they're whispering into each other's ears and looking at me. Jake makes it sound like whatever he had with her was casual, but I get the sense that she thought or hoped it was more than that. Logic tells me that it's odd she would be here, but I've noticed that in Wheaton, people show up when there's a party, whether they've been invited or not.

Jake comes up behind me and wraps me in his arms. "Are you having a fun birthday party?"

I turn and put my arms around his neck. "I am. You?"

He presses his soft lips to mine. "I am. Happy twenty-fifth, Camilla."

"Happy thirty-fifth."

Jake holds me for a moment.

"Go on and be with your friends," I tell him. "I'll be fine. Continue with your host role."

He smiles and looks happy. "I get you all to myself tomorrow. I have big plans."

"Can you give me a hint?" I pull at his shirt.

"I think you'll love your gift."

I think Jake will love what I got him as well. I smile and wave him off, then watch as he joins a group standing by the firepit.

As the night turns cooler, people begin to congregate around the fire Jake has started. The crowd has thinned, and Jake's parents left hours ago with Kylie. Jake is talking to Malik and Dax by the fire. I shiver and go inside to find warmer clothes.

I grab a sweatshirt from the closet in Jake's bedroom. It's nice to be alone for a moment. Everyone has been so nice, but I can't help but feel like I've stepped into Jake's life, a place where I'm not yet sure how I fit. I feel like an impostor. A toilet flushes. I peek out of the closet and see Tiffeny and her friend leaving the bathroom.

Tiffeny looks me up and down and then fixates on the sweatshirt I'm holding. "Hi, Camilla."

I feel territorial. Like her energy should no longer be in this room. In his house that I decorated. "Hi?" I say, making it sound like a question.

"Greta and I were just talking about you. Isn't that right, Greta?"

Her friend smirks in my direction.

"You know," I say, gesturing toward the door, "there are two bathrooms downstairs."

Tiffeny laughs as she smooths out her shirt. "I know, but I'm used to going up here from when Jake and I were together."

"I'm going to go back outside," I say as I try to leave.

Tiffeny steps in front of me, and I can tell from the cunning grin on her face that she has other plans. Her hand clasps my shoulder. "I was wondering out loud to Greta whether or not Jake has shared with you some important details about his life."

"I'm sorry," I say, my body stiffening. "I don't know what you're talking about." I try again to step past her, but she holds me firm. My heart feels like it's going to escape through my mouth.

"So Jake hasn't mentioned the fact that he's married?" she asks, holding back laughter.

I'm dizzy. Like I'm experiencing this conversation out of my body. Electricity prickles my nerves.

I'm sure I'm going to faint. All the color drains from my face. "I don't know what you're talking about."

"From your expression, I can see he hasn't told you. Haven't you looked him up on the internet? I mean, you know he played professional football, right?"

My mouth is so dry that I don't know how I manage to get the words out. "No, I've never looked Jake up. Why would I?" This isn't me. Usually, I can hold my own better than this. I'm wilting under the pressure.

Tiffeny laughs. "Because everything you need to know is out there. He was quite the internet celebrity a few years back."

I turn away and don't even remember my feet hitting the stairs as I go down them. A few people congregate inside, but not anyone I know. I open the back door and see Jake standing by the fire, off in the distance. I stalk toward the back of his place, where I find that my car is blocked in by other vehicles. It's dark at the end of the driveway. When I get far enough to where no one will see me, I turn on my phone's flashlight. Then I start off for the cottage.

The ground feels like it moves under me. I can't catch my breath. The sky spins. I stop walking for a moment to put my hands on my knees and try to catch my breath, but it feels like an elephant is sitting on my chest. Finally, I collect myself and complete the journey home. There is no way that Jake won't come looking for me once he realizes I'm gone, so I do something I've never done before at the cottage. I lock the door and pull the shades shut. I'll have to go to his place tomorrow to get my car.

Tiffeny isn't trustworthy. She lied about Jake wanting to buy the cottage from me. Well, technically, she didn't lie because Jake admitted to saying that to her. Remembering that makes me feel even worse. Tiffeny hasn't been my favorite person, but I have no reason to doubt her.

I slide onto my bed, bring up an internet browser, and type "Jake Abram Oakland Rockets." Who looks people up on the internet? Has anyone ever looked me up? It's never something I've done or thought about doing. I click on the first link, and the headline reads, "Former Oakland Rockets quarterback Jake Abram weds a mystery woman in Las Vegas."

Against my better judgment, I read on, where it details that Jake and the woman both appeared intoxicated as they walked into a Las Vegas chapel. Logic tells me that I need to stop going down this rabbit hole, but I continue to click on articles.

*Former Oakland Rockets quarterback Jake Abram can't be found. Estranged wife distraught.*

It's the final article I click on that sucks all the air out of the room and makes it hard for me to breathe.

*Former Oakland Rockets quarterback Jake Abram spotted in Los Angeles with estranged wife. Sources confirm the couple has reunited.*

A picture is attached to the article. The print date coincides with the weeks-long period when Jake said he was out of town for work. I knew something felt off, but I gave him space and never asked. I had no right at the time. A picture shows him in an embrace with a tall, willowy woman with long, straight black hair. Her sunglasses are as big as her head. She wears bright-red lipstick. She looks like she just stepped out of a fashion magazine, and her head rests comfortably on his shoulder.

I hardly recognize him, but I know it's Jake. He looks like anyone you would see in Los Angeles—not at all like someone from Wheaton. He wears dark-wash jeans that hug his legs, a fitted blue polo shirt, and loafers. His sandy-blond hair brushed off to the side. His muscular frame. His hands. He's holding her, his arms around her waist just like he always does with me. She's stunning.

*If Jake is with a woman that looks like her*, I think, *then what has he ever seen in me?*

None of this makes sense. Jake is into me, I can tell. I know what men in love look like. He's not that good of an actor to be able to fake it, but these headlines and the photo…it's all right there in front of me. It's proof that whatever this is, Jake has been lying to me since day one.

I do the math. He was gone for two and a half weeks, and here he was, in Los Angeles the whole time. Tiffeny may have disclosed all of this to me for all of the wrong reasons, but I'm glad to have learned it all now instead of later.

I lie in bed, the articles replaying in my head, along with the picture of Jake and that woman. I feel like I'm going to be sick. I wait for the knock on the cottage, but it never comes. I spend most of the night in bed crying until eventually I fall asleep.

# CHAPTER 29

Happy birthday to me.

At the first sign of light, I throw clothes on and splash water on my face. My eyes are red and puffy, and my face still has yesterday's makeup smudged all over. My only goal is to walk down to Jake's, get my car, and never look back. Last night was the worst and most restless night of my life, and although I told myself I didn't want Jake to show up, the fact that he never came speaks volumes. I don't remember ever feeling this way. I suppose there's a reason we call it a crush. My heart literally feels like it's been crushed into a million pieces.

I knew. For whatever reason, I felt like things were going to end badly. I want to scream that I allowed myself to feel something. I know better than this.

Only a few other cars remain in the yard alongside mine. I don't see Tiffeny's car, but what do I even care at this point? It's over, and Jake is free to do what or whoever he wants. I slide into my car and pound my fist on the steering wheel. I wish that whatever we entered into had never started. Nothing that happened is worth how I feel at this moment.

I back up, and once I'm turned around, I head down the driveway as fast as I can, dust from the gravel flying up on both sides of the car like great plumes of smoke. I want to call someone to vent, cry, something, but no one would be up at this hour, and the person I really want to talk to is the one person I can't.

When I get to the house, my grandparents are still sleeping, so I tiptoe into the bedroom I've been calling mine. I turn my phone off, pull the quilt up to my chin, and let the tears flow.

When I finally wake, I turn my phone on and see that it's early afternoon. Several texts pop up, most wishing me a happy birthday, and then I have several from Jake.

*Happy birthday, City Girl! I don't know where you went last night. I was busy catching up with people and assumed you went up to the room to sleep. Imagine my surprise when I went to bed and you weren't there.*

*I have a lot of fun plans for us today! I can't wait to give you your gift.*

*Camilla, are you there? I'm starting to get worried.*

*Now I AM worried. I'm heading to town and will stop at your grandparents' house.*

*Sunny said you're sleeping. Why did you leave? And why are you sleeping? What happened?*

*Did I mess this up?*

Downstairs, I find Grandpa sitting in the living room.

"Happy birthday, Cammy." He starts to get up, but I motion for him to sit back down.

I pull up the chair next to him.

"Your grandma just went up for a nap, but I wanted to wait for you. Is everything okay? I was surprised to see you here this morning and not at the cottage."

I try to smile, but the tears pool in my eyes. I blink them away. "I'm fine, Grandpa. I had a hard night. But I'm fine."

Grandpa puts his hands on his knees. "Jake was here looking for you. I told him you were sleeping, and he asked if he could come up and talk to you. I told him he better not."

I wipe my eyes. "Thanks, Grandpa."

His expression crumples at the recognition of my tears.

"I'm sorry," I say. "I'm just feeling a little emotional right now."

Grandpa leans over the coffee table and squeezes my arm. "Can I treat you to the tavern tonight for your birthday? If you don't have any other plans."

I pat my grandpa's hand and cry. I try to hide my face, but it's no use. He pushes himself out of his chair and pulls me into a hug. Who makes the rules about who can take care of whom? Rules are meaningless. There are moments when I need to take care of Grandma Sis, and at this moment, I need Grandpa Sunny to take care of me. I bury my face in his shirt, and at the smell of his mint snuff, I let go fully and start sobbing.

Grandpa pulls out a handkerchief and hands it to me. "No one is supposed to cry on their birthday."

I blow my nose. "I'm fine. Dinner at the tavern sounds good."

"Cammy, sweetheart," Grandpa says in a lowered voice. "I've been married to my bride for over sixty years. I know that fine never means fine."

We compromise and decide to order pizza and watch *The Birds* by Alfred Hitchcock. Grandma pulls out paper plates, television trays, and three cans of RC Cola. The pizza arrives at five, and we start the movie early, too, because I know that by seven thirty, my grandparents will retire to bed.

When the movie starts, I go through my phone and thank my parents and Robby for the birthday wishes. Some friends have reached out too. I have a couple of missed calls from Robby, and I let him know that I'll try to call him tomorrow because I'm too busy today.

I have always loved this movie, but I can't concentrate on anything. Grandpa makes popcorn on the stove top, and now he and my grandma start eating it. Both of them watch me more than they watch the movie. Every time I glance at them, they stare at me for a moment before returning their attention to the television.

All I can think about is Jake.

I jump when I hear a knock at the back door.

Grandpa looks at me, and I mouth, "Let me get this."

Jake stands outside, holding a bouquet of vibrant wildflowers and a box. "Happy birthday, Camilla." He hands me the flowers.

I don't smile as I take them from him. "Um, yeah. Happy birthday to you too."

Jake looks at me, trying to read the situation. Then he starts pacing. "I can tell you're upset, Camilla. What's going on?"

With a sigh, I turn as if to leave him on the doorstep.

"Did something happen last night?" he asks.

I take a deep breath, but I can't seem to think of anything to say.

"I was hoping to get to spend the day together," he says. "I had a great day planned."

He takes the flowers and gift from me and sets them on the table on the patio. I step outside and let the door close behind me.

"I'm sorry I left early," I say. "I should have said something, but I didn't want to ruin your night."

Jake reaches his hand to mine, but I pull back. "Did I do something wrong?" he says.

I point to him and then me. "You and I aren't going to work."

Jake looks uncomfortable. "I don't know what you mean."

I shake my head. "I'm so much younger than you." Every word I speak is meaningless and absent of truth. I tiptoe around my hurt and pain, leaving Jake to decipher the bad clues I'm leaving him.

"We've talked about our age difference. It is what it is. Who cares?"

"Ten years is a lot. But it's more than that."

He straightens up abruptly. "I don't get it. Are you breaking up with me?"

I think to last night and the headlines I read. Jake is married. I was never his. More importantly, Jake was never mine. I let my guard down, and this is what happened. I knew he was trouble the first time I saw him this summer. And I still ended up in his bed. I've never fallen for someone. Is this the pain the men I left behind felt? If so, then I deserve this pain.

"You make it sound like we were together," I say. "We were hanging out. And now I think it's best if we don't hang out anymore."

Jake slams his fists on the patio table, and I jump. "What's going on, Camilla? None of this makes sense."

He's not wrong. None of this makes sense. When we were together, he made me feel like I was the only one in the room. That he's been leading a double life makes no sense to me.

I put my hands on my hips. "I'll send you money for everything you've done."

"You're maddening, Camilla. And I already told you I don't want your money. Are you going to tell me what happened?" His voice cracks.

My grandparents' neighbors live close by. I have to do everything in my power not to yell when that's all I want to do. I want to ask the question. I want to hear the words from Jake, but I can't bring myself to say it. Even thinking about him being married makes my heart break.

"You and me?" I point to both of us. "We were never supposed to be together. We don't even like each other that much. I'm doing the grown-up thing and calling out the inevitable."

"We don't like each other that much?" My skin burns when he touches me. "You know that isn't true."

My mind flashes to the magnetism from the first time I saw him this summer. No matter what words we shared or arguments we had, there were so many times I wanted to grab his face and kiss him, and I know he felt the same way. But none of that matters anymore. I refuse to cry, and if I call Jake out on the fact that he's a married man and was with his wife a couple of weeks ago, I won't be able to hold back the tears. I'll scream and I'll end up in the local newspaper. I have to show restraint and not give in to the emotion.

"Camilla." He steps closer. "What do I need to do to fix this?"

I stare into his eyes. I love his eyes. "You could start by being honest with me," I say, trying with all of my energy to keep the tears at bay.

"The truth is, you're right." He looks at me with a pained expression. "We were never supposed to be together, but I couldn't stay away from you. I know I haven't always been kind, but I wanted to. You mean everything to me."

"Then be honest with me. Right now, Jake. Here's your chance."

"The truth is—"

The door to my grandparents' house swings open before Jake has a chance to finish his thought.

It's Grandpa. "Is everything okay out here, kids?" He looks at me and then Jake.

I put my hand on my grandpa's shoulder. "Everything's fine. Jake is leaving."

Jake tries to speak again, but I go inside and slam the door behind me. Low mumbles of a conversation between Jake and my grandpa can be heard through the window, and then Grandpa comes inside. I look out the window. Jake continues to stand there, looking stunned. The pain in the middle of my chest is piercing. *Why do I feel sad for him?* I wonder. *This is his fault.*

I've walked away from too many men to count. I've never felt like I was going to suffocate afterward. But right now, I feel like the walls are closing in on me and that nothing will ever be the same from this point forward.

Jake accepts defeat and returns to his truck. Once I'm sure he's gone, I head out, grab the flowers and the gift, and bring them inside. Against my better judgment, I decide to open the card. There aren't many words, but the ones he writes further break and confuse me.

*Camilla,*

> *Happy birthday. This isn't the first we've spent together, and I hope it's not our last. I know it will be my favorite. You have my entire heart.*

> *Yours always,*
> *Jake*

Nothing makes sense anymore. Why would he write this to me? How can he be so good at living a double life that he can have a wife while also writing me such a personal note?

I open the first of two packages. Hemingway's *The Sun Also Rises*. When I open the front cover, I'm stunned to see that it's a first edition. I can't even imagine how he got this or how much he spent. I run my hand over the binding. The book is in flawless condition. I rip open the smaller gift. The picture of Jake and me from his graduation has been restored into a beautiful five-by-seven frame.

I wipe the tears from my face as I look at this picture. Jake looks so young, like he's about to venture off to college and create a life for himself. I'm eight and innocent and infatuated with a boy who will never be mine. Oh, I wish I could go hug that naïve girl and tell her that everything will be okay. I can't believe that Jake still has this picture so many years after it was taken.

I fold my hands over my chest and lean over and cry. Happy birthday to us.

# CHAPTER 30

Two days pass, and I barely get out of bed. Light drips in from the windows. Then darkness comes again. My grandparents check on me often. I tell them that I think I caught a bug and will need a few days to recover. Grandpa Sunny tries to get me to go to the doctor, but I don't think the doctor can fix what's ailing me.

On the third day, I shower and put on clothes for the first time. Then I send money to Jake and get a receipt that he's received it. I know he told me he doesn't want my money, but making our summer transactional will help bring me peace. I sent him almost everything in my checking account, and I know it's not even close to enough. Not only did he put in countless hours leading the work, but he also bought the flooring, the paint, the roofing materials, and the shower. The list goes on. He cut down trees and landscaped the lawn. He worked tirelessly.

I tell myself I shouldn't feel this sad. I've had three men before Jake tell me that they love me, and I walked away from every one of them. I always had a reason. The summer was almost over. We lived too far away. We were just having fun. I'm moving again.

Not that Jake told me he loves me, not that I would have let him if he tried. Love ruins everything.

After walking away from Anders, Leif, and José, I barely thought about them. I wished them well—I still do—and I hope they've found what they were looking for, but I have never felt sad about no longer having them in my life. It was a relief to be free of them.

I leave Grandpa and Grandma a note on the kitchen table. I slept so late that they are already napping. I've missed tea with Grandma and coffee with the men several days in a row.

I drive to the cottage, my mind racing. My mood was better back when I first decided on a Labor Day gathering with my family. But now, planning for family to be here feels like a chore. Does it make sense to stay in Wheaton anymore? I was never staying for Jake—had told myself that I was staying despite him. But I'm not sure if Wheaton is big enough for both of us. I already planted the seed with Robby, but I haven't said much of anything to anyone else. I don't know if leaving my grandparents is possible. I like being near them, and they are going to need me more with each passing day.

As I pull into the cottage, my stomach leaps to my throat at the sight of Jake's truck. It's so unexpected, but it appears that while I've been lying in bed, Jake has been finishing the cottage. I'm sure he heard my car, so now I have no choice but to go inside. I refuse to run like a scared rabbit.

I open the door to the cottage. Jake must not hear me over his drill. He's crouched down and drilling on the underside of the new stone countertops. The cupboards are done and painted. They're beautiful. But the countertops put the finishing touch on the cottage. They are gray with hints of white. The cottage has never looked as beautiful as it does right now.

The drill stops.

"Hey," I say.

I see his face for the first time. His eyes look red and tired, his hair swept beneath his backward ball cap, several days of stubble on his face.

"I didn't know you were going to be here," he says. "I'm nearly done, and then I'll be out of your hair."

He leans against the counter, and I stay by the door. We're separated by space, unspoken words, and regret.

"It looks great in here, Jake. I mean, I don't have words." The place is unrecognizable from the way it looked when I first arrived to Wheaton, but the feeling it used to give me has also changed.

"I received the money. It's insulting. I told you I didn't want it."

I lean against the table. "You've put in so much time and labor. I'll never be able to express how much this means to me, to my family."

Jake pushes off the counter and leans against the other side of the table. "I did this for you."

"Jake, please." I stare at the floor, unable to look into his eyes. "And my birthday gift was beautiful, but it was too much. I can't accept it."

"Well, I refuse to take it back. I got it for you." He slumps. "I don't like what's happening here. If I did something to hurt or offend you, I'm sorry, but I deserve an explanation."

"We spent days and nights talking," I say haltingly. Blood rushes to my face. My hands ache from all the weight I'm putting on them as I lean over the table. "But you being married never seemed important enough to mention?"

His face turns the color of the sun on a hot June day. "You looked me up on the internet?"

"Not at first," I yell. "The night of your birthday party, Tiffeny told me. And then, yes, I looked you up."

"You knew I had a past, and you knew I was in the public eye for years, and instead of giving me the respect I deserve, you spied on me."

"Don't turn this on me, Jake. You told me you were out of town for work. I saw the photo of you and her."

"You want to know the truth, Camilla? You could have asked." He pounds his fist into the table, and I flinch. "After my injury, I went off the deep end. Before, I was someone who drank rarely and never did drugs. But after, I lost my identity. Everything I thought I was going to be ended on that field. The pain pills they prescribed me made everything seem better. Until they didn't. Mixing them with alcohol was the perfect escape from reality."

When I don't respond, he turns away from me.

"I was so consumed with self-pity that I surrounded myself with users who didn't care about me. A group of us were in Vegas, and I wasn't in the right frame of mind when we walked into a chapel and got married. Because of that stupid decision, I've spent the past five years giving this woman money she doesn't deserve and trying to annul the relationship. That's why I was in California."

"Jake—"

"No, wait, Camilla." He rubs the stubble on his face. "I don't think I would have survived another year the way I was living, but my dad showed up in California and insisted that I get on a plane with him, come home, and work on myself. It was our relationship—me and you—that motivated me to start working with my lawyers again to move this along and to put my past behind me once and for all."

Jake takes his hat off and brushes his hair back with his fingers.

"I needed to be free to move on with you fully. Free from the trap I've lived in for the past few years." The words pour out of his mouth, rendering me speechless. "The thing is, Camilla, I'm in love with you. But you know that already. I tried to tell you, and you couldn't cut me off fast enough."

"You should have told me all of this," I say as I strain my neck to look at him.

"I was going to!" he shouts. "And you should have respected me enough to talk to me instead of invading my privacy and searching for me online."

I barely register that the door to the cottage opens, except that Jake glances toward the door before he looks back to me.

"And do you know what I really think? You're using this new information about a wife I was never actually in a relationship with as an excuse not to get close to me. All you do is run away."

"That's enough."

I look toward the door. Robby stands there, bag in hand. "Robby, what are you doing here?" I cry.

Jake goes into the kitchen and grabs his tools. "I'm right, Camilla, and you know it. You were looking for an out. Congratulations, you found it."

When Jake tries to leave, Robby steps in front of him and puts his hand on his arm.

Jake brushes it away.

"Jake, calm down," Robby says.

"Stay out of it, Robby," Jake and I say in unison.

My brother stands between us, providing a buffer.

"I would never have looked you up, Camilla," Jake says, "even if you were a public figure. But here's what I've learned—all from you. You studied in Savannah but couldn't stay put for four years, so you studied abroad. And then when that ended, you decided to spend a summer in Israel. And when things got too real there, you decided to go back to

Savannah, only until you decided to study abroad in Barcelona."

Robby tries to interrupt. "Jake, stop—"

But Jake doesn't stop. Instead, he puts his hand out to silence Robby. "And then, instead of settling down after college, you decide that the Peace Corps was calling your name, and you moved to Cambodia. Let's call a spade a spade, shall we, City Girl? You aren't running away from me. You're running away from you."

"That's enough!" Robby screams with more force than I've ever heard from him.

Jake pushes past Robby and slams the door of the cottage. I sit down, needing to catch my breath. At first, I'm numb, but then the tears start to roll down my cheeks.

"What did I walk into?" Robby asks as he sits in the chair next to me, hand on my arm.

I glare at him. "What are you doing here? I wasn't expecting you for days."

"Grandpa called. He said you needed your big brother."

I snort through my next cry, and Robby pulls me into his neck.

"Can you believe he said those things to me?" I ask.

"Um—"

"I mean, the nerve," I interrupt. "And then he dares to tell me he loves me."

We move to the couch. I lay my head back on the armrest and prop my feet on Robby's lap.

"And you looked him up online?"

I kick at Robby. "He should have told me about his past."

"Perhaps." Robby squeezes my foot. "And he was probably going to at some point."

"Don't take his side," I warn.

"Cam, I'm always on your side. But let's break this down for a moment. Jake had a tough couple of years, did something stupid, and has been paying for it ever since. It sounds like he went out to California for closure."

"It still sounds like you're taking his side."

"It's not like he cheated on you, right?" Robby searches for his phone and types something into the screen. The photo of Jake and the mystery woman pops up. "All right, she's hot."

I kick him in the side.

"My read on this," he continues, "is that Jake and this woman grabbed a cup of coffee and said their final goodbyes. And can I just say that I'm surprised at your restraint in not doing an internet search on him earlier? I mean, the guy was a profes- sional athlete."

I sit up and put my head in my hands.

"Cam, if you don't want to be with Jake, then don't be. But at least be honest about why."

"I've never married someone in Vegas while drunk and on pain meds," I say into my palms.

Robby shakes his head. "No, you haven't. But you have run from every potentially serious rela- tionship that's ever presented itself to you. So don't sit over there acting like you're some put-together grown-up."

"Ouch." I fold my arms over my chest.

"Are you still going to stay in Wheaton?" he asks with one raised eyebrow.

"For a while."

"Good."

I lie back on the couch, bring my knees to my chest, and close my eyes, trying to regulate my breathing after being yelled at and called out.

I feel broken. This all started with my anger at Jake, then with me breaking things off with him, and now he's mad at me. Robby can say what he wants about me, but relationships aren't supposed to be this complicated this early on. And Jake is wrong. This isn't about me looking for an excuse. This is about Jake not being honest with me.

\*\*\*\*\*

The next morning, Robby and I get up early enough to have coffee with the men at the café. Robby drives us in his rental because he says he refuses to ride in my death trap of a car. It's already a beautiful day with the promise of warmth.

"Have you talked to Jenna since you arrived?"

"We've texted, but I haven't seen her."

"Robby, that's stupid," I say. "You and Jenna have nothing to do with this mess. Talk to her."

"Why do you care if I go and see Jenna? We're friends."

"If you say so." I shove Robby in the arm.

The café is full.

Walt sees us first and waves us over. "We get both of you this morning. What a treat."

Juan grabs an extra chair, and the six of us sit around the square table, shoulder to shoulder.

After we all have our cups in front of us, Walt leans over to me. "How much longer do we have you in Wheaton, Camilla? It's nearly Labor Day."

I look to Grandpa, as I haven't brought this up to him yet. "Funny you ask, Walt. I was planning on talking to Grandpa. I'm hoping I can stay awhile and live at the cottage. I mean, now that it's insulated, it could be a year-round place, right? With a furnace, that is."

Grandpa nearly chokes on his coffee. "I've heard a rumor that you were looking into staying. So it's true?" His eyes are big, and it feels like minutes and not seconds as he anticipates my response.

"I don't know for how long, but this summer has gone too fast, and I'm not ready to leave. I mean, if you'll have me."

"Of course, Cammy," he says.

Walt whoops with excitement, and Juan whistles. Lawson pounds on the table. Grandpa dabs at his eyes as if he's crying. Robby takes us all in and laughs.

Lawson speaks, food flying out of his mouth. "We could take Camilla duck hunting!"

The outburst is so loud that everyone in the café looks at our table in wonder. Though I'm happy that my best friends in Wheaton want me to stay, I laugh at the thought of me wearing camouflage and holding a gun—or worse, a dead duck.

"What about you, Robby?" Walt asks. "Can you stay too?"

Robby coughs and dabs his lips with a napkin. "Unfortunately, my job requires me to live in Chicago. But I'll have more reasons to visit Wheaton now that Cam is staying."

"I guess that's a win for us," Juan says, and we all laugh.

After coffee, Grandpa, Robby, and I walk back home. Robby walks in front of us, and Grandpa slides his arm over mine for support.

"I'm so happy I don't have to say goodbye to you yet," he says.

"Me too, Grandpa." I lean my head against his shoulder. "And I've been thinking of ways I can make some money. I want to try to start my design business. I've talked to Carrie, who owns the thrift store. We haven't been able to connect live, but I'm hoping I can rent it."

"That would be great if it works out."

"It would, but it'll come down to how short of a lease I can get. I want to stay longer. I just don't know how long."

A truck slows next to us. Jake parks and hops out. He doesn't look at me as he approaches us. "Sunny, I'm hoping you and I can chat. Do you have a minute?"

"Jake," Grandpa says. He gestures to Robby and me. "You guys go ahead. I'll make sure Jake gets me home."

I glance back, as does Robby.

"What do you think that's all about?" Robby asks when we're out of hearing distance.

"Maybe Jake's going to try to turn Grandpa against me."

Robby pokes me in the arm and shakes his head.

We get back to the house just as Annie is on her way out. I talk to her for a few minutes before going inside. Robby heads upstairs, leaving me alone with Grandma.

"I'll put the kettle on, Grandma."

The wind coming in through the open kitchen window serves as another sign that this summer is almost in the books.

Grandma smiles hopefully. "Do you have time for tea with me, Camilla?"

"Of course."

When the pot is ready, I pour our cups. I dip my teabag into the steaming hot water. Grandma smiles and looks out the window, rollers still in her hair with a clear plastic cap over them. She places her hand over mine and holds it there.

"Did I ever tell you that when Jake moved back to Wheaton, he stayed at our cottage?"

My throat tightens at the sound of his name.

"Oscar and Eleanor were already gone, and their cottage was falling apart. I told him he could stay at ours, although it was only in slightly better shape."

I chuckle to myself, thinking of how much Jake obsessed over the fact that none of the Bergland relatives kept up the cottage, but it seems like the Abram family didn't do much better. It's like I'm Jake ten years later.

"Why didn't he stay with his parents?" I ask.

"Oh, when he got here, so many of those pesky newspeople came too. Everyone wanted a piece of the famous Jake Abram. They were parked outside of his parents' home, so he stayed at our cottage to hide out."

"Jake never mentioned that to me," I say.

Grandma blows into her tea mug. "And then he insisted on taking care of the lawn at the cottage. He's never stopped since. Your dad and Larry tried to hire a kid who would come out weekly and take care of it, but Jake always insists he'll do it. And he has never accepted money."

"I didn't know that," I say into my mug.

"I know you're hurting, but Jake is one of the good ones." Her hand rests over mine.

"Did you know?" I ask my grandma. "About his struggles?"

"We all knew. But it isn't my business or anyone else's in this town. There are always two sides to every story, and the news painted an awful picture. But that's not the Jake I've known."

"He should have told me, Grandma."

She dips her teabag into her cup. "Imagine the worst things you think about yourself. Do you openly share those things with the people you love?"

She removes her glasses and wipes her eyes. I hand her a tissue, which she uses to blot away the tears. Then she stands and goes to the sink.

"I know I have *that ailment*," she says over her shoulder. "And I know I've almost burned this house down on more than one occasion. I know that, recently, I didn't recognize my own husband. I can admit these things to almost everyone, but saying them to Sunny is too hard."

A shudder of sympathy ripples through me.

"I love him too much," Grandma says, her voice raised to be heard over the water pouring from the faucet as she rinses her cup. "And if I don't say these things to him, part of me can continue to believe that these parts I don't like about myself aren't real."

I go to her and wrap my arms around her shoulders. The tears fall over my cheeks. I can sense when Grandpa enters. We must look like quite the spectacle.

"Is everything okay?" he asks.

"Yes, we're fine," I say tearfully. "What did Jake want, Grandpa?"

"Oh, nothing much. Did you tell Sis about your plans to stay longer?"

Grandma puts her hands up to her face and then pulls me into a hug.

# CHAPTER 31

The Berglands will arrive today. My grandparents seem to have permanent smiles on their faces. Grandma and Grandpa can't wait to have everyone here. Liam is between jobs and moving to New York City the first week of September, and he has told us that he can't wait to spend a long weekend in Wheaton. And David told me that he will be happy to stay in Wheaton for a few days, as the Florida heat has become unbearable.

Uncle Larry and Aunt Diane have said that they are excited and eager to see the cottage's transformation. Then there are my parents. I'm sure they're excited to all be in Wheaton at the same time, as it's been a while.

As cars start to arrive, I wonder if this excitement I'm experiencing is how my grandparents felt every time they would see us pull up to their home or cottage. I see my parents first, and I run to them. It has only been a summer since I last saw them, but it feels good to embrace them.

"You look great, Camilla." Mom is beaming, the kind of smile where her heart touches mine and we become in sync for a moment.

"I'm so happy you guys are here," I say.

The next car bears Uncle Larry and Aunt Diane, whom I haven't seen in more than a year. I run over to greet them. We've decided that my parents and Larry and Diane will stay at the cottage with my cousins, Liam and David, while Robby and I will stay in town. Or he'll sleep on a mattress on Jenna's floor, as that seems to be the new normal for him.

I help everyone get settled inside the cottage.

Robby walks in. "Liam and David just pulled up."

I run out of the cottage once again. Liam sees me first. He grabs me around the waist and spins me. David follows his lead, lifting me off the ground with his embrace.

"It's so great to see you," David yells.

"I know! I can't believe we're all here together. It's been ages!"

"It's about time someone made this happen." Liam pats my back.

I help them bring their bags inside the cottage.

"Thank goodness for one girl in the mix," David says. "Us boys would never have been so organized."

Everyone seems shocked by the transformation of the cottage. I still can't believe how beautiful it turned out. I think about Jake and wish that he could be here to see their reactions.

As everyone gets settled, I pull out the food I prepared. It's so good to have the Berglands all here together. I look forward to tomorrow, when my grandparents will join us and we can spend the whole day living in the past in Grandma Sis's favorite place.

Liam leans into me. "The parents are starting to wind down. How much longer do we need to stay before we ditch them?"

I look at Robby, who shrugs.

"Jake reached out and invited us to his place," Robby says. "Said he'd love to see everyone."

"Man, we haven't seen Jake in years." David stands up. "I'm up for that plan."

The four of us load up on drinks and walk down the gravel driveway to Jake's. Ending up at his place tonight was not originally part of the plan. Liam and David stride a few feet in front of Robby and me.

"This is going to be awkward," I whisper. "Think anyone would miss me if I disappeared to town?"

"Yes. We never get to see Liam and David. It'll be fine. Jenna will be there and hopefully Dax too."

Jake greets everyone and welcomes us in. Our gazes linger on each other. His lips turn up in a smile, but I look away. I walk over to the island, where Liam has started arraying the bottles of liquor he brought. Dax and Jenna are already here.

Jake is friendlier than I've ever seen him as everyone catches up. He must have been taking a dip in the lake because he's wearing only swimming trunks. His skin looks warm as the beads of water melt on him. It occurs to me as I watch them that all the other Berglands are so much taller than me.

Jenna claps her hands. "I know this is going to sound ridiculous, but I found the most amazing photo we should recreate. Please humor me."

Everyone groans.

"Remember the pictures of us all lined up, oldest to youngest," she says with a grin. "What do you say?"

Jenna hands me a photo. I look to be about five, as I'm missing a front tooth, my wild hair is pulled into two braids, and my stomach sticks out of my two-piece, which unfortunately cuts a few inches below where it should. I hand the photo to Dax.

"I'm only doing this if Camilla replicates the two-piece look," he says.

I swat his arm.

"Seriously, though, who's going to take the picture?" Liam asks.

"Self-timer," Jenna says. She looks at Jake. "Are you ready?"

We all begrudgingly line up in front of his fireplace. Jake stacks books on a table to get the phone high enough to take the picture. Once he's done, he takes his place as first in line, as he's the oldest. After Jake comes Liam, who is twenty-nine but turns thirty next month. Dax stands right next to him, as he's still twenty-nine for three more months. At the ripe age of twenty-seven, Robby goes next, followed by the two twenty-six-year-olds, first David and then Jenna. Finally, the new twenty-five-year-old me steps in at the end. With the seven of us all lined up, Jake hits the button for the picture and runs back to the line. We all wait for the flash to go off.

We all look at the photo, which immediately sparks memories for me. Liam and Dax were always best friends. Robby and David were thick as thieves, only a year apart, and Jenna and I would be together constantly. Jake was always the loner, as he was older than all of us. But as the picture shows, he and I are the bookends of a group that has been connected since the beginning. The oldest and the youngest, two Leos who ended up being so similar.

"Jake." Liam pats him on the shoulder. "I saw a headline about you today. Congrats, man."

I take a sip of my wine and look around at everyone, confused.

"Yeah, thanks man," Jake says. "It was a long time coming."

"Sounds like it," David says.

My eyes cut to Jake's, but he looks down. I take another drink of wine. "What was the headline? I must have missed it."

"Surprising, City Girl, as you spend so much time on the internet looking me up." His gaze pierces holes in me.

Liam looks at Jake and then back at me, his expression riddled with confusion. "His estranged wife finally signed the annulment papers."

I laugh too loudly. "So you're finally single?"

"I've been single for years, Camilla," Jake says through gritted teeth. "But you already know that."

David leans in and whispers in my ear, "Wow, you guys don't seem to like each other very much."

"We don't," I say, biting into my lip.

The sky is a beautiful orange when we stroll outside with our drinks and gather around the fire-pit. Without a cloud in the sky, tonight's sunset will be gorgeous. The fire starts with a roar, and we all settle into our chairs.

"It's so beautiful out tonight." Liam plops into the chair next to me. He pulls a sweatshirt over his head, crosses his legs, and looks out at the lake.

David sits down next, followed by Jenna and Robby and then Jake and Dax.

We watch as a pelican swims by, illuminated orange by the pending sunset.

"I'm not going to get sunsets like this in the city," Liam says as he stares straight ahead.

"Florida has some of the best sunsets," David interjects.

Jake straightens his legs and crosses them at the ankles. "California had some of the most beautiful sunsets over the Pacific. But I'd argue that Lake Traverse's are the best I've seen."

No one looks at one another. We all watch the dimming sun slowly inch toward the hills. A few grab their phones and start clicking away.

I brace myself when Jake takes a breath because I know he's going to say something about how they should put their phones away. Instead, he surprises me.

"At some point in life," he says, "the world's beauty becomes enough. You don't need to photograph, paint, or even remember it. It is enough."

I say, "No record of it needs to be kept, and you don't need someone to share it with or tell it to. When that happens—that letting go—you let go because you can."

Jake and I look at each other.

"Seriously, City Girl," he says. "Is there any piece of literature you don't know?"

"Sorry," I say. "Toni Morrison's *Tar Baby* is one of my favorites."

Before Jake has a chance to respond, David says, "Wow, you're both really bookish."

I look at Jake. "I bet women who aren't well read are impressed by all of your soliloquies."

Jake leans toward me, and it's as if everyone else fades to the background. "You have no idea."

"Ugh," I retort. "You disgust me."

Robby jumps in, eager to change the subject. "We live all over the country. Remarkably, we all ended up here at the same time."

Jenna looks at me and smiles. "Thanks to you, Camilla."

Liam puts his hand on mine. "I think we should commit to all coming back here every couple of years at the same time. It's been too long since our trips have brought us all together. I mean, I've been back a few times, but we haven't seen the Abrams on those trips."

Jake chuckles under his breath. "The Abrams live here. It's the Berglands that ended up so far away."

"I can commit to coming back every two years at the same time," David says.

"I'll come back a lot," Robby adds, looking at Jenna.

The sun's bottom grazes the hill, the oranges and yellows spreading into the sky.

"How about you, Camilla?" Dax turns to me. "Would you come back every so often for an Abram-Bergland reunion?"

I realize that I haven't told anyone besides Robby, my parents, and Grandpa and Grandma about my plans to stay. Although I don't know if I'll stay forever, I'm not ready to say goodbye yet. "I'm actually going to stay in Wheaton, at least for a while."

Almost all the voices ring out at the same time. "What?"

I feel Jake's eyes on me, but I avoid looking at him.

"I don't know for how long," I say, "but why not? It's not like I have anywhere else to go."

"But what will you do here?" Liam asks.

"I want to start a design business." I shrug. "I wanted to rent the most perfect storefront on Main Street, but I found out earlier today that someone beat me to it. Hopefully, I can find another space."

"Do your parents know?" Liam asks.

"Yes. And Grandpa and Grandma."

Everyone goes silent and looks back at the lake. The most vibrant colors peek out behind the hills.

Moments like this, I feel one with the earth. No one pulls out a phone this time. Instead, we focus on the beauty in front of us. We sit in silence for a while as the sky goes from orange to pink, to deep blue, to black.

"We're going to walk back to the cottage," David says with a nod in Liam's direction.

Robby follows Jenna into her bedroom. Lilly who? Dax takes the other. I look around, not knowing where I'll go. There isn't enough room for me at the cottage tonight, and I can't drive back to town.

Jake reads my mind. "You can stay here."

"I'll sleep on the couch," I say.

"No, you take my room. I'll sleep on the couch."

I go to argue, but Jake leads me upstairs. Every conversation we've had lately has ended in a fight, and I'm exhausted from the arguments and the heartache. He goes into his closet and throws a shirt and shorts onto the bed as I sit down. Then he goes back into his closet. I hear him digging around for something.

"I need to say one thing to you, Camilla." He stands in front of me as I sit on his bed. "The picture you saw of me in California was after we met with our lawyers and signed the papers. Gwen asked me to get a cup of coffee, and we went to the coffee shop next door to the lawyers' office. She apologized. For everything. She's a broken person, and she made her amends. That picture was our goodbye."

"Okay," I say as I look down at his comforter and smooth my hand across the surface.

"Okay," Jake says. He goes to the door and closes it behind him.

I lie in the dark room and look at the ceiling. This summer is the first time I've allowed myself to feel love. And I don't just mean with Jake. I mean with Sis and Sunny too. All those years I've avoided Wheaton, the only place that has ever felt like home, simply because having a front-row seat to their aging seemed more difficult than staying away altogether. But this summer, I allowed myself to fall back in love with them and with Wheaton. And Jake? That feels like love too. I keep telling everyone that I don't truly have a home base. But I do and I always have. Wheaton is home.

# CHAPTER 32

I'm the first to leave Jake's in the morning. When I get outside, I notice that his truck is gone. I head to our cottage, where the grown-ups have most likely been up for hours. I laugh to myself that I'm twenty-five, but it's still my parents and aunt and uncles who have reached grown-up status. I don't feel like I have quite yet.

My mom sits outside alone, having a cup of coffee by the lake, a blanket draped over her lap.

I stand next to her. "Hey, Mom."

She turns to me and smiles. "You're here early. Is everything okay?"

"I guess so." I pull up a chair and sit by her. There is no wind, and the lake looks like glass.

"I'm not convinced." She reaches over to touch my arm.

I sigh. "I'm starting to have a lot of big feelings about staying in Wheaton."

"Will you walk with me?"

I stand up. We walk down the gravel road, my arm looped in hers. The air is cool this early in the morning, the grass wet from dew.

"I said I'll stay for a while," I begin, "so I will. But it's going to be quiet once you all leave. And I don't know if living here will feel like enough of an adventure for me."

"Adventures come in all forms."

"What do you mean?"

Mom bends down to grab a walking stick on the grass near the road. "I mean that whether you stay here or go on a faraway adventure, you'll still need to deal with who you are and what you want."

Jake's tattoo flashes in my mind. *You can't get away from yourself by moving from one place to another.*

"Robby told me what happened between you and Jake," Mom says as we reach the bench that Grandma and I consider our own. "Sunny mentioned something to me about it too."

We sit. I scoot as close to my mom as possible and rest my head on her shoulder.

"I worry about you, Camilla," she says. "You're so independent, but deep down, I know you want to be grounded somewhere, and I know you're scared. I worry that you're going to run again."

I close my eyes and hold them tight. "Robby told you about Jake?"

"He did. I had no idea you were having such a lovely summer romance."

"So then Robby told you about his past?" I lift my head off her shoulder.

Mom wraps her arm around me and pulls me in tighter. "Yes. It's a past that you should have let Jake

341

tell you about when he was ready. It must have felt like a violation to him that you looked it up."

I look away.

"I don't regret the way we raised you and Robby," she continues. "We gave you opportunities, adventure, and culture. And although we moved all the time, we all had each other. You and Robby reacted so differently to your upbringing, though. I should have recognized it sooner. I thought Robby was the one who wanted to find a home base and that you wanted to remain our wild child. But in hindsight, you've been looking for a place that felt like home too."

She wipes a tear off my cheek.

"You always find a reason to leave," she says. "I don't second-guess the decisions you've made, but do you feel differently about Jake than you have in your previous relationships?"

I sigh. I don't have the words yet, but I do feel differently about Jake. I mean, it's Jake. That makes it different. But it's so much beyond my feelings for him. I feel so paralyzed, and if I'm honest with myself, nothing he's done should prevent me from giving him another chance. Our nearly month-long romance was magical. Scary magical. Sure, he didn't tell me everything, but I left a few things out too.

"He's my Jake," I say as I sit up straight on the bench. "But I'm scared about how I feel. I don't know if I could handle it if things don't work out."

"But imagine what your life will look like if you're brave enough to try. Maybe things will work out. Maybe Jake is your person. And maybe he's not. But there's only one way to know for sure." Mom stands up. "You're stronger than you think, Camilla, and you need to stop living your life like everyone in it is going to disappear." She squeezes my shoulder. "Go get him."

\*\*\*\*\*

The Abrams begin trickling to the cottage in the late afternoon. My grandparents arrive, their faces alight with joy. When Sis's parents built this cottage almost seventy years ago, their dream was days like today, with family spending time together, breaking bread, and enjoying one another's company.

Walt shows up in his silver thunderbird, and Annie is with him. I run to help him out of the car. I'm happy to see Lawson and his wife, Georgia, and then Juan and his wife, Emma, get out of the back seat. Dax and Kylie get out of Jenna's car. Jake is nowhere to be found.

The energy is lively as people play croquet with Grandma Sis. She always beats everyone, never showing mercy to the less skilled players among us. George and Lucy Abram sit with my parents, laughing and catching up like no time has passed at all. Liam and Dax stand at the grill with beers in hand. The bratwursts and burgers come off the grill in bulk. David scrolls through his phone, showing Grandpa and Grandma photos. Robby and Jenna keep going into the cottage to bring everyone drinks. The Coffee Crew ladies sit in the shade with their iced teas.

It doesn't feel right that Jake isn't here. The only reason we're out here enjoying this space is because of Jake and his hard work.

Walt, Juan, and Lawson sit near the dock, fishing poles nearby. I go to them and pull up a chair.

"The fish are biting," Juan says. "I picked up some crawlers and am thinking about throwing a line in."

"You can't use crawlers this time of year," Lawson interjects. "Let's use my leeches. It's the only thing that works this late in the season."

I need the wisdom of my best friends right now. "I'm going to take a raincheck on fishing. I'm hoping you can help me with something."

Walt moves his chair closer to me. "Sure thing, Camilla. What can we help with?"

"Remember when we all talked about looking for a local boy in town for me?" I take a deep breath and go for it. "You were right to suggest Jake."

Everyone leans in.

"I like him," I say, "but I'm afraid I messed things up. I don't know how to make it right."

"I knew it!" Walt yells, cookie spewing from his mouth in every direction. "You two seem to have something special. I could tell."

"*Had*, Walt," I correct. "I messed it up, remember?"

Lawson turns his head so fast that his braid nearly whips me in the face. "Where is he? He isn't here."

"I think he's not here because of me," I confess.

"Oh," they all say in unison.

"Sunny, get over here!" Walt hollers across the lawn.

Grandpa gets up and walks over to us.

"Cammy is having boy trouble, Sunny."

"Oh, guys," Grandpa says. "Let's not get in Cammy's business."

"But, Sunny," Juan whispers as he leans forward, "Camilla asked for our help. Trust me. We're as surprised as you."

Walt pulls his chair closer so we all sit in a circle. "Here's what we do. We all get in the boat and troll down to Jake's house."

"And then what?" Juan asks.

"And then Camilla can profess her love to him."

"Stupid," Juan and Lawson say at the same time.

"Is that what you did to get Annie to be your girl?" Lawson adds.

Walt huffs. "Well, I don't hear any better ideas."

Juan puts his hand on my arm and then looks at the guys. "We could catch some fish and then we can cook it for Jake and Camilla and get flowers and play romantic music, and we'll stay away while they talk."

Lawson nods. "It's not the worst idea."

I agree that the idea could work. I could ask Jake to talk, and then the men could cook and serve us. Jake would have to hear me out because Sunny,

---

Walt, Juan, and Lawson would be present. He would have to forgive me.

Grandpa leans back and crosses his legs at the ankle. "Camilla, do you want to make a grand gesture?"

"I was thinking more along the lines of saying I'm sorry," I admit. "But I'm open to anything at this point."

My grandpa stiffens and looks at his watch. "I have an idea, but it involves all of us going to town, and no one can ask questions on the drive."

"I'll drive!" Walt yells.

We walk to Walt's Thunderbird. Grandpa whispers into Walt's ear, and then they both look back at me. The five of us manage to fit into the little car. Walt drives, Grandpa takes the passenger seat, and I sit in the back between Juan and Lawson. Walt never goes over ten miles per hour. The men all talk over each other as they try to give me ideas about what I can say to Jake when I find him. I don't even bother to ask where we're going or what my grandpa's plan is. And I don't know what I'm going to say. I just know that I'll be honest and put my heart on the line.

I'm sure it's the longest drive of my life, but Main Street finally comes into view.

Grandpa looks back. "Cammy, I think that's Jake's truck in front of the thrift store. Let's look there first."

Walt stops in front of the store, and we all get out of the car.

"Well?" Grandpa says, gesturing to me. "Look in there for Jake."

"In the thrift store?" I ask, the confusion written all over my face.

"Yes," they all say in unison.

"Why would he be in there?"

From the way they look at me, I can sense that they won't be answering any further questions. Nothing makes sense right now. Why would I have to go into the thrift store of all places to make my grand gesture? I try to look in the windows first, but there's something blocking them from the inside. I glance back at the gentlemen. They stand in a line, watching me.

"See if the door's unlocked," Walt shouts.

I turn the knob, and the door slides open. I hold my breath at what I find. The place has been transformed. The wood beams above my head shine and the walls are a perfect shade of gray. The original hardwood floors have been polished. Shelves have been hung, and large canvases of pictures I took of Jake's finished designs hang on display.

The desk we took out of the cottage during the remodel stands in the corner. On it rest binders full of design options. The space is small but perfect. The sign hanging above me reads *S&S Designs*.

Jake stands in the corner, watching me take it all in, a bouquet of flowers in his hand.

"What are you doing here?" I ask.

"I've been conspiring with Sunny to get you here. I have a few things I want to say to you."

I turn back toward the entrance. The four men have the door open. They're watching everything.

I put my hands over my mouth. "They were supposed to be taking me to find you so I could say a few things to you."

"Really?" Jake looks down at the bright red roses he holds and smiles. "I'm listening."

"Okay. But first, what is all of this?" I look around again. This space looks like mine. It's full of my pictures and favorite colors.

He takes a step toward me. "I rented this space for you. I wanted to fix it up as a surprise. Sunny told me about your interest in this place, and I got ahold of Carrie before you had a chance to."

"This is mine?"

"Yes. *S&S Designs*. Sunny and Sis. I rented this for you. And I know a general contracting business in town who has been dying to start a partnership with an interior designer." He takes another step closer. "Now your turn. What did you come to say?"

"I came to say I'm sorry. I should have let you explain. The thing is, I knew that if I let you talk I'd lose all reason to stay mad at you. And I wanted to stay mad." My heart beats so fast and erratically it feels like it's going to explode out of my chest. "You were right about everything. All of it. It was never even about you or your past or going to California. I was looking for an out. I was scared, but I don't want to run anymore." I pause and bite my lip, suddenly nervous. "And…"

"And what?"

I look down at my feet and put my hands on my warm cheeks. "I love you." I've never said these words to a romantic partner, and so I find myself slightly surprised that I didn't spontaneously combust.

"You love him?" Walt shouts from the door.

Sunny grabs his arm and shushes him.

I can't help but laugh.

Jake smiles and wipes his eyes. "I love you too."

"And he loves you too!" Walt says, pulling at his suspenders. "This is too much."

"Kiss her already!" Juan yells from behind me.

Jake and I laugh at how we somehow find ourselves with an audience for all these very personal things we're saying to each other.

Jake hands me the flowers and lifts me off the floor. When our lips connect, he feels like home. The men start clapping.

"I knew we'd find someone for Camilla," Lawson says through his smile.

Jake puts me down, but I keep my arm tightly around his waist and rest my head on his chest.

"Let's go back to the cottage and let these kids have some alone time," Grandpa says as he ushers the men to Walt's car.

"You were really coming to find me?" Jake asks, taking my hand.

"I talked to my besties, and they said that I needed to do something big so you'd forgive me."

"I panicked because Sunny had you here thirty minutes too early. I nearly wasn't ready."

I laugh. "That's why Walt was driving so slow."

Before we leave the old thrift store, I take one more look at the space. It's beautiful.

"I'm sorry," we say at the same time. We embrace in front of his truck for what feels like a long time. From all the cars that go by, I can imagine that the headline in the next *Wheaton Happenings* is going to be about the out-of-town woman who has snagged Wheaton's golden boy.

Jake kisses me and holds his forehead against mine. "You made today so easy. I had a whole speech planned."

"Yeah?" I say as I place my hands on his arms.

Jake opens the door to his truck and lifts me in. He kisses me as he leans in and buckles my seat belt, bent over me. "The CliffsNotes version is that I fell in love with you the moment I saw you on my woodpile, and that I would have built you a brand-new cottage if it meant getting to spend every waking moment with you this summer and beyond. I've been yours since the very first moment."

I choke up.

"There's more," he continues, "but now I'm feeling shy." He shuts the passenger door, hurries around the front, and gets in on the driver's side.

My heart explodes when he looks at me. "I want to hear the rest later," I say.

We drive out to the cottage as the sun nearly sets. Jake drives with one hand, his other hand holding mine. The windows are down, the wind blowing back our hair as I switch between smiling out at Wheaton and smiling at him. Fear may set in tomorrow, but tonight I feel free. I told a man that I love him, and the earth didn't shatter, and the floor didn't fall out from under me.

Most importantly, I'm going to let him love me and trust that moving forward is part of being an adult. I don't want to run anymore. As we turn down the gravel driveway, I notice that the corn is taller than Jake. In a few weeks, it will all be harvested.

Jake throws the truck into park and hurries over to my side to open my door. He leans down and kisses me. "I love you, Camilla Bergland."

I blush and cover my face with my hands. Baby steps. "I love you." My eyes meet his.

We walk toward the group. Everyone is sitting at the lakefront in their chairs or on blankets, waiting for the Lake Traverse fireworks to start. For decades, it has been a Wheaton tradition to have fireworks on Labor Day weekend, as it marks the end of one season and the start of another. Grandpa Sunny and his buddies prefer the theory that the fireworks signal that duck season is coming soon. I think they're all right. As we approach, people turn to us, and Jake never lets go of my hand.

My mom is wearing an expression that says, "It's about time." Robby elbows Jenna, and they both look relieved. Liam and David have the funniest reaction. Last night, they clearly believed that Jake and I hated each other, but here they see how wrong they were. It has always been love.

Jake takes one of the extra blankets and spreads it on the lawn. I fall back on my elbows, and he does the same. He gets closer to me and rubs my arm. Even when the fireworks start, I can feel his eyes on me more than the display. Kylie comes over and sits next to me, and I put my arm around her. Everyone oohs and ahhs and grabs their cell phones to take pictures. I reach down for mine as well.

Jake takes it and puts it back down. "Let's be in the moment."

I look over at him and kiss his cheek, which is full of soft stubble. We're all here. The six Abrams. Uncle Larry, Aunt Diane, Liam, and David. My parents and Robby. Walt and Annie sit next to each other, and I don't think my eyes are fooling me when I catch them holding hands. Lawson has his arm around Georgia. Juan and Emma sit close to each other. I have Jake by my side, which is right where I want him.

In the middle of all of us sit Sunny and Sis. Right where they belong.

# EPILOGUE

"Hey, City Girl, will you stir the chili?" Jake yells at me from his balcony.

I shake my head that he still thinks it's funny to call me City Girl. I grab a spoon and stir the chili that he spent all morning making. The aroma has reached every part of his home. Jake assures me that I've never had better chili, and from the smell of it, I don't doubt him.

He comes up behind me and kisses my cheek. His hair is damp from his shower. I loop my fingers into his jeans and pull him in for a kiss.

"You haven't snuck any of my chili, have you?" he asks with a grin.

"I promise I'm waiting."

I mix up the ingredients to Grandma Sis's famous cornbread as Jake turns on the TV and switches to a pregame show. I put the cornbread in the oven and set the timer.

"I'll be right down," I say as I take to the stairs. "I'm going to go get dressed."

It's the most beautiful day on Lake Traverse. The autumn air is crisp, with a promise of winter lingering in the air. I've never been in Wheaton this

353

time of year. The beauty rivals the summer. The trees are all starting to change their hues with their red, yellow, and orange leaves. Every night, Jake and I get to sit by the fire in our sweatshirts and look out at the lake while he plays the guitar and sings for me. It turns out that I never hated this time of year because of the cold. In hindsight, I hated the end of summer because it meant I was leaving. It feels good not to be going anywhere this time.

Jake's front door swings open. Jenna walks in with their parents. Next comes Dax and Kylie, who runs to me. I get on my knees to hug her. Grandpa Sunny enters with Walt, and I go greet them, my hand intertwined with Kylie's.

"I'm making Grandma's famous cornbread, Grandpa. You'll have to take some home to her."

Grandpa puts his arm around me. "She'd love that. I tried to get her to come out, but she's never been one for football. Plus, she was having too much fun knitting with Annie. You're going to have enough winter gear to last you several winters."

"Hey, Walt." I kiss him on the cheek. "At least you came."

"I wouldn't miss a free meal and a football game between the Minnesota Thunder and the Oakland Rockets."

Everyone sits around the TV. I help Jake bring people drinks. Jake stirs his chili as I pull the cornbread out of the oven.

His hands grip my waist as he nuzzles his head into my neck. "My jersey looks good on you."

I look down at his Oakland Rockets jersey, number five. It hangs almost to my knees. As I look at the TV, it's hard to believe that Jake once played for this team or that people once sat around their televisions to watch my boyfriend play football.

I knit my fingers in his, and he leans in and kisses me. We jump when Jenna coughs from just behind us.

"Jake, get your hands off Camilla, please. The game's starting."

Jake winks at me and goes to the couch.

"What can I help you with?" Jenna says through a laugh.

"I think everything's good. I'm going to set out the bowls and condiments, and people can come in here and help themselves."

Jenna grabs the onions and shredded cheese while I cut the cornbread.

"I was talking to Carrie the other day," Jenna says. "She said the design work you did on Malik's house is beautiful."

My heart swells as I think about how I've started to pick up more clients. "That's so great to hear. Speaking of design, I'm thinking of heading into Minneapolis for a day next weekend to go to some specialty shops. Any interest in coming?"

Jenna spoons chili into a bowl. "That actually works out perfectly because I have a job interview there the week after."

"A journalism position?"

Jenna does a little dance. "Yep. I'm ready to dive into finding out what's next for me."

"Yay," I clap my hands together. "Although I'd prefer if you stay in Wheaton."

I finish laying the food out.

"The chili is ready for anyone interested," I call out to the room of football watchers.

I take the empty spot on the couch next to Jake. He pulls me into him. I tuck my knees up and lean against his chest. Scrolling on the bottom of the television, I see the words, "No Rockets quarterback has beaten Jake Abram's single-game passing record of four hundred yards."

I grab Jake's waist and shake him. "Did you just see your name?"

He pulls me closer and puts my hand under his shirt. "I did. It's no big deal. Did you really not know I played football professionally?"

"I swear. I've never even seen an NFL game until I started watching with you this season."

Jake kisses my forehead. "And that's one of the reasons you're the perfect person for me."

I put my hand on his face and whisper into his ear, "I love you too."

# About the Author

When she isn't writing novels featuring strong female leads on a path to self-discovery, Leah Omar makes her career at a global medical device company. From Eyota, Minnesota, she holds bachelor's degrees in communications and English literature and a master's in business administration from Augsburg University in Minneapolis.

As a writer, Leah is devoted to giving her readers contemporary love stories that make us remember that we have more similarities than differences and that love can conquer all. When Leah is not busy writing women's fiction and romance, she can be found watching a basketball game on TV, traveling somewhere far away, eating something spicy, or trying to shape the lives of her two amazing kids.

Her breakout novel, A Labor of Love, was published in April of 2021. Leah now calls Minneapolis home, which she shares with her husband and two kids.